REVELATION UNSEALED

Donald A. Salerno Jr.

Published 2004 by Virtualbookworm.com Publishing Inc., P.O. Box 9949, College Station, TX, 77842.

Published in the United States of America

Cover Illustration: David Ingram
All artwork and design: Anne Perretta.
Chart theologies: Donald A. Salerno Jr.

Library of Congress Catalog Card Number:
95-69193

ISBN 1-58939-541-7

TABLE OF CONTENTS

ACKNOWLEDGMENTS

MANY PEOPLE HAVE CONTRIBUTED to make this book a reality. I would like to first thank my editors: Dr. Anthony Bennardo, Elise Weinstein, and Robert Perretta for their absolutely huge effort in helping to create a highly readable manuscript. I also would like to thank Marvin Rosenthal, Dave Rosenthal, and Kevin Howard, for some of the insights and encouragements they offered. Jeff Weinstein, Pastor Tom May, Frank and Cindy Watychowicz, Renee Bennardo, Kevin Piech, and Jim Matkovich deserve special recognition for their many efforts and input into this project. Special thanks goes out to my Pastor Phil Ballmaier whose supreme reverence for the word of God has inspired me to concentrate more on the clear teachings of Scripture and less on my own personal theologies and opinions. This careful approach has helped me to reach a comfortable (and sometimes not so comfortable) resolution of many difficult prophetic passages. I would also like to acknowledge all those Bereans at Calvary Chapel of Elk Grove Village whose tenacious questions encouraged me to keep heading back to the Scriptures for logical biblical support of my positions. To Ann Perretta, my artist, I express my gratitude for the many charts, maps, and illustrations that help make this book truly unique. Your diligent efforts were much appreciated. And to James Ellis who provided me a copy of his personal studies on the Antichrist I am deeply indebted, for without your work I would have lacked some integral pieces in solving the enigma of the Antichrist. I am also grateful for all those who have taken the time to read the manuscript and offer suggestions, as well as constructive criticisms. To my parents, Cathy and my late father Don as well as my brothers Anthony and Michael, and to the rest of my family, I express my appreciation for putting up with my numerous ramblings over the years about Bible prophecy, as well as my preoccupation with the creation of this book. Without your support, patience, love, and criticisms this book would have never been written. I would also like to express my gratitude to my lovely wife Rosario and the whole Caceres family for their graciousness and assistance. Finally, to my publisher who decided to take a chance on Revelation Unsealed when it seemed that no one else would. I cannot thank you enough.

Dedicated to the late Donald A. Salerno Senior

&

my son Donald A Salerno III

TABLE OF ILLUSTRATIONS

1. Concept A.W. Pink, The Antichrist {Grand Rapids: Kregel, 1988} 88-89.
2. Concept E.W. Bullinger, Companion Bible {Grand Rapids: Kregel, 1990} 5-6.

PREFACE

THIS BOOK IS THE CULMINATION of over fifteen years of intense study in God's word concerning the return of Jesus Christ. I choose the word culmination not in the sense that I have all the answers, but in the fact that I feel confident enough to present the results of these studies to the body of Christ.

It has often been said that we stand upon the shoulders of giants. In the case of this book, this saying eloquently applies. My salvation was a result of reading a book on Bible prophecy, and from that day forward the main thrust of my biblical studies was focused in the area of eschatology, or end-time prophecy. This study led me to numerous books, tapes, and commentaries on literally every aspect of Bible prophecy. Although I began with my own theological viewpoints, I chose to study other viewpoints for bits and pieces that could help me understand God's prophetic timetable. As a result, I have greatly benefited from the work of the many eminent researchers and biblical scholars who have preceded me. The insights that many of these godly men have offered have been essential in my overall understanding of end-time events. In particular, the works of Robert Van Kampen and Marvin Rosenthal assisted me in harmonizing many difficult scriptures into the Lord's prophetic chronology.

More important than any of the books I have read in my years of research is the one book on which all of them are based: the Bible. There is no greater authority than God's word. It has always been my belief that if your theology does not line up with the word of God then one must abandon their theology. Many of the problems associated with the study of Bible prophecy are due to the fact that there are those who try to make it fit their own theology. When it does not, there is a tendency from some researchers to ignore or gloss over important scriptures. Other scholars often take scriptures out of context, applying them to present situations, when they should not be doing so. All of this has led to great confusion in the body of Christ concerning Bible prophecy. Because of the apprehension created by date setting and other unsound practices, many in the church have avoided the book of Revelation.

It is my belief that Satan is doing everything in his power to make the church believe that the book of Revelation is not relevant for today. Of course, to those who believe it is relevant, he will convince that they are not able to even comprehend it. Due to all the uncertainty created, many will not even attempt to understand Revelation. The problem is that the book of Revelation may be more relevant today than ever. This will become extremely evident in the following pages. We must all realize that God has not written His word to confuse us, but so that we may have understanding. I am thoroughly convinced that God has clearly outlined His end-time plan for us in Scripture. In order to discover it, we must let what Scripture says take precedent over what we feel it should say.

In his letter to the Thessalonians the Apostle Paul writes this concerning the end times:

> But you brethren are not in darkness, that this Day should overtake you as a thief. You are all sons of light and sons of the day. We are not of the night nor of darkness. Therefore let us not sleep as others *do*, but let us watch and be sober. (1 Thessalonians 5:4-6)

Paul tells us to "watch" and "be sober" so that this day will not overtake us like it will for those who walk in darkness. If, then, we do not study what God has written concerning these events, how are we to understand what is to occur? There are many that will argue that when it all happens they will be prepared, but for now they need to concentrate on more important issues. In turn, I need to point out the Pharisees of Christ's day, who knew all the prophecies concerning His first coming, and not only did not recognize Him as Messiah, but crucified the Lord of Glory. It is vitally important that we understand end-time issues as well as every other doctrinal issue of God's word. The time has come when all believers must know God's word for themselves. This is because many of those in today's pulpits are teaching things contrary to what God has said. We must be like the Bereans who searched the Scriptures daily to see if what they were taught was indeed true (Acts 17:10-12).

I, myself, am not very comfortable with many of the conclusions that my study of Scripture has brought me to concerning the return of Christ. Yet, I must remain uncomfortable because Scripture judges me; I do not judge Scripture. The bottom line is truth, and that is what I have been after since the first day I began studying God's word. I hope that this volume presents the truth of God's prophetic plan with integrity and the highest regard for His word. This book is not a new revelation, nor do I claim that I have all the knowledge there is to have concerning this matter. Although some of my views may seem controversial, I have not written this book to cause division. Unfortunately, God's word is a sword that will divide. If one wants to teach God's word uncompromisingly, he or she will encounter those who will not be pleased. It is my hope that the contents of this book will stir the church to open their Bibles and begin to check for themselves what may shortly come to pass. The message is of such importance that if we truly are in the last days the very salvation of millions of souls is at stake. I do not state those words lightly.

As our Lord Jesus has said:

Therefore you also be ready, for the Son of Man is coming at an hour when you do not expect *Him*. (Matthew 24:44)

1
THE SIGNIFICANCE OF REVELATION

THERE ARE FOUR MAIN REASONS why the book of Revelation is relevant for today. One of the most important of these reasons is that it is the only book in God's word that promises a blessing to all who read it. In Revelation 1:3 the Apostle John writes:

> Blessed is he who reads and those who hear the words of this prophecy, and keep those things that are written in it; for the time is near. (Revelation 1:3)

Since God has offered a special blessing to all that read Revelation, it is for the edification and spiritual well being of every believer to do so. The conditions for this blessing by the Lord are twofold; it is not only to those who read, but also to those who "keep those things that are written in it." The Lord wants believers to obey the words that are written in Revelation. One cannot obey what one cannot understand. Therefore, it is the personal responsibility of every believer to read Revelation, and pray that God gives him or her wisdom to understand and obey its contents. This has been my prayer for the past fifteen years of my study of the Apocalypse. I have discovered that God is very faithful in giving understanding when one remains diligent and persistent in the study of His word.

The second reason why Revelation holds such importance is that God specifically outlines what is going to happen to believers and unbelievers as His final plan for the ages unfolds. In the Olivet Discourse in Matthew chapter 24, our Lord states that there will come such a great deception that if it were possible the very elect could be deceived (Matthew 24:24). The only way to guard oneself against any type of religious heresy or deception is to know God's word. It will be no different for those who will be around when these things take place. During this great deception, it will be absolutely crucial that every believer knows, for his or herself, what the scriptures say concerning Satan's final plan. When the last period of human history unfolds there will arise much confusion for those who are not aware of what lies ahead. In order to avoid any of these deceptions, every Christian should read and study what God has written in the book of Revelation.

It is my firm belief that it is Satan's intention to keep us from reading Revelation. To accomplish this, he will tell the believer that what it reveals does not concern him at this point in time, or its contents are too hard to understand, when in actuality, the complete opposite is true. Satan will do whatever it takes to lull the church of Jesus Christ to sleep before making his final stand against God. If the devil can keep the church out of the word of God, the church will be caught unaware as the end closes in. Satan has always sought to thwart God's plans for both Israel and the church. I cannot stress enough how vital it is to know exactly what God's word says concerning the Devil's tactics. Satan, himself, is a student of Scripture who is able to twist its meaning in order to deceive untold millions. He did this in the Garden of Eden (Genesis 3:1-5), as well as in the temptation of our Lord (Matthew 4:1-11). These exercises in Scripture twisting were only warm-ups for his ultimate deception.

The third reason we should study Revelation is that it is relevant to our time in history. So much so, that it is extremely urgent that every believer has an overall understanding of just what this prophetic book has to say. Alarmingly, there is nothing left to be done prophetically, before Revelation's predictions begin to take place. When looking at the present political, social, and religious climate of our day one can begin to see how it eerily parallels what the scriptures say would take place in the days preceding the return of Christ. In the following chapters we will see some very compelling reasons why we may indeed be very near to the return of Jesus Christ.

The fourth reason why Revelation is relevant is because, contrary to what Satan and others would like us to believe, the book of Revelation is not difficult to understand. God has not written this book to conceal, but rather to reveal what is going to occur. Therefore, it is not God who has made this book difficult to comprehend. It has been men with preconceived theologies that tend to make Revelation difficult. These "scholars" try to make the book of Revelation fit their own doctrine of end times. In doing so, many difficult scriptures that do not fit into their framework are allegorized, dispensationalized, or discarded altogether. Many great scholars who insist on a literal reading of inspired Scripture fail, themselves, to hold to this view when teaching Revelation. This book is not an indictment against them, but rather a call to be consistent in the interpretation of Scripture, even if the conclusions reached fly in the face of one's own theology. It must be kept in mind that there are essentials of the Christian faith that are not up for debate, such as the Trinity, redemption at the cross, and the resurrection. Non-essentials, such as who authored the book of Hebrews or the timing of the rapture, should be debated but only in a genuine search for biblical truth. The edification and preparedness of the body of Christ should be the ultimate focus of any study of prophetic Scripture.

We have approached an era where God has taken off the blinders and has begun to reveal to His faithful what the book of Revelation is saying. Over the past 150 years there has been an incredible explosion of interest in the study of Bible prophecy. This is because recent generations have had the benefit of history, which has helped to unlock many of the difficult scriptures. With each passing decade the church has gained a clearer understanding of the events that will unfold, as the return of Jesus appears to draw closer. The very fact that men are now able to understand God's prophetic timetable, is in itself a fulfillment of the words of Daniel, concerning the study of Bible prophecy:

> But you, Daniel, shut up the words, and seal the book until the time of the end; many shall run to and fro, and knowledge shall increase. (Daniel 12:4)

In context, one of the Lord's angels is telling Daniel that at the time of the return of Jesus, knowledge concerning the prophecies outlined in his book would increase. What Revelation is to the New Testament, the book of Daniel is to the Old Testament. In fact, it would be quite impossible to comprehend many of the symbols used in Revelation, without understanding their interpretations as given to the prophet Daniel. It is interesting that today there is a great amount of understanding about what the book of Daniel reveals concerning end-time prophecy. The book of Daniel is, in a sense, the Revelation of the Old Testament. Within its pages are contained the most extensive details concerning the empires that would persecute Israel, the rise of the Antichrist, and the great tribulation. Because of the incredible amount of understanding God has granted concerning Daniel's writings, there has been a great unveiling of the words of Revelation. Daniel was specifically told by God to seal his book. The Apostle John is told to do just the opposite, with the book of Revelation:

> And he said to me, "Do not seal the words of the prophecy of this book, for the time is at hand." (Revelation 22:10)

Because of the wisdom of many great men who have spent their lives studying these prophecies, and the benefit of our place in history, we are at a point where the words of Revelation have literally opened up. This is the very reason why Satan does not want believers to read and understand what is written in Revelation. He knows that his time is short and his ultimate defeat is almost upon him. Satan would like nothing better than to catch the church of Christ unaware as he spins his awesome web of deception. Hopefully, this book will help believers to study Revelation, as well as the rest of God's word, in order to be better prepared to stand against the enemy.

AUTHOR'S APPROACH TO REVELATION

Hermeneutics For Our Study

The word "Hermeneutic" comes from the Greek word "Hermeneuo," which means to interpret or explain.[1] Hermeneutics is the science of studying Scripture. One's hermeneutic will determine one's view of how a biblical text is to be understood. Being that the Bible is the Holy Word of God, one must choose a very strict hermeneutic. There are many differing views when it comes to the study of Revelation. Because it would take a book in itself to explain these many viewpoints, I am just going to relate my specific approach to Revelation.

Literal Interpretation: I believe that the book of Revelation is to be interpreted literally, in its most natural sense. One needs to pursue the clearest, simplest, and most obvious meaning of each passage. If symbolism is employed, then the symbol's literal meaning must be interpreted in comparison with other Scripture. It is the author's belief that unless the text itself indicates that it should be interpreted symbolically or figuratively, Revelation should always be interpreted literally. Too many commentators have created bad teaching on this book by allegorizing it. We should not look for any hidden meanings. Only one meaning should be given to any text unless it is assigned another meaning from a different portion of Scripture. When a second meaning is assigned, independently, it is often subject to the theology of the interpreter, and not to the sovereignty of God's word. If God states a symbol represents something, we cannot say that what we are told it is to represent, really represents something else. The word of God must speak for itself. It means what it says, and it often says exactly what it means.

Context: One of the most important aspects of a proper biblical study involves the context of a scripture. The book of Revelation must be understood in its overall context, along with each individual scripture in Revelation being understood as to how it relates with the overall context of the entire book. Therefore, one must compare scripture with scripture, not with just any scripture, but only with that scripture to which the same context applies. Also, seeming contradictions in God's word are never accepted. God's word does not, and cannot, contradict itself. If the prophet Daniel sees one thing, and John, in Revelation, sees another, and they seem to contradict one another, it does not negate the truth of God's word. It is just that there has not been found a common denominator that harmonizes what seems to be a contradiction. One must not, however, attempt to contrive a system in which all these verses harmonize; the word of God itself should reveal this system.

Chronological Order: It is my firm belief that the very context of Revelation demands that it be interpreted chronologically. There are chapters in which John goes back to re-describe events that have previously taken place. These are commonly known as parenthetic chapters. When one comes upon these parenthetic chapters, they also should be interpreted chronologically as they relate to the overall context of the entire book. As we will see, John will give enough information within these parenthetic chapters to tell us where on God's outline they are to be applied. Basically, if one remembers that there are seven seals, and the opening of the seventh seal reveals seven trumpet judgments, and the blowing of the seventh trumpet, reveals seven bowls and all the parenthetic chapters give greater details on these judgments, one will be able to understand the basic outline of Revelation.

Futurist/Pre-millenal: I believe that the prophecies outlined in the book of Revelation are still future. None of the events presented therein have yet taken place. We are presently seeing their preparation, but we have not seen their fulfillment. I also hold to the pre-millenal view presented by the book of Revelation. This is the belief that Jesus Christ will return before the 1000 year Millennium: first to take His church (the rapture), to restore the nation of Israel, destroy Antichrist, and to set up a literal (1000 year) Millennial Kingdom that will rule the earth.

Pre-Wrath Rapture: I am convinced that Revelation teaches that before the great outpouring of God's wrath, Jesus will come to gather His church from the earth. Unfortunately, before this gathering takes place, the church will undergo a tremendous time of persecution from the Antichrist. I know many sincere Christians do not like this view, neither do I. For ten years I lived, believed, and taught, a Pre-tribulation rapture (the view that Jesus takes His church out prior to the persecution by Antichrist). But often, certain scriptures that did not coincide with my 'beliefs" were just not addressed, or had to be glossed over and "dispensationalized". My study of the church fathers along with books written by Marvin Rosenthal, and Robert Van Kampen forced me to deal with those scriptures in ways that were not comforting. I truly believe that if one listens unbiased to the statements of Jesus, along with the words of Paul and the Apostle John, the Pre-wrath view is evident and it harmonizes the difficult scriptures that I, along with many others, used to struggle with. If the Pre-wrath view is the correct view, then it is imperative the church of Jesus Christ awake out of its spiritual slumber. If we do not prepare ourselves now, we may be like the five foolish virgins who were also not prepared. Jesus told them " . . .' Assuredly, I say to you, I do not know you.' "(Matthew 25:12). These are not the words one wants to hear when brought before the throne of the Lord Jesus Christ. Concerning the timing of the rapture, I am going to stay consistent with my proposed chronological view of Revelation. When John says the rapture occurs, that is where it should occur and it must agree with all other scriptures that are concerned with the timing of the rapture. Basically, I am going to stay consistent with where Scripture places the rapture, and not where I would prefer it to be placed. This will become evident as all the scriptures are presented.

I hope and pray that I will remain completely congruent with the above views presented. I am not claiming any type of new or special knowledge about the book of Revelation, only a desire to unveil the truth of what God has said about the second return of Christ.

The purpose of this book is neither to sensationalize nor to trivialize the word of God. By this work, I hope to present a sound scriptural base for others to study this amazing prophetic text. If the results of what I write are not pleasing to men, then so be it. I would much rather be true to the word of God than to be revered in the eyes of men. I also wish to present an outline of end-time events that correlates completely with all the other scriptures that also refer to these same events. This chronology should be completely consistent, not contradicting what God has said. Hopefully, what is presented will make clear many of the more difficult verses of Revelation. Most of these difficult passages were solved when I stayed inside of scriptural history instead of going to what is known from secular history (This will be very evident especially when Revelation chapter 17 is presented).

Finally, the primary endeavor of this book is to help believers prepare for the great wrath of the Antichrist. A time is coming where every Christian will have to choose whom he will serve: Jesus Christ or the Antichrist. It will be a period when brother will turn against brother, and those in the church will be scrambling to the leadership for answers. Unless we know the truth of God's word, we may very well believe the lies of Satan's false messiah. I cannot stress enough that each believer must read and know these things for themselves. We can no longer listen to man's words; we must listen to God's words. It is my desire that our study of Revelation will be consistent with all of God's word.

> And those of the people who understand shall instruct many; yet *for many* days they shall fall by the sword and flame, by captivity and plundering. Now when they fall, they shall be aided with a little help; but many shall join with them by intrigue. And some of those of understanding shall fall, to refine them, purge them, and make them white, *until* the time of the end; because it is still for the appointed time. (Daniel 11:33-35)

2
SOME PROPHETIC BACKGROUND

BEFORE NARROWING OUR FOCUS to the book of Revelation, it would be beneficial to cover some of the biblical events that have occurred which show that we are possibly in the last days. In order to have a confidence in the reliability of the prophetic signs given by the Bible, it would be wise to know exactly what God's standard for a prophet was. There are many today, who claim to be prophets from God. Most of these individuals have made various inaccurate predictions concerning the second return of Christ. By claiming that they know the exact day and hour of the return of Jesus, they have led many believers astray. Christians have sold their belongings and hunkered down in bomb shelters, awaiting the predicted destruction. Upon the realization that the predictions were inaccurate some have lost faith, while others blindly continue to follow the "prophet," who awaits for further instructions from above. The disturbing thing is that a majority of these so-called "prophets" are not prophets of God at all. They are, in effect, false prophets who lead those who believe them into false doctrines. These difficulties with false prophets will continue to increase as the second advent of Jesus approaches.

THE TRUE PROPHET

Scripture makes a clear distinction between a true prophet of God and a false prophet, as well as what was to be done when someone prophesied in the Lord's name falsely. In the book of Deuteronomy the Lord tells Moses very clearly how to tell who is a false prophet:

> I will raise up for them a Prophet like you from among their brethren, and will put My words in his mouth, and He shall speak to them all that I commanded Him. And it shall be *that* whoever will not hear My words, which He speaks in My name, I will require *it* of him. But the prophet who presumes to speak a word in My name, which I have commanded him to speak, or he who speaks in the name of other gods, that prophet shall die. And if you say in your heart, **"How shall**

> **we know the word which the Lord has not spoken?"-** when a Prophet speaks in the name of the Lord, if the thing does not happen or come to pass, that *is* the thing which the Lord has not spoken; the prophet has spoken it presumptuously; you shall not be afraid of him. (Deuteronomy 18:18-22) {*Emphasis Mine*}

The only way to know a true prophet from a false prophet is to test whether or not what is predicted comes to pass. A biblical prophet had to be one hundred percent accurate one hundred percent of the time. There was absolutely no room for error; if the prophecy failed, the prophet was to be killed. The Lord also warned Israel about false prophets who would prophesy accurately but promote false gods:

> If there arises among you a prophet or a dreamer of dreams, and he gives you a sign or a wonder, and the sign or the wonder comes to pass, of which he spoke to you, saying, "Let us go after other gods which you have not known, and let us serve them," you shall not listen to the words of that prophet or that dreamer of dreams, for the Lord your God is testing you to know whether you love the Lord your God with all your heart and with all your soul. (Deuteronomy 13:1-3)

Many would do well by applying the rules concerning false prophets that have been given to us by God. In recent decades there have been scores of people, both religious and secular, who are claiming to give prophetic utterances. God strictly warns believers to test these prophets to: one, see if they are prophesying with one hundred percent accuracy, and two, to check the religious beliefs and theology of these individuals. If the God they promote is not the God of the Bible, then no matter how accurate they are, one is not to listen to them. If the above rules had been carefully adhered to, many followers of false prophets like Jim Jones or David Koresh would be alive today. In light of these passages, one may ask how God's word, itself, has done as far as its prophetic accuracy.

THE ACCURACY OF BIBLICAL PROPHECY

Although the prophecies contained within the book of Revelation have not yet come to pass, we can believe that they will, based on the amazing track record of the fulfillment of Bible prophecy. Probably the most astounding of these, are the over three hundred specific prophecies that were made concerning the life, death, and resurrection of Jesus Christ. These prophecies were fulfilled in the exact manner that the scriptures predicted they would be. For example, in Isaiah 7:14, the prophet states that Jesus would be born from a virgin. Meanwhile, the prophet Micah, in chapter 5:2, declares that His birth would take place in the city of Bethlehem. What's astounding is that both these men predicted this, literally, hundreds of years before the birth of Christ! King David predicts, in Psalms 22:16-17, that Jesus would suffer death by crucifixion. This was a method of execution that would not be developed until hundreds of years after David even penned Psalm 22. The unbelievable precision of Bible prophecy has led many to a critical study in the statistics of biblical accuracy. In looking at the statistical likelihood of just eight of these prophecies being fulfilled in the life of Jesus, Professor Peter Stoner, using the modern science of probabilities, concluded that the chances would be 1 in 10^{17}, or 1 in 100,000,000,000,000,000.[1] The odds of just eight of these prophecies coming true are absolutely staggering. In light of these incredible odds, it must be remembered that there were over three hundred of these prophecies fulfilled in the life of Christ alone; all with one hundred percent accuracy.

In addition to prophecies concerning the first coming of Jesus, there are those that have already been fulfilled that pertain to world history. One of the best known of these is the prophet Ezekiel's prediction of the destruction of the ancient city of Tyre. In Ezekiel chapter 26:3-7, the prophet states that the armies of the king of Babylon, Nebuchadnezzar, would come and destroy the city of Tyre. Eventually, it is stated that the entire city would be thrown into the sea. In fact, Ezekiel states that the very dirt would be scraped off to the bare rock, and Tyre would become a place for fishermen to cast their nets. A study of ancient history reveals that three years after this prophecy was made, Nebuchadnezzar laid siege and eventually captured the mainland city of Tyre.[2] The second part of the prophecy, concerning the tossing of the city into the sea, remained unfulfilled until the time Alexander the Great. Alexander wanted to conquer the island city of Tyre, which was off the coast of the previously destroyed mainland city of Tyre. Since he did not have a fleet to attack this island city, he quickly ordered his men to throw the debris from the destroyed city into the sea to make a causeway. In doing this, his armies even scraped the ground down to the bare rock; throwing it in the sea to create this causeway. Today, the city of Tyre has not been rebuilt and a small fishing village exists where it once sat.[3] It is the accurate fulfillment of scriptures such as the one above, that put the Bible on a prophetic level of its own. God has also made many detailed prophecies concerning the land of Israel and the state of its people preceding the return of Christ. It is the prophecies that deal with the nation of Israel, that unlock the key to the whole end-time prophetic scenario.

GOD'S GREAT PROPHETIC TIMETABLE

In His dealings with Israel, God always gives specific prophetic time frames. For example, God told Abraham that his people would be slaves in Egypt for 400 years, and then they would be delivered (Genesis 15:13). He also informed Jeremiah that the Jewish nation would be led away in captivity to Babylon for 70 years, before finally being restored to the land (Jeremiah 25:11). History shows that both of these prophecies were fulfilled with incredible precision.

The Seventy Weeks

The most crucial prophecy in all of Scripture, concerning God's dealings with Israel, is Daniel's prophecy of the Seventy Weeks. A proper understanding of this prophecy will make the study of Revelation much easier to grasp. In Daniel chapter nine, after a long prayer petitioning God about His plans for the nation of Israel, an angel reveals to Daniel that:

> Seventy Weeks are determined For your people and your holy city, To finish the transgression, To make an end of sins, To make reconciliation for iniquity, To bring in everlasting righteousness, To seal up vision and prophecy, And to anoint the Most Holy. (Daniel 9:24)

The word used here for week is the Hebrew word for weeks, or heptads: "Shabuwa".[4] The word in this context has the meaning of "a seven," or literally a week of seven years. The angel is basically telling Daniel that 70 weeks of seven years, or 490 years, are determined upon Israel for God to complete His redemptive work with them. It is interesting to note that in the gospel of Matthew when Peter asks Jesus how many times one should forgive his brother, He answers seventy times seven, or 490 times (Matthew 18:22). This is the exact amount of time that God has given Israel to atone for their sins in rejecting their Messiah. In this prophecy, Daniel is also given specific information as to when the countdown for the 490 years is to begin:

> Know therefore and understand, *That* from the going forth of the command to restore and rebuild Jerusalem until Messiah the Prince, *There shall* be seven weeks and sixty two weeks; The street shall be built again, and the wall, even in troublesome times. (Daniel 9:25)

The prophecy states that from the issue of the decree to restore and rebuild Jerusalem, until the advent of the Messiah, there will be 69 weeks of years (69*7). (One must remember that Israel was in captivity to Babylon at the time that Daniel was writing this prophecy). This would then amount to 483 prophetic Hebrew years, (a prophetic year consisted of 360 days), or 173,880 days (483*360), from the date of the decree. It is known from history, and from the biblical book of Nehemiah (Nehemiah 2:1), that this decree was issued by King Artaxerxes Longimanus in the first day of the Jewish month of Nissan in the twentieth year of his rule. This exact day was computed by the Royal Observatory, Greenwich, United Kingdom as being March 14, 445 B.C.[5] If one counts forward the 173,880 days from date of this decree, it would bring one to the tenth day of the Jewish month of Nissan A.D. 32, or April 6 A.D. 32. This was the exact moment that Jesus Christ marched into Jerusalem on a donkey, presenting Himself as Israel's Messiah. The Jewish government rejected Jesus as their Messiah, and only days later had Him crucified by the Roman government. His rejection and crucifixion were predicted in the following verse of Daniel's prophecy:

> And after the sixty-two weeks Messiah shall be cut off, but not for Himself; And the people of the prince who is to come Shall destroy the city and the sanctuary. The end of it *shall be* with a flood, And till the end of the war desolations are determined. (Daniel 9:26)

As stated above, after Jesus was rejected He was to be "cut off" or killed. Then, just as predicted, the city and the Temple (Sanctuary) were completely destroyed by Titus and the Roman legions, only 40 years later, in A.D. 70. The Jewish people were then dispersed into all nations just as Moses had revealed many years earlier (Deuteronomy 28:64-66). When Israel rejected their Messiah, God's countdown on the prophetic timetable stopped at the 69th week. For it was stated to Daniel, that the 70 weeks were "For your people and for your holy city"(Daniel 9:24). God's prophetic clock would not begin again until the people of Israel were back in their land and in possession of Jerusalem.

Since Israel's rejection of their Messiah, God has shifted His work primarily to the Gentiles. We are now in what is known as the church age, God's great parenthesis so to speak. The church age was a mystery that was not revealed in the Old Testament; this is pointed out by the Apostle Paul:

> the mystery which has been hidden from ages and from generations, but now has been revealed to His saints. To them God willed to make known what are the riches of the glory of this mystery among the Gentiles: which is Christ in you, the hope of glory. (Colossians 1:26-27)

Because the church age was not revealed until the resurrection of Jesus, many of the Old Testament prophecies concerning the coming of the Messiah tend to meld His first and second advents into one verse or verses. An excellent example to show that the two comings are often linked together is found in the Lord's reading of Isaiah, as is recorded in Luke's gospel. In his text, Luke writes that Jesus stood to do a reading in the synagogue. Jesus turned specifically to the book of Isaiah and read the following:

> *The Spirit of the Lord is upon Me, Because He has anointed Me to preach the gospel to the poor. He has sent Me to heal the broken hearted, To preach deliverance to the captives And recovery of sight to the blind, To set at liberty those who are oppressed, To preach the acceptable year of the Lord.* (Luke 4:18-19)

After reading these words, the Lord told the congregation that on that very day was the fulfillment of Isaiah's predictions. Curiously, Jesus stops His reading in the middle of verse two. This is because the second half of the verse refers to the Lord's second coming, in which He will take vengeance on God's enemies (Isaiah 61:2). Jesus ends His reading there, because the fulfillment of the remainder of the prophecy would not occur until His second advent. The complexity of this particular type of biblical prophecy was one of the main reasons that the Jews failed to recognize Jesus as their Messiah. Because of this, they also failed to discern the signs of the times; even though Daniel gave the exact day of the Messiah's coming to them. The ancient Rabbis could not rectify the verses that spoke of a suffering Messiah, with those that spoke of a conquering Messiah. In fact, Rabbis began to postulate that there would be two Messiahs: A suffering Messiah, called Messiah Ben Joseph or Messiah son of Joseph, along with a conquering Messiah, called Messiah Ben David or Messiah son of David. This is why, in the scriptures, Jesus was often referred to as the Son of David.

The Jews, at the Lord's first coming, were looking for a Messiah to destroy Rome and return Israel to its former glory. When Jesus failed to do this, He was rejected by the Jewish government (the Sanhedrin) and crucified. To this day the Jewish people, as a nation, fail to recognize that Jesus was their Messiah. God is going to use the last remaining week (7 years) of Daniel's Seventy Weeks to bring the nation of Israel to believe in Jesus as their Messiah. This last week of seven years is what is often referred to as the Seventieth Week of Daniel. The beginning of the Seventieth Week is contingent upon two factors:

1. The Jewish people must be back in the land of Israel, as a nation. (Daniel 9:24)

2. The Jewish people also must be back in possession of the Holy City of Jerusalem. (Daniel 9:24)

Back In The Land

Amazingly, God told the prophet Ezekiel nearly the exact day that Israel would return to the land of Israel, as a sovereign nation, before the Seventieth Week would begin. This prophecy's fulfillment, summarized below, is fully documented in author Grant Jeffrey's book Armageddon Appointment with Destiny. In the book of Ezekiel, God gives the prophet some strange instructions:

> . . . This *will be* a sign to the house of Israel. Lie also on your left side, and lay the iniquity of the house of Israel upon it. *According* to the number of days that you lie on it, you shall bear their iniquity. For I have laid on you the years of their iniquity, according to the number of the days, three hundred and ninety days; so you shall bear the iniquity of the house of Israel. And when you have completed them, lie again on your right side; then you shall bear the iniquity of the house of Judah forty days. **I have laid on you a day for each year**. (Ezekiel 4:3-6) {*Emphasis Mine*}

The Lord told Ezekiel that God would judge Israel a total of 430 years (390 + 40) for their iniquity. The judgment would involve them being thrown out of the land of Israel. The first portion of this judgment began in 606 BC when the Jews were carried away to Babylon for 70 years. They were then allowed to return to the land in 536 BC. If one deducts the 70 years of judgment from the total number of years given to Ezekiel (430), one is left with 360 years of remaining disbursement for Israel. In the book of Leviticus God states that if Israel does not repent after being punished, her judgment would be multiplied seven times:

> I will set My face against you, and you shall be defeated by your enemies. Those who hate you shall reign over you, and you shall flee when no one pursues you. And after all this, if you do not obey Me, then **I will punish you seven times more for your sins**. (Leviticus 26:17-18) {*Emphasis Mine*}

Since Israel did not repent after coming from the land of Babylon, the remaining years of God's judgment would be multiplied by seven, yielding 2520 Hebrew years (360*7), before Israel would once again be restored as a sovereign nation. 2520 Hebrew years of 360 days would be a total of 907,200 days (2520*360). If one then converts this to solar years, by dividing 907,200 by 365.25, one ends up with 2483.8 solar calendar years of remaining judgment. The Jews returned from Babylon in the spring of 536 BC after the decree of Cyrus. If one takes the spring 536 BC and adds the 2483.8 remaining years of judgment, one is brought to the spring of the year of 1948. Incredibly, the nation of Israel was restored in the spring of 1948 on May 14th.[6] The nation of Israel was reborn in exact fulfillment of Ezekiel's prophecy.

The Seventy Weeks of Daniel

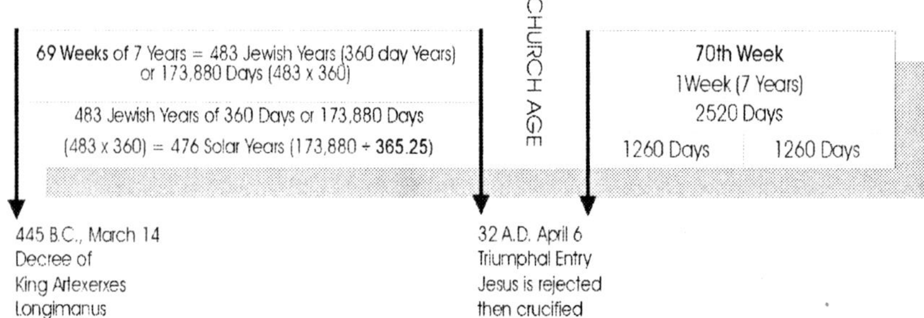

The Years of Judgment Predicted by Ezekiel

Judgment Predicts 430 Years of chastisement (Ezekiel 4:3-6)

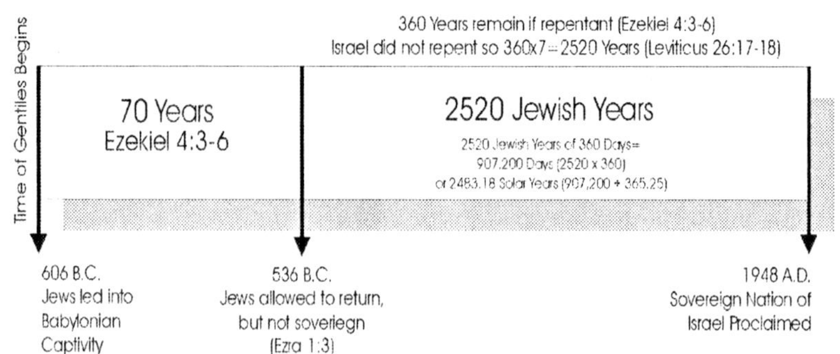

The Possession of Jerusalem

Since the Jewish people had returned to the land in 1948, one of the requirements for the prophetic clock to start ticking again had been accomplished. Yet, they were still not in possession of the city of Jerusalem. Then, in 1967 the unimaginable occurred. Israel was about to be attacked by her surrounding Arab neighbors and it looked like there would be no hope for the tiny nation. Incredibly, in a daring preemptive strike Israel virtually wiped out the entire military of her aggressors. In six short days, Israel's armies had totally defeated the Arabs and had taken new areas of land that included the Golan Heights, the Gaza strip, the West Bank, and most importantly the city of Jerusalem. Since that time, Israel and Jerusalem have become a trouble spot upon which all the eyes of the world have been focused. The six-day war, in 1967, brought Israel into possession of the city of Jerusalem. With its capture, the world was brought one step closer to the greatest fulfillment of Bible prophecy that will ever be witnessed. Soon, the last week of Daniel's prophecy will begin. Israel will come to believe in their Messiah and the whole world will witness it.

So when does the countdown of the last seven years of God's plan begin? Again, the prophet Daniel is very specific as to the commencement of the Seventieth Week:

> Then he shall confirm a covenant with many for one week; But in the middle of the week He shall bring an end to sacrifice and offering. And on the wing of abominations shall be one who makes desolate, Even until the consummation, which is determined, Is poured out on the desolate. (Daniel 9:27)

The "he" referred to is the "prince who is to come" of Daniel 9:26. As we will later see, this person is none other than the Antichrist. According to Daniel, the last seven-year period for Israel begins with a confirmation of a covenant, or treaty, by Antichrist with Israel and many other nations. Isaiah refers to this covenant as Israel's treaty with death:

> Because you have said, "We have made a covenant with death, And with Sheol we are in agreement. When the overflowing scourge passes through, It will not come to us, For we have made lies our refuge, And under falsehood we have hidden ourselves." (Isaiah 28:15)

There are many more details concerning this treaty and Antichrist, which will be discussed in-depth at a later time. At this point, let it suffice to say that Scripture reveals that a man with great political powers will enter into a peace alliance between Israel and her Arab neighbors. When this treaty is confirmed, or enforced, God's prophetic timetable for the last seven-year period, and the return of Jesus Christ will begin. One only needs to read the news to understand that the world is extremely close to seeing this type of treaty come to pass. Israel has already made serious attempts to broker a final peace agreement with the Palestinians and Jordanians, and is working to achieving similar peace agreements with Syria, and the rest of her Arab enemies. It is very likely that Jerusalem may become a divided city, with the east portion going to the Arabs, and the west to the nation of Israel. In this agreement it is foreseeable that Israel, in exchange for the east portion of Jerusalem, will be allowed to rebuild their temple. The outcome, however, remains to be seen. What most people fail to recognize is that these agreements and concessions do not just happen. When two nations want to make peace they will often have a third nation act as a neutral arbitrator. In the case of the Oslo peace accord with the Palestinians, representatives from Norway helped to get the two opposing parties to hammer out a peace accord. Without the behind-the-scenes negotiations with Norway, this agreement may have never come about. It will be no different with the Antichrist. He will be the political master who will capture the attention of the entire world when he is able to confirm a peace agreement with Israel and her enemies. God tells Israel that this is not only a big mistake for them, but it is also a big mistake for the entire world. What takes place during the seven years following this treaty is outlined with incredible detail in God's word, most specifically in the book of Revelation. With the above prophetic background in mind, let us enter God's final plan for the ages: **REVELATION**.

3
REVELATION UNSEALED
(The things, which you have seen)

THE BOOK OF REVELATION, also known as the Apocalypse, is the final book of the Bible. It contains the very last of the inspired words of our Lord Jesus Christ. Revelation closes the cannon of Scripture. Any written words that are attributed to be from the mouth of God, coming after the book of Revelation, are nothing more than lies. As we read previously, God has promised grave consequences to those that would add or take away from the Apocalypse, (Revelation 22:18-19) or any book of Scripture for that matter.

THE DATE OF REVELATION

Most evangelical scholars place the date of Revelation's writing somewhere between 90-95 A.D.. This was the accepted period given to us by the early church fathers. Early believers like Irenaeus, Clement of Alexandria, Origen, Victorinus, Eusebius, and Jerome all confirm this date.[1] There are those who would like to see Revelation's inception at an earlier date before A.D. 70. These scholars feel that all the events described in Revelation were fulfilled in the destruction of Jerusalem at the hands of the armies of Rome. While there was tremendous bloodshed and death during this siege, it does not even begin to compare to the type of destruction that will begin to unfold when God's wrath arrives. I could cite many reasons why the events outlined in Revelation were not fulfilled in the destruction of Jerusalem, but once one begins to see the absolute immensity of the judgments of God, one will realize the inconsistencies of holding to an early date. The earth has not yet seen the period of destruction depicted within Revelation.

ITS AUTHORSHIP

The author of Revelation is Jesus Christ. Its message was entrusted to His Holy Angel, to be recorded by the beloved Apostle John. John basically transcribed what Jesus revealed would occur as the events of the Seventieth Week unfolded. The Apocalypse was accepted by virtually all the early church fathers as being a genuine writing of the Apostle John. Of late, there has been much speculation that John could not be the author of Revelation because the book's internal writing style is very different from that of John's previous texts. The Apocalypse contains a unique literary style that extensively employs Hebrew idioms. These idioms are often not expressed grammatically correct when translated into the Greek language. One of the reasons for the large volume of these Hebrew idioms, is that there are over 285 references to the Old Testament within the book of Revelation; the most of any New Testament book.[2] Concerning the question of Revelation's authorship, based on internal evidence, Robert Thomas Professor of New Testament language and literature at Masters Seminary states:

> One's use of internal criteria can and often does become quite subjective, allowing him to prove just about anything he sets out to prove. Sometimes, when there is no such consensus among the ancients, one must rely on internal matters, as is the case with the epistle to the Hebrews. But to use internal evidence to counteract a consistent tradition coming from the earliest period of church history is ill advised.[3]

As stated above, the early church fathers almost unanimously accepted John's authorship for Revelation. It is also interesting to note that John's gospel does not include the events preceding the Second Coming, revealed in Christ's Olivet Discourse, as is found in the other three gospels. It may be that the Holy Spirit did not have John record the Olivet Discourse in his gospel because, at a later time, Jesus would give him even greater details concerning those end-time events. Revelation is in complete agreement with the Olivet Discourse, where Christ revealed the events what would occur before His return (Matthew 24). Revelation goes past the events outlined at Olivet into details concerning the Day of the Lord and the Millennial kingdom.

THE INTRODUCTION

The Revelation of Jesus Christ, which God gave Him to show His servants things which must shortly take place. And He sent and signified *it* by His angel to His servant John, who bore witness to the word of God, and to the testimony of Jesus Christ, and to all things that he saw. Blessed *is* he who reads and those who hear the words of this prophecy, and keep those things that are written in it; for the time *is* near. (Revelation 1:1-3)

John reveals that his text is really the Revelation of Jesus Christ. It is important to observe as we proceed that what Christ reveals in the Revelation is in complete agreement with what is revealed in the gospels. An angel is sent to John to assist him in recording and understanding what Jesus is about to disclose. Of what is to be revealed, it is said that it would "shortly take place." I am persuaded that, within the context of Revelation, this verse is referring to the actual duration of time for the scenario outlined to occur. That is to say that, these events that are detailed will take place in a very short span of time (Seven Years). It is then disclosed that what is written has been "signified." The use of the particular Greek word "semaino," for "signified" carries the suggestion of something being expressed by signs.[4] Jesus has chosen to reveal what would occur through the use of symbolic code. Revelation is symbolized or "signified" in such a way that only one, who has an overall knowledge of the Old Testament, as well as the New Testament, can completely understand its symbols. Every symbol used in Revelation can have its interpretation found in other portions of Scripture. It is absolutely vital that in properly interpreting Revelation, one employs the meaning that has been given to these symbols by God's word. To do anything else opens Revelation up to loose interpretations, rather than concrete truths. It is also important to remember that world events should never dictate Revelation's interpretation. Only through other portions of Scripture can the Apocalypse be properly understood.

John then states that he is one who has "bore witness to the word of God, and to the testimony of Jesus Christ." The words John uses to describe himself are extremely important. We will see this same phrase used many times throughout the Apocalypse. In every instance, it always refers to those who are genuine believers in the Lord Jesus Christ, whether they are Jewish or Gentile. While progressing through Revelation, we will begin to see what happens to all those who keep the witness of God and have the testimony of Jesus Christ. The apostle also states that he is writing down the things which he "saw." There are many times in Revelation where John states "I saw" or "I heard"; he also holds entire conversations with those whom he was seeing and hearing. Because of this, I am thoroughly convinced that John did not have a mystical vision. Rather, he was catapulted forward in time to the days preceding the return of Jesus Christ.

Next, as was explained previously, John pronounces a blessing on all those who read and keep the words of the prophecy. Revelation is the only book in all of Scripture, which pronounces this blessing. It is to the advantage of every believer that he or she reads the book of Revelation. This blessing may occur because one needs to understand the entire Bible in order to comprehend Revelation. In trying to gain insight on the Apocalypse one is led to read the entirety of God's word, thus being greatly blessed.

THE SALUTATION

> **John, to the seven churches which are in Asia: Grace to you and peace from Him who is and who was and who is to come, and from the seven Spirits who are before His throne, and from Jesus Christ, the faithful witness, the firstborn from the dead, and the ruler over the kings of the earth. To Him who loved us and washed us from our sins in His own blood, and has made us kings and priests to His God and Father, to Him *be* glory and dominion forever and ever. Amen. Behold, He is coming with clouds, and every eye will see Him, and they *also* who pierced Him. And all the tribes of the earth will mourn because of Him. Even so, Amen. "I am the Alpha and *the* Omega, the Beginning and *the* End," says the Lord' "who is and who was and who is to come, the Almighty."** (Revelation 1:4-8)

The destination of this letter was to seven churches in the region of Asia Minor. There were many churches at the time of Revelation's writing, but John was told to write specifically to these seven churches. The Apocalypse however, was not written for only the eyes of these seven churches. This is evident that in verse one, it is said to be written for all of Christ's servants. Jesus chose these particular congregations, because He was going to address issues in these churches that would be important for all believers; especially those who will be around to witness His return.

John then extends greetings from the seven Spirits before the throne, and from the Lord Jesus. There has been much debate as to the identity of the seven Spirits since there is only one Holy Spirit. Many feel that this represents the sevenfold ministry of the Holy Spirit as portrayed by the prophet Isaiah (Isaiah 11:2). While this view is interesting, I believe there is a better explanation. In Revelation 5:6, the seven Spirits are equated with being the seven eyes of the Lord Jesus Christ. These seven Spirits are said to be ". . . sent out into all the Earth." The second book of Chronicles and the Prophet Zechariah, also refer to these seven eyes or Spirits:

> For the eyes of the Lord run to and fro throughout the whole earth, to show Himself strong on behalf of *those* whose heart is loyal to Him . . . (2 Chronicles 16:9)

> For who has despised the day of small things? For **these seven** rejoice to see the plumb line in the hand of Zerubbabel. They are the eyes of the Lord, Which scan to and fro throughout the whole earth. (Zechariah 4:10) {*Emphasis Mine*}

It seems safe to conclude that these are, very likely, seven spiritual beings that help to play a part in God's governing over the affairs of men. It is quite possible that they may be the seven angels who will pour out God's wrath upon the earth. They also may be a special class of angelic beings who are created just for the purpose of being the eyes of the Lord.

John then describes the Lord Jesus as being the faithful witness and the firstborn of the dead, whose blood has cleansed us from our sins. This description of Jesus, Himself, as being a faithful witness unto death, is of great importance to those believers who will suffer the persecution of Antichrist. Because of Christ's faithful witness and resurrection, those who will remain faithful to Him during this time also will take part in the resurrection. Since Jesus is the "ruler over the kings of the earth," He has the authority to make His faithful servants "kings and priests" in His kingdom.

The apostle then relates a brief description of the glorious return of Jesus Christ, when "every eye shall see Him." He will be seen by the nation of Israel ("those who pieced Him") and the rest of the unbelieving world. When this occurs, there will be a great mourning because the Day of God's Wrath will commence. This will be seen in greater detail as Revelation unfolds. Jesus is next spoken of as being the "Alpha" and the "Omega." These are the first and last letters of the Greek alphabet. Jesus is implying that He is everything that God has to say about Himself. In the gospel of John, Jesus is referred to as being the Word of God incarnate (John 1:1-5).

Finally, Jesus is described in terms that indicate His eternal existence, ("The Beginning and the End" and the one "who is and who was and who is to come"), as well as terms that describe Him as being "the Almighty." In using these terms, Jesus equates Himself with God with such deliberate terminology that no other meaning can be concluded.

THE REVELATION OF JESUS

> **I, John, both your brother and companion in tribulation, and in the kingdom and patience of Jesus Christ, was on the island that is called Patmos for the word of God and the testimony of Jesus Christ. I was in the Spirit on the**

Lord's Day, and I heard behind me a loud voice, as of a trumpet, saying, "I am the Alpha and the Omega, the First and the Last," and, "What you see, write in a book and send *it* to the seven churches which are in Asia: to Ephesus, to Smyrna, to Pergamos, to Thyatira, to Sardis, to Philadelphia, and to Laodicea." (Revelation 1:9-11)

In verse nine, the Apostle John identifies himself as a companion in tribulation, because of "the word of God and the testimony of Jesus Christ." Since this book is written to believers who will see the great tribulation, John desires to relate to them that he is also one who has suffered as a believer in Jesus Christ. In fact, because of his Christian witness, the Roman emperor Domitian exiled him to the prison island of Patmos. This island, in the Icarian Sea off the coast of Asia Minor, was a rocky barren place that was chosen as a penal settlement by the Romans.[5] John was worshipping here, on the Lord's Day, when he states that he was "in the Spirit." John seems to be detailing, for his readers, a description of how the Holy Spirit inspired God's servants to write the Holy Scriptures. As the Apostle Peter declares:

for prophecy never came by the will of man, but holy men of God spoke *as they were* moved by the Holy Spirit. (2 Peter 1:21)

John is then told by Jesus, who reemphasizes His divinity, to record what he sees in a book and send it to seven specifically named churches in Asia Minor.

Then I turned to see the voice that spoke with me. And having turned I saw seven golden lampstands, and in the midst of the seven lampstands *One* like the Son of Man, clothed with a garment down to the feet and girded about the chest with a golden band. His head and *His* hair *were* white like wool, as white as snow, and His eyes like a flame of fire; His feet *were* like fine brass, as it is refined in a furnace, and His voice as the sound of many waters; He had in His right hand seven stars, out of His mouth went a sharp two-edged sword, and His countenance was like the sun shining in its strength. And when I saw Him, I fell at His feet as dead. But He laid His right hand on me, saying to me, "Do not be afraid, I am the First and the Last. I *am* He who lives and was dead, and behold I am alive forevermore. Amen. And I have the keys of Hades and Death. (Revelation 1:12-18)

John now relates to us, an incredible image of the resurrected Jesus Christ. This Jesus is far more awesome than the son of a carpenter that John knew in his younger days. When Jesus was on earth He was the "Son of Man," a prophet. In this vision He is "the Son of Man," a priest, and when He returns to rule the nations, He will be "Son of Man" reigning as a king.[6] Jesus is dressed in a High Priest's robe as one who is about to judge. He is not, at this point, going to judge the world but to judge His church and not only those named in Asia Minor, but also those who bear the name of Christ during the days preceding His return. Every detail of this description of Jesus has meaning for His church. The Prophet Daniel saw this very same portrait of Jesus:

> I watched till the thrones were put in place, And the Ancient of Days was seated; His garment was white as snow, And the hair on His head *was* like pure wool. His throne was a fiery flame, Its wheels a burning fire; (Daniel 7:9)

Jesus is explained to be in the midst of seven golden lamp stands as a priestly judge. The seven lamp stands, we are told in verse 20, represent the seven churches that Jesus will now be addressing. These churches are representative of the seven types of churches that will exist on earth at the return of Christ. The lamp stand is an appropriate symbol for the churches, because Jesus has told us, that as His followers, we are to be a light to the world (Matthew 5:14-15).

Christ's hair is described as being dazzlingly white, which refers to His being the Ancient of Days, or the Eternal One (Daniel 7:9). This also alludes to His eternal nature, and His perfect wisdom. His eyes are like a burning flame of fire that is able to reveal the inner thoughts of men. Before Him nothing will be hidden, but all things will be brought into the light (Matthew 10:26). His feet of brass are indicative of His impending judgment of the churches. Brass is often times used in Scripture as a symbol of judgment. In fact, many of the temple implements used in the Old Testament sacrificial system were made of brass.

Seen in the Lord's right hand are seven stars; in verse 20 these are said to represent the seven Angels of the seven churches. Because the Greek word used for angels "angelos" also can be interpreted "messenger," there are many who believe that Jesus is referring to seven pastors or leaders of these congregations. I favor the view that the letters are written not to pastors per se, but to men who were representatives of the seven churches without a unique leadership role. These would be men like Epaphroditus and Epaphras who were representatives of Churches in Philippi and Colosse. Although they held no official title that we are aware of, they went to Rome in the name of these churches to assist the Apostle Paul.[7] If, as some believe, the seven stars are really referring to seven Angels, it seems an illogical progression for John to receive a Revelation from an angel of Christ so that he could relay it to other angelic beings.[8] If God wanted to address other angels, He could have eliminated the middle man by speaking directly to these angelic beings, or by having other heavenly servants relay the message.

Seen coming out of Christ's mouth is a two-edged sword representing the word of God, which is said to be:

> . . . living and powerful, and sharper than any two-edged sword, piercing even to the division of soul and spirit, and of joints and marrow, and is a discerner of the thoughts and intents of the heart. (Hebrews 4:12)

This is appropriate symbolism, because in the next part of Revelation Jesus is going to judge the thoughts and intents of the heart of those who claim to carry His name. It also said that His "countenance was like the sun shining in its strength." This statement brings to mind the appearance of Jesus on the Mount of Transfiguration, where as Matthew states, "His face shone like the sun" (Matthew 17:2). Because of the unbelievable magnificence of Christ, John falls down as if dead. The Lord then strengthens John and calms his fears, thus showing His great mercy even in the midst of judgment. After these reassuring words, Jesus continues with statements that reinforce His deity. He stresses His eternal existence by being the "first and the last." Jesus also brings to remembrance His death on the cross, reminding believers that He did partake of death, but is "alive forevermore." The death and resurrection of Jesus is a guarantee of the resurrection of all His servants (Romans 6:5-9). This promise is especially important for the churches because there will be many who will lose their lives for their faith in Christ, during the great tribulation of Antichrist. In the midst of this persecution, believers must always remember that it is Jesus who has the "keys of Hades and Death." He is in complete control at all times and no one can harm a hair on His believers' heads unless he allows it. Satan can throw everything he has against the church of Jesus Christ. In the process he may kill many believers, but he will never prevail against the Lord's elect.

> **Write the things which you have seen, and the things which are, and the things which will take place after this. The mystery of the seven stars which you saw in My right hand, and the seven golden lamstands: The seven stars are the angels of the seven churches, and the seven lampstands which you saw are the seven churches.** (Revelation 1:19-20)

Verse nineteen is extremely important, because it gives us the outline of the book of Revelation. This three-part division relates the past vision of the glorified Christ (Rev. 1:1-20) as "the things which you have seen." The present condition of the churches of Asia Minor (Rev. Chapters 2-3) are described as "the things which are," along with the future events about to begin (Rev. Chapters 4-22) as being "the things that will take place after this." This division of this prophetic book is the most simple and natural way of understanding its contents.[9]

In verse twenty, Jesus explains the meaning of the seven stars and the seven lamp stands. Often, God interprets the symbols used in Revelation for us within its very text. It is crucial to stay with the interpretation that is given. God knows what the symbol means; so why double guess God?

It is of great importance to understand the message that Jesus will now speak to the seven churches.

4
THE SEVEN CHURCHES
(The things, which are)

THE LETTERS TO THE SEVEN CHURCHES hold enormous significance for all those who follow Jesus. In these short epistles, a picture of how the Lord views those who follow Him is presented. They demonstrate that Jesus is always active and knows the motives behind those that say they are His followers. Our Lord does not let sin go unnoticed or unpunished, but He is long-suffering; hoping to bring all to repentance. In Peter's writings, the apostle states that judgment will first begin in the house of God, and then God will judge the world (1 Peter 4:17). Jesus is not judging His believers for their sinfulness, as this was accomplished fully at Calvary. It must be understood that Jesus is using this judgment to separate the true disciples from the false disciples. His true disciples will hold true to Him no matter how great the persecution or deception. One could literally write an entire book just on these seven letters, and, in fact, there are some excellent works that do just that. The scope of this section is to briefly outline the strengths, weaknesses, judgments, and promises given to these seven churches. While many commentators concentrate on the historical aspects of these seven churches, I will focus primarily on the message the Lord speaks to these assemblies.

WHY THESE SEVEN CHURCHES?

There have been many that have asked why Jesus addressed these seven particular assemblies. Surely there were larger or more prominent churches that He could have written. The churches Jesus speaks to were located in an area known then as Asia Minor; equivalent to the western half of modern day Turkey. It seems that this area may play an important role in the rise of the Antichrist, as will become evident in the study of his ascension to power.

The Cities

The seven cities in which these churches were founded formed a circle of approximately one hundred miles in diameter. Ephesus was a center for the worship of the goddess Artemis[1], while Smyrna was a beautiful city known to be a leader in the sciences and medicine.[2] Pergamos was notorious for its intense Caesar-worship, and well known for its extensive library.[3] Thyatira was a commercial city, in which the dyeing and manufacturing of woolen goods was their most prominent industry.[4] Sardis was a place of incredible wealth where the Acropolis had once been the center of all city life.[5] Philadelphia was the hub of Greco-Asiatic civilization and used to spread the Greek language to Lydia and Phrygia.[6] Laodicea was the location of a famous school of medicine that developed a salve to cure eye diseases.[7]

The Near/Far Prophetic Theme

It is crucial to understand that it is not the cities that make these churches special, but it is the churches themselves. Each of these churches has strengths and weaknesses that have been inherent in the body of Christ throughout all of church history. Some have good teaching, while others are filled with bad doctrine and false prophets. Several persevere and overcome under persecution, while others compromise their dedication to Christ. What Jesus is doing in these letters, is preparing His end-time church to face the great deception and persecution of the Antichrist by showing them how these seven churches also faced persecution, deception, and false teachers. In understanding that this is the reason that these letters were written, it is easier to see their relevance to the overall theme of the Apocalypse.

The prophetic style of these letters consists of what are commonly termed near/far prophecies. This particular type of prophecy takes a present happening and applies it to a future situation. This style of prophecy is used in the Old Testament book of Joel. Joel describes a present invasion of locusts and likens it to the future day of God's judgment. The Lord reveals to Joel that His future judgment will make the plague of locusts pale in comparison. In the same manner, Jesus is using the success and failures of these churches to warn the church entering the last days about what is about to come to pass upon them ("The things which will take place after this").

I should note that there is many that hold the view that each of these churches represents a particular age of church history. Although this view is interesting, it opens up a Pandora's Box of possible bad exegesis. For example, if the seven churches are really representative seven church ages, then what does the Isle of Patmos really represent, or what does the Apostle John really represent? One must stay consistent to the view that the most natural, plain meaning of Scripture must be taken. Anything else is open to ones own subjective interpretation of what a passage really means.

Jesus stresses, in Matthew chapter 24, that the deception perpetrated ıntichrist will be so incredible that if it were possible it could deceive the very elect. (Matthew 24:24) Our Lord is giving us ample warning in these letters to test everything and to not deny the faith, no matter what the situation. As was seen in John's vision of Christ, He stands as a judge and He is going to use His judicial discernment to separate the "wheat" from the "tares": the false disciples from the true disciples. In looking at these important words of Christ to the seven churches, let each of us, as individual believer's, examine ourselves as to whether we are really in the faith (2 Corinthians 13:5).

The Seven Churches of Asia Minor

EPHESUS: LOST FIRST LOVE

To the angel of the church of Ephesus write, "These things says He who holds the seven stars in His right hand, who walks in the midst of the seven golden lampstands; I know your works, your labor, your patience, and that you cannot bear those who are evil. And you have tested those who say they are apostles and are not, and have found them liars; and you have persevered and have patience, and have labored for My

name's sake and have not become weary. Nevertheless I have *this* against you, that you have left your first love. Remember therefore from where you have fallen; repent and do the first works, or else I will come to you quickly and remove your lampstand from its place-unless you repent. But this you have, that you hate the deeds of the Nicolatians, which I also hate. He who has an ear, let him hear what the Spirit says to the churches. To him who overcomes I will give to eat from the tree of life, which is in the midst of the Paradise of God." (Revelation 2:1-7)

Jesus introduces Himself as the One "Who holds the seven stars in His right hand, who walks in the midst of the seven golden lamp stands." This shows that Jesus is actively involved in the affairs of His disciples.

He is genuinely concerned as to how His church is progressing. It also reveals that Jesus controls every aspect of His body of believers; nothing happens without His authority. According to our Lord, this assembly has lost its first love (Jesus), and they are in danger of losing their life as a church. They have become a church of routine; going through the motions of Christianity without a love for Christ. This body is made up of Christians who serve out of obligation, and not out of love and dedication. This is a back-slidden church in which false apostles have seen an opportunity to lead away the weak. Paul in His last words to the church at Ephesus, forewarned of this happening:

> For I know this, that after my departure savage wolves will come in among you, not sparing the flock. Also from among yourselves men will rise up, speaking perverse things, to draw away the disciples after themselves. (Acts 20:29-30)

This church is commended as being wise, in that it was able to recognize that these men were false apostles. There is a movement where men are also claiming that they are the "apostles" of the last church age. These so-called "apostles" are claiming the same authority as the original twelve apostles. This is in contrast with the word of God, which states that Jesus built His church upon the foundation of the apostles and prophets (Ephesians 2:20). A foundation, once laid, has no need to be built again. There is therefore, no longer any need for apostles on the level of those who began the early church. There may be those who have been gifted apostolically or prophetically, but there is no one who holds the office of an apostle or prophet as it was held when the church age began. Many arguments can be made in favor of this position, but the strongest one is found in Revelation 21:14, where it is stated that the New Jerusalem is to have twelve foundations. We are further informed that these twelve foundations are to have the names of the Lord's twelve apostles written upon them. It seems rather cruel of the Lord to leave out the great "apostles" of the last church age by only including the first twelve apostles names on the foundations. We would do well to test these men, like the church at Ephesus did. Along with these false apostles is a group that Jesus refers to as the Nicolaitan's. Nikao in the Greek means "to conquer," and laos "People": or conquerors of the people.[8] Some suggest that this was a group who attempted to establish a church hierarchy based on the Roman priesthood. Others say that they were those who practiced immorality under the guise of Christianity. Whatever the case, the thrust of the Lord's message is that all believers must test these men's teaching against the word of God.

This church is also said to have "persevered," and has had "patience" for the name of Christ. These are important terms that are often used in Revelation when the true disciples of Jesus are being spoken of. As the end-time church undergoes the persecution of Antichrist, believers will be called upon to "persevere" and have "patience" in the midst of this persecution.

To those who do not persevere or repent, it is stated that Jesus will come quickly and remove their lamp stand. This indicates that those who deny their faith in Christ will be discarded as being those who were never truly His disciples. Notice that Jesus is also alluding to His Second Coming in reference to this church. This shows that, although He is talking about what is taking place in their specific congregation, it does also apply to what will be happening to the congregations preceding His return. This is confirmed by the fact that Jesus then admonishes them to "hear what the Spirit says to the Churches." This makes the scope of His message apply to all His churches; not just specifically to this small congregation in Asia Minor. The phrase "He who has an ear, let him hear what the Spirit says to the Churches," applies only to those who are true disciples of Jesus. As Paul states:

> But the natural man does not receive the things of the Spirit of God, for they are foolishness to him; nor can he know *them*, because they are spiritually discerned. But he who is spiritual judges all things, yet he himself is *rightly* judged by no one. (1 Corinthians 2:14-15)

Only one who is truly of Christ can have the spiritual ears to comprehend what He is saying.

For those who do persevere and overcome the Antichrist, Jesus promises eternal life. One will be able to partake of the tree of life, which was taken from man's presence after his fall into sin. The tree of life will be restored when Jesus begins His kingdom. Those who have shown themselves to be true followers of Jesus will given open access to the fruit of this tree.

SMYRNA: THE PERSECUTED CHURCH

And to the angel of the church in Smyrna write, "These things says the First and the Last, who was dead, and came to life: I know your works, tribulation, and poverty (but you are rich); and *I know* the blasphemy of those who say they are Jews and are not, but *are* a synagogue of Satan. Do not fear any of those things which you are about to suffer. Indeed, the devil is about to throw *some* of you into prison, that you may be tested, and you will have tribulation ten days. Be faithful until death, and I will give you the crown of life. He who has an ear, let him hear what the spirit says to the churches. He who overcomes shall not be hurt by the second death. (Revelation 2:8-11)

Jesus next addresses a church that is undergoing tremendous affliction. This assembly is a perfect example of how the Lord's church needs to be during the great tribulation of Antichrist. Jesus told His followers that:

> . . . In the world you will have tribulation; but be of good cheer, I have overcome the world. (John 16:33)

Our Lord has never promised that He will take us out of this world's tribulation, but rather He has prayed that we would be kept from the evil one (John 17:15). He promises to give us the strength to overcome, since He also overcame. Jesus addresses this congregation as the one "who was dead, and came to life." This is because there are going to be those in this church who will pay with their life for their faith in Christ. It is interesting to note that Jesus does not tell these disciples that He is going to snatch them out of this situation, but rather that they need to "be faithful unto death" This phrase "be faithful unto death" is in direct contrast with those who claim the end-time church will not see the great tribulation of Antichrist. The argument most often presented is that Jesus stated that the gates of hell would not prevail against His church (Matthew 16:18). Therefore, if the church were to undergo the persecution of Antichrist, it would amount to Satan or the gates of hell prevailing over the church. This line of reasoning ignores the great multitude of believers, across the span of church history, who have undergone incredible persecution. In the first century, the affliction of the church was so great that the floor of the Roman coliseum was literally stained with the martyr's blood. In reading great classics like, Foxes Book of Martyrs, one is often overwhelmed by the tremendous faith and resolve shown by these Christians while under persecution. Yet, in all of this, Satan has not been able to destroy the church of Jesus Christ. The true disciples entering the great tribulation, likewise, may also pay with their lives in resisting the Antichrist. As the prophet Daniel states:

> I was watching; and the same horn (Antichrist) was making war against the saints, and prevailing against them, until the Ancient of Days came, and a judgment was made *in favor* of the saints of the Most High, and the time came for the saints to possess the kingdom. (Daniel 7:21-22)

When it seems that Satan and the Antichrist are going to destroy God's elect, Jesus will cut short the great tribulation and initiate the Day of the Lord. Although Satan may win some battles, he will never win the war. He will not prevail! To "overcome" is to keep the faith and not deny Jesus even in the face of death. Those who resist and overcome will have no fear of the second death. Those who deny Jesus and take the mark of the Antichrist will suffer the second death and there will be no crown of life for them. The faithfulness and perseverance of this church, holds great meaning for the church that enters the last days and the great tribulation.

PERGAMOS: THE LICENTIOUS CHURCH

> **And to the angel of the church in Pergamos write, "These things says He who has the sharp two-edged sword: I know your works, and where you dwell, where Satan's throne is. And you hold fast to My name, and did not deny My faith even in the days in which Antipas *was* My faithful martyr, who was killed among you, where Satan dwells. But I have a few things against you, because you have there those who hold the doctrine of Balaam, who taught Balak to put a stumbling block before the children of Israel, to eat things sacrificed to idols, and to commit sexual immorality. Thus you also have those who hold the doctrine of the Nicolatians, which thing I hate. Repent, or else I will come to you quickly and will fight against them with the sword of My mouth. He who has an ear, let him hear what the Spirit says to the churches. To him who overcomes I will give some of the hidden manna to eat. And I will give him a white stone, and on the stone a new name written which no one knows except him who receives *it*."** (Revelation 2:12-17)

Jesus introduces Himself to this church as "He who has the sharp two-edged sword" Within this church are some real spiritual problems, and Jesus is going to use the sword of the word of God to separate the thoughts and intents of certain members of this assembly. There are, however, true disciples within this congregation who have not denied the faith, even under intense persecution. This church is also said to reside near the throne of Satan. This statement is extremely important. Many scholars make the argument that temple worship was so intense in Pergamos that this is why the Lord referred to it as the throne of Satan. I feel the reference to the throne of Satan goes beyond that argument. This is because there were many other areas in Asia Minor where Satan worship was much more prevalent. I believe that when Jesus said that within this area was the throne of Satan He meant it. Satan's center of operations is in the region of Asia Minor, near the city of Pergamos. I intend to show later that the throne of the Antichrist, himself, will also be in this area. There is, within Pergamos, a true remnant that has not denied their faith. The Lord mentions specifically a man name Antipas as one of His faithful martyrs. Not much is known about Antipas, but legend has it the he was put into a golden calf and roasted alive. In speaking of this man, Jesus again reiterates that this area is "where Satan dwells."

Unlike the assembly at Sardis, who were only commended for their service to the Lord, Pergamos has some problems. The church has allowed those who hold to the doctrine of Balaam, as well as the Nicolaitan's, to be in their midst. The doctrine of Balaam is a reference to the Book of Numbers, chapters 22 to 25. In these passages Balaam, an evil prophet, suggested to Balak, the king of Moab, to invite the children of Israel to an immoral feast. The Israelites accepted the invitation and committed all kinds of sexual immorality with the daughters of Moab. Because of this, God judged Israel and sent a plague that killed 24,000. In a similar manner, this church has allowed false brethren to infiltrate and promote a false doctrine that combines sexual immorality with the eating of things sacrificed to idols.

Jesus states to these false teachers that when He returns it will not be to take them to heaven, but to fight against them with the sword of His mouth. They are not true disciples, and will be judged as such at the Second Coming. Again, we see a shift from the near aspect to the far situation of the Lord's Second Advent employed within these letters.

To those true believers that are able to recognize this false doctrine, and overcome persecution, Jesus promises to give them some of the hidden manna, along with a white stone with a new name written on it. This manna may refer to Jesus as being the true manna, or an allusion to the manna that is in the heavenly Ark of the Covenant; of which the earthly one was patterned after (Revelation 11:19). [9] It also may be a reference to His provision of sustenance for believers during the great tribulation period. It is later disclosed in Revelation, that during this time, no one will be able to buy or sell unless they worship the Antichrist and take his mark. To worship the Antichrist for food would, in a very real sense, amount to eating food in exchange for idolatry. During this period, the Lord will be faithful to provide His believers with food. The promised white stone may be speaking of an ancient practice where white stones with one's name on it, were used for admission to special events and feasts.[10] These true believers who did not spot themselves by unholy feasts, shall be given entrance to the marriage feast of Christ (Revelation 19:7-9).

THYATIRA: THE COUNTERFEIT CHURCH

> **And to the angel of the church in Thyatira write, "These things says the Son of God, who has eyes like a flame of fire, and His feet like fine brass: I know your works, love, service, faith, and your patience; and as for your works, the last are more than the first. Nevertheless I have a few things against you, because you allow that woman Jezebel, who calls herself a prophetess, to teach and beguile My servants to commit sexual immorality and to eat things sacrificed to idols. And I gave her time to repent of her sexual immorality, and she did not repent. Indeed I will cast her into a sickbed and those who commit adultery with her into great tribulation, unless they repent of their deeds. And I will kill her children with death. And all the churches shall know that I am He who searches the minds and hearts. And I will give each one of you according to your works. But to you I say, and to the rest in Thyatira, as many as do not have this doctrine, and have not known the depths of Satan, as they call *them*, I will put on you no other burden. But hold fast what you have till I come. And he who overcomes and keeps My works until the end, to him I will give power over nations--*'He shall rule them with a rod of iron; as the potter's vessels shall be broken to pieces-*-'as I have also received from My Father; and I will give him the morning star. He who has an ear, let him hear what the Spirit says to the churches."** (Revelation 2:18-29)

To this church, Jesus describes Himself as having eyes like flames of fire and feet of fine brass. This is an indication that He is going to uncover the false teaching prevalent within this congregation. He is also going to exert tremendous judgment on those who refuse to repent. First, Jesus commends the true disciples of this church for their works, service, and patience, or perseverance. Unfortunately, they have allowed a false prophet, referred to by the name of Jezebel, to cause those in the church to commit sexual immorality, and to eat things sacrificed to idols. It is my feeling that there was a literal woman named Jezebel, within this assembly, who claimed to be a prophetess. She is much like the Jezebel of the Old Testament who caused Ahab king of Israel to worship idols and commit sexual immorality (1 Kings 21:25-26). This assembly is faced with a false prophet, whereas the congregation at Ephesus was faced with false apostles.

Today, there are many Christians who are looking to, so-called, prophets and prophetesses to find out what God has for their life. Personally, I believe that believers can operate in the prophetic when the Holy Spirit so wills, but I am not convinced that there are any men today with a ministry like that of the prophets. If there are any prophets, they had better be one hundred percent accurate. If they are not one hundred percent accurate, then what they say is not from God. Remember, prophets always claim that their message is directly from the Lord. If what the Lord supposedly spoke through them does not occur, then either they are lying, or the Lord is lying. There is no alternative excuse, or explanation, for their inaccuracy. False prophets, who seemingly have a hot line to God today, like those in Thyatira, have beguiled many believers. Jesus warns, that as the deception of the Antichrist unfolds, many false prophets will arise and they will lead astray many believers (Matthew 24:11). Disciples, who have based their faith more on "signs" and "wonders" from prophets, and less on God's word, will be the first to be deceived.

Jesus also discloses that He has given time for this false prophetess to repent, but that she has refused to do so. Because of this, her, those who commit adultery with her, and all her offspring are going to be thrown into the great tribulation, where they will be killed. The text of the letter now moves forward into its near/far application to the time of the great tribulation. Jesus will use this period to bring destruction to all who prophesy falsely, as well as their followers. Jesus declares that when they are cast into the great tribulation "all the churches shall know that I am He who searches the minds and hearts." This is important, because it shows that the other churches also will be around during this time of tribulation, and they will realize that it is Jesus who has judged these false disciples. It is only the Lord who can judge the hearts and the minds of those who claim to follow Him. He knows the false prophet's motives, and will, Himself, put to an end their fraudulent deceit. In verse 24, Jesus tells the other churches, along with the few faithful in Thyatira, to hold fast until He returns to take them out of the great tribulation.

To those who overcome, they will be given the authority to rule the nations. This authority will be given to believers as they rule with Jesus. They also will be entrusted with the morning star. Believers who overcome are often likened to stars in Scripture (Daniel 12:3). This gift of the morning star enforces the promise of the faithful being rulers alongside of Jesus.

SARDIS: THE DEAD CHURCH

> **And to the angel of the church in Sardis write, "These things says He who has the seven Spirits of God and the seven stars: I know your works, that you have a name that you are alive, but you are dead. Be watchful and strengthen the things which remain, that are ready to die, for I have not found your works perfect before God. Remember therefore how you have received and heard; hold fast and repent. Therefore if you will not watch, I will come upon you as a thief, and you will not know what hour I will come upon you. You have a few names even in Sardis who have not defiled their garments; and they shall walk with Me in white, for they are worthy. He who overcomes shall be clothed in white garments, and I will not blot out his name from the Book of Life; but I will confess his name before My Father and before His angels. He who has an ear, let him hear what the Spirit says to the churches."** (Revelation 3:1-6)

To this congregation Christ describes Himself as the one who has the "seven Sprits of God." These seven Spirits were those that were explained previously as being the eyes of the Lord upon earth. Jesus says that although this church has a prominent name that they are alive, they are really dead. There are many churches today that have extremely large congregations. Many within these churches attend merely because of the incredible worship team, or the magnificent building, but not because of Christ. The age of television has created a mentality among believers that a church service must be fast paced and flashy in order to hold the congregation's interest. Pastors and evangelists are pushed to be charismatic, while preaching sermons that are current and catchy. This worship style breeds a fast food type of church, which is quick in its service, but short in spiritual nutrition. Christianity of this type may create large congregations, but the lack of solid biblical teaching is the very evidence of its deadness. The church at Sardis was just such a church. They were known as being alive for their large congregation and many works, but Jesus pronounces that they are dead spiritually.

Jesus is warning the spiritually dead members of this congregation to be watchful, because they have no idea what is about to come upon them. They are told to remember what they have received and heard, and to get a hold of it and repent. It seems that the Lord is referring to people who have heard the gospel, but have not mixed what has been heard with faith (Hebrew 4:2). Because of this, there are those that attend but are not true disciples. This is evidenced in the next statement, that for these, Christ will return as a thief, and they will not have any warning that this is about to occur. In the Apostle Paul's letter to the Thessalonians, he states that Christ comes as a thief only to the unbelieving world (1 Thessalonians 5:2-4). The true disciples will be looking for the coming of Christ, and will not be caught by surprise. In fact, the elect are commanded to be ready for the Lord's return (Matthew 24:44).

There are said to be those, even in this dead church, who are true believers. To these Jesus promises to provide the white garments that only the righteous will be allowed to wear. Jesus also will not blot their name out of the Lamb's Book of Life, but will confess their name before His father. The unbeliever's names will be blotted out and to them Jesus will pronounce, "I never knew you" (Matthew 7:23). It is interesting to note that those to whom Jesus states "I never knew you," will be the same ones declaring to Him the great works they did on His behalf:

> Many will say to Me in that day, "Lord, Lord have we not prophesied in Your name, cast out demons in Your name, and done many wonders in Your name? And then I will declare to them, "I never knew you; depart from Me, you who practice lawlessness!' (Matthew 7:22-23)

Because they do not truly know the Lord, their works will not be "found perfect before God" (Revelation 3:2). These false disciples will not be numbered among those who are to escape the wrath of God. They will be left to endure the wrath of God along with the rest of the unbelieving world.

PHILADELPHIA: THE FAVORED CHURCH

> **And to the angel of the church in Philadelphia write, "these things says He who is holy, He who is true, *'He who has the key of David, He who opens and no one shuts, and shuts and no one opens'*: I know your works, See, I have set before you an open door, and no one can shut it; for you have a little strength, have kept My word, and have not denied My name. Indeed I will make *those* of the synagogue of Satan, who say they are Jews and are not, but lie-indeed I will make them come and worship before your feet, and to know that I have loved you. Because you have kept My commandment to persevere, I also will keep you from the hour of trial which shall come upon the whole world, to test those who dwell on the earth. Behold, I come quickly! Hold fast what you have, that no one may take your crown. He who overcomes, I will make him a pillar in the temple of My God, and he shall go out no more. And I will write on him the name of My God, and the name of the city of My God, the New**

> **Jerusalem, which comes down out of heaven from My God.** ***And I will write on him*** **My new name. He who has an ear, let him hear what the Spirit says to the churches."** (Revelation 3:7-13)

The Lord begins this letter by revealing that He is holy and true. This is an appropriate description of Himself to a group of believers who are being commended by the Lord as being true and holy disciples. Jesus also introduces Himself as one who has the keys of David (Isaiah 22:22). By this, Jesus is stating that He alone has the authority to let the true saints into His eternal kingdom while withholding entrance to those who are not really His disciples. To this church, because of their faithfulness, He promises an open door into His Messianic Kingdom. There are those who suggest that the Lord is speaking of an open door in terms of spreading the gospel. The problem with this view is that the keys of David are indicative of the Millennial Kingdom and not evangelism. It seems appropriate that these who have kept His word, and not denied His name will be given open access to the kingdom of Jesus Christ. No one will be able to stop them from entering; not even those of the "synagogue of Satan." These are those who call themselves Jews, but are not, because they reject Jesus as Messiah. At the culmination of the Seventieth Week many of these unbelieving Jews will, as a nation, come to believe that Jesus was their promised Redeemer. When they do this, they will then also realize that Jesus indeed loved the Christian believers whom they have persecuted. One day Israel will understand that God also loved the Gentiles and, although kept hidden, did have a plan for their salvation.

The next verse is probably one of the most controversial, and debated, of all of Christ's words to the seven churches. This passage is very easily understood if it is taken, in context, in its most natural sense. The believers Jesus is addressing are those who have kept His "command to persevere" and have not denied His name. They are a group of disciples in the midst of incredible testing, who has shown themselves to be faithful. As more of Revelation unfolds it will be revealed that there will be a period where Satan, through the Antichrist, will vent his fury upon the nation of Israel and the church. It is during this moment where the faithful saints must persevere. Because this church has persevered through the great tribulation, Jesus has promised to keep them from "the hour of trial which shall come upon the whole world to test those who dwell upon the earth." The Apostle Peter declares that judgment will first begin with the house of God, and then it will be upon the world (2 Peter 4:17). This time of judgment, or trial that is to come upon the world, is none other that the Day of The Wrath the Lamb, or the Day of the Lord. This day is referred to as being the "hour of His judgment" by the announcement of the second angel of Revelation 14:7. This is the moment when God will pour out His wrath on the unbelieving world. In this passage, Jesus references the term "those who dwell upon the earth." This phrase, without exception, refers to unbelievers, as well as to those who will give their allegiance to Antichrist. Christians are not "earth dwellers," for we are not of this world (John 17:16). Therefore, it can be simply concluded that, in this passage, Christ is promising the believers who persevere through the persecution of Antichrist that they will be taken off the earth before the Day of God's Wrath begins. For as true disciples, we are to "... wait for His Son from heaven, whom he raised from the dead, *even* Jesus who **delivers us from the wrath to come**."(1 Thessalonians 1:10) {*Emphasis Mine*}

Jesus also tells this church to hold fast because He is coming quickly. Those whom He takes will be a part of the people who populate the new heavenly city, and will receive a new name from the Lord. They will have the very name of God written upon them to show that they belong to Him. This is to contrast true believers with those who accept the mark of the beast, in allegiance to the Antichrist.

LAODICEA: THE LUKEWARM CHURCH

> **And to the angel of the church of the Laodiceans write, "These things says the Amen, the Faithful and True Witness, the Beginning of the creation of God: I know your works, that you are neither cold nor hot. I could wish you were cold or hot. So then, because you are lukewarm, and neither cold nor hot, I will spew you out of My mouth. Because you say 'I am rich, have become wealthy, and have need of nothing'--and do not know that you are wretched, miserable, poor, blind, and naked--I counsel you to buy from Me gold refined in fire, that you may be rich; and white garments, that you may be clothed, that the shame of your nakedness may not be revealed; and anoint your eyes with eye salve, that you may see. As many as I love I rebuke and chasten. Therefore be zealous and repent. Behold, I stand at the door and knock. If anyone hears My voice and opens the door, I will come in and dine with him, and he with Me. To him who overcomes I will grant to sit with Me on My throne, as I also overcame and sat down with My Father on His throne. He who has an ear, let him hear what the Spirit says to the churches.** (Revelation 3:14-22)

To the Laodiceans Jesus describes Himself as "being the faithful and true witness." This description is used to contrast Himself with the lukewarm faithless members of the Laodicean church. Within this assembly are those who "professed Christ hypocritically, but do not have in their hearts the reality of what they pretend to be their actions."[11]

Because the false piety of these so-called "disciples," Jesus states that He will spew, or vomit, them out of His mouth. The Lord also reveals that these members have the audacity to think that they are rich. The members of this assembly felt that they had it all spiritually, because they were blessed materially. The health and wealth gospel, of today's Christianity, preaches that we are rich because we are "the King's kids." Anything that one wants from God is theirs for the asking. Often a believer's spiritual standing is judged by the material wealth he or she possesses. Those who are rich, charismatic, and influential, are given higher priority in the church. This thinking implies that those who are wealthier have somehow gained more favor from God. The very opposite is shown to be true, as the Lord exposes the true spirit of this congregation. Jesus tells them that they are wretched, poor, blind, and naked. Spiritually, these believers are destitute, while materially they are wealthy. Instead of earthly gold, Jesus challenges them to buy from Him gold that has been refined in fire. This brings to remembrance what the Apostle Paul said concerning believers works as the fire of the Lord's judgment tests them. Those that are made of gold, silver, and precious stones will survive, while the worthless will be burned (1 Corinthians 3:12-15)

Jesus is telling this church to purchase heavenly treasure that will pass His scrutiny. With this heavenly treasure they are encouraged to purchase garments to cover their nakedness, as well as salve, so that their spiritual sight is again restored.

There seems to be a miniscule number of truly faithful disciples who are within this congregation. Jesus tells them He is knocking, and if there is anyone who can hear His voice He will let them in. This is very likely the same door that Christ has left open for the believers in the church at Philadelphia. The Laodicean disciples are like the five foolish virgins who forgot to take extra oil with them while waiting for the bridegroom's return. When the door to the wedding entrance was shut they came saying:

> . . . Lord, Lord, open to us! But he answered and said "Assuredly, I say to you, I do not know you." Watch therefore, for you know neither the day nor the hour in which the Son of Man is coming. (Matthew 25:11-13)

The five wise virgins were those who heard His voice and were allowed to enter into the wedding feast. To those within this assembly who overcome, if any, they will be seated alongside Christ on His throne.

It is important to see that Jesus is revealing these problems out of His genuine love and concern for His disciples. The Lord will often rebuke and chastise believers who have lost their way. He does this in order to bring that person, or persons, to repentance and restoration so they may enjoy eternal life.

FINAL THOUGHTS ON THE SEVEN CHURCHES

From what is presented in these seven short epistles, it seems that the body of Christ entering the last days will be weak and sickly. It also will be overwhelmed by false teaching. Many believers will be able to discern these false teachers, while others will openly accept them and be led astray. Idolatry, greed, and sexual immorality also will be prevalent. As the days of the tribulation of Antichrist begin, there will be disciples who persevere and become overcomers. There also will be those who deny their faith and the name of Christ, failing the test of a true disciple. Other heretical congregations will be thrown headlong into the great tribulation, so that the other faithful churches will see the justness of God against these false believers. Finally, there will be those who will be left to enter the Day of the Lord, and they will be destroyed by the wrath of God, Himself.

These words of Jesus have incredible meaning for us as we see many similar types of churches existing in our day. The body of Christ is currently seeing an attack on the Bible from its own members that have been unequaled in church history. We are in a time where the word of God has become secondary to the word of man. May God help us to persevere. "He Who has an ear, let him hear what the Spirit says to the churches."

5
THE THRONE
(The things, which will take place after)

THE APOSTLE JOHN, having just recorded Christ's words to the seven churches of Asia Minor, will now be transported to heaven for a birds eye view of what will happen to the end- time church, as well as, what will occur when the wrath of God is poured out.

> **After these things I looked, and behold, a door *standing* open in heaven. And the first voice which I heard *was* like a trumpet speaking with me, saying, "Come up here, and I will show you things which must take place after this." Immediately I was in the Spirit; and behold, a throne set in heaven, and *One* sat on the throne. And He who sat there was like a jasper and a sardis stone in appearance; and *there was* a rainbow around the throne, in appearance like an emerald. Around the throne *were* twenty-four thrones, and on the thrones I saw twenty-four elders sitting, clothed in white robes; and they had crowns of gold on their heads. And from the throne proceeded lightnings, thunderings, and voices. And *there were* seven lamps of fire burning before the throne, which are the seven Spirits of God. Before the throne *there was* a sea of glass, like crystal. And in the midst of the throne, and around the throne, *were* four living creatures full of eyes in front and in back. The first living creature was like a lion, the second living creature like a calf, the third living creature had a face like a man, and the fourth living creature was like a flying eagle. And *the* four living creatures, each having six wings, were full of eyes around and within. And they do not rest day or night, saying: "Holy, holy, holy, Lord God Almighty, Who was who is and is to come!" Whenever the living**

creatures give glory and honor and thanks to Him who sits on the throne, who lives forever and ever, the twenty-four elders fall down before Him who sits on the throne and worship Him who lives forever and ever, and cast their crowns before the thrown, saying: "You are worthy, O Lord, To receive glory and honor and power; For You created all things, And by Your will they exist and were created." (Revelation 4:1-11)

John now begins to record the heart of the book of Revelation. In the outline given of the Apocalypse, he is now relating "the things which will take place after this." This is evident, because the apostle starts chapter four with the phrase "After these things." After what things? The things that pertain to Christ's words concerning the churches of Asia Minor. John is then summoned into heaven to be shown exactly what is going to occur as the Seventieth Week of Daniel begins.

There are many who suggest that this call to heaven is indicative of the rapture of the church occurring at this moment in the book of Revelation. It is argued that because John is said to hear a shout, as well as a voice like a trumpet, that what is presented is a clear reference to Paul's rapture passage in 1 Thessalonians:

For the Lord Himself will descend from heaven with a shout, with the voice of an archangel, and with the trumpet of God. And the dead in Christ will rise first. (1 Thessalonians 4:16)

While the parallels in the language are intriguing, the events that occur to John do not relate with the events that occur in 1 Thessalonians. First, nowhere in the text of Revelation do we see the Lord descending to bring John into heaven. He is merely summoned. The second inconsistency is that John is taken in the spirit, and not bodily, as would occur if this were paralleling the rapture. The third problem is that John is the only one who is taken. Nowhere is there any description of the rest of the heavenly saints being with John as he is summoned into heaven. Finally, John's summons is for that of receiving spiritual revelation, while the rapture is for receiving the redemption of the body.[1] In light of these inconsistencies, it is then often claimed that John is merely symbolic of the entire body of Christ. Unfortunately, we are never told in Revelation that John symbolizes anything other than himself. In order to stay with a literal hermeneutic, one must accept the fact that John is only representative of a single Apostle of the Lord, and not a symbol of the redeemed of the ages.

Once in heaven John begins to describe the majestic throne of Almighty God. He states that the presence of the one on the throne was like "jasper and a sardis stone in appearance." The ancient jasper stone was crystalline or opaque in appearance, while sardis was fiery red. This description is indicative of the holiness and justness of God. These brilliant colors present a picture of the righteous and holy anger that God is about to pour out on the sinfulness of mankind.[2] It is also stated that there is an emerald rainbow around the throne. The rainbow was a symbol of God's promise to Noah that there would never be another flood that would destroy the world (Genesis 9:7-17). The rainbow around God's throne thus, is a reminder to the Lord to remember His great mercy even in the midst of His divine wrath.

THE ENIGMA OF THE ELDERS

Described next, are 24 thrones upon which 24 elders sit. There has been much controversy as to just who these elders really are. Many feel that they are representative of the church, which has just been raptured. It is pointed out that the elders have already received their thrones, white robes, and crowns. Therefore, they must be resurrected saints that have received their rewards from the judgment seat of Christ. The error with this approach is that the number of the elders (24) is not said to represent a larger number. If the numbers used in Revelation really represent larger numbers then the whole book becomes utter confusion. This is because John is very specific about numbering things correctly. Later, we will see a great host of angels and a great multitude of believers. John is very specific in describing these as being such. Also, it is not said that these elders represent anything, merely, that they are beings before the throne of God. They are not in any way said to represent the church. In fact, throughout the book of Revelation they are always distinguished from the saints (Revelation 7:13-14, 14:3, 19:4-8).

The view that the elders are resurrected saints who have received their rewards from the judgment seat of Christ is also not likely. This is because the Judgment seat of Christ is not said to take place until after the seventh trumpet judgment (Revelation 11:17-19). If, as I propose, Revelation is chronological, then the seventh trumpet judgment has not yet taken place; therefore, neither has the Judgment seat of Christ. The believers that these elders are often said to symbolize are usually the twelve Patriarchs of Israel and the twelve Apostles. It is argued that after the rapture these two groups will be fused into one people. While it is true that there is no distinction between Jew and Gentile in the Church of Jesus, it does not necessarily follow that a fused group of Old and New Testament believers will represent the redeemed of the ages. If this group does, one may ask why then are there not 24 gates and 24 foundations, instead of 12 in the New Jerusalem (Revelation 21:12-14)? [3] It is specifically told to us by John that the gates and the foundations are representative of the twelve Old Testament Patriarchs and the twelve New Testament Apostles. To have twelve gates for the Patriarchs and twelve foundations for the Apostles does not represent a true fusion of Jewish and Christian believers. Declaring that the elders represent the twelve Patriarchs and twelve Apostles merely reads too much into the text.

It is more likely that these elders are a special class of angels that have a high authority before the throne of God. The elders are later shown to be offering incense (Revelation 5:8), which is one of the same functions that are performed by another angel (Revelation 8:3). This angelic assembly is mentioned in Isaiah 24:23:

> Then the moon will be disgraced And the sun ashamed; For the Lord of hosts will reign on Mount Zion and in Jerusalem And before His **elders**, gloriously" (Isaiah 24:23). {*Emphasis Mine*}

No matter what the case concerning these 24 elders, it is safe to say that they are a special class of 24 created beings that have been given the honor of serving God before His throne. They do not represent or symbolize anything else.

THE LIVING CREATURES

As if the elders were not puzzling enough, John next introduces the four living creatures. Before these living creatures are mentioned, the apostle sees seven lamps burning before the throne of God. Many propose that these seven burning lamps are the seven lamp stands that represent the seven churches of Asia Minor (Revelation 1:20). It is then argued that the presence of these burning lamps in heaven proves that the church is to be raptured before the Seventieth Week begins. So that one does not reach the conclusion that these are the same lamp stands that were representative of the churches in Asia Minor, John tells us that they are the "seven Spirits of God" (Revelation 4:5). These spirits were described previously as those whose eyes run to and fro upon the earth as the eyes of the Lord. John next sees a sea of glass like crystal, and in the midst of it are four living creatures. These beings each have distinct features: one is like a lion, the second is like a calf, another has the face of a man, the fourth is like a flying eagle, and all have six wings. They are said to constantly worship God, and their hymn "Holy, Holy, Holy Lord God Almighty Who was and is and is to come" is recorded for us in verse eight. The proper identification of these beings is important because they will play a major role in chapter six of Revelation.

There are three main details that should be observed about these living creatures. They are before the throne of God, they each have six wings, and they constantly sing the song cited above. With these features in mind, it becomes extremely easy to identify who these creatures are, and what their purpose is. In Isaiah chapter six the prophet has a vision of the throne of God and he sees these very same creatures:

> In the year that King Uzziah died, I saw the Lord sitting **on a throne**, high and lifted up, and the train of His *robe* filled the temple. Above it stood, seraphim; each **one had six wings**: with two he covered his face, with two he covered his feet, and with two he flew. And one cried to another and said: **"Holy, Holy, Holy, *is* the Lord of Hosts; The whole earth is full of His glory!"** (Isaiah 6:1-3) {*Emphasis Mine*}

These creatures that Isaiah refers to as Seraphim or "burning ones" (in the Hebrew), are exactly the same beings that John describes. They are before the throne, they have six wings, and they sing a similar song.

When Isaiah sees the throne of God, although a servant of God, he realizes his absolute sinfulness. The Seraphim then does something extremely interesting to Isaiah:

> Then one of the seraphim flew to me, having in his hand a live coal *which* he had taken with the tongs from the altar. And he touched my mouth *with it*, and said: "Behold, this has touched your lips; Your iniquity is taken away, And your sin purged." (Isaiah 6:6-7)

It seems evident from Isaiah that the role of the Seraphim is to purify those who are about to enter before the throne of Almighty God. As the "burning ones" they will test by fire (live coals) and cleanse believers before they enter God's presence.[4] We will later see that they will perform this role, of purifying the true disciples from the false disciples, as the seals of Revelation are opened. This is done in order to bring the true body of Christ before the throne of God.

In the final verses of chapter four the 24 elders and the living creatures are shown worshipping the absolute majesty of God.

THE SCROLL OF DOOM

> **And I saw in the right hand of Him who sat on the throne a scroll written inside and on the back, sealed with seven seals. Then I saw a strong angel proclaiming with a loud voice, "Who is worthy to open the scroll and loose its seals?" And no one in heaven or on earth or under the earth was able to open the scroll, or to look at it. So I wept much, because no one was found worthy to open and read the scroll, or to look at it. But one of the elders said to me, "Do not weep. Behold, the Lion of the tribe of Judah, the Root of David, has prevailed to open the scroll and to loose its seven seals." And I looked and behold, in**

> **the midst of the throne and of the four living creatures, and in the midst of the elders, stood a Lamb as though it had been slain, having seven horns and seven eyes, which are the seven Spirits of God sent out into all the earth. Then He came and took the scroll out of the right hand of Him who sat on the throne. Now when He had taken the scroll, the four living creatures and the twenty-four elders fell down before the Lamb, each having a harp, and golden bowls full of incense, which are the prayers of the saints. And they sang a new song saying: "You are worthy to take the scroll, And to open its seals; For You were slain, And have redeemed us to God by Your blood Out of every tribe and tongue and people and nation, And have made us kings and priests to our God; And we shall reign on the earth." Then I looked and heard the voice of many angels around the throne, the living creatures, and the elders; and the number of them was ten thousand times ten thousand, and thousands of thousands, saying with a loud voice: "Worthy is the Lamb who was slain To receive power and riches and wisdom, And strength and honor and glory and blessing!" And every creature which is in heaven and on earth and under the earth and such as are in the sea, and all that are in them, I heard saying: "Blessing and honor and glory and power *Be* to Him who sits on the throne, And to the Lamb, forever and ever!" Then the four living creatures said, "Amen!" and the twenty four elders fell down and worshipped Him who lives forever and ever.** (Revelation 5:1-14)

At the beginning of chapter five John sees a rolled scroll that has writing on the inside and on the back, and is sealed with seven seals. The prophet Ezekiel is shown a scroll exactly like this one and is told what is contained within, as well as its significance for Israel:

> Now when I looked, there was a hand stretched out to me; and behold, a scroll of a book *was* in it. Then He spread it before me; and *there was* **writing on the inside and on the outside**, and written on it *were* lamentations and mourning and woe. (Ezekiel 2:9-10) {*Emphasis Mine*}

It is absolutely critical that we understand how this scroll was sealed, because contained inside the scroll is the wrath of God Almighty. The Greek word John uses for scroll is "biblion" which is indicative of a scroll that was made of "either animal skins or dried papyrus fibers."[5] A rolled up scroll was sealed for numerous reasons, but mainly to keep those who were not authorized to do so, from reading it.[6] In ancient cultures to break the seal of the scroll of an official or a king, would often result in death. This was why Christ's tomb was sealed by the Romans (Matthew 27:66). Anyone who broke the Roman seal, who did not have the authority to do so, would have been killed. These scrolls were rolled and then sealed across usually with clay or string seals.[7] Each of the seals carried a condition, and could only be loosened by the one who had met the condition. What John then is seeing is a scroll in the hand of the Almighty with seven seals placed horizontally along the outer edge, so that no one could unroll and read its contents until all the seals were broken.

It was not, as some propose, a scroll that had seven sections of writing which would then be rolled up to the end of the first section and a droplet of wax placed to seal that section. The scroll would then be rolled up further to the end of the next section with the placing of another droplet of wax, and so on, until all seven sections were sealed. One would then unroll the scroll reading up to the end of the first section; break the droplet of wax and proceed with the following section, breaking each droplet until all the contents were read. The above-proposed method would have been contrary to all the known customs of John's day, as well as the archeological evidence of the sealing of ancient scrolls. Unfortunately, for some, this goes against their view of how Revelation should be interpreted; so contrary to historical knowledge, they fabricate their own scroll sealing methods.

The Seven Sealed Scroll of Revelation

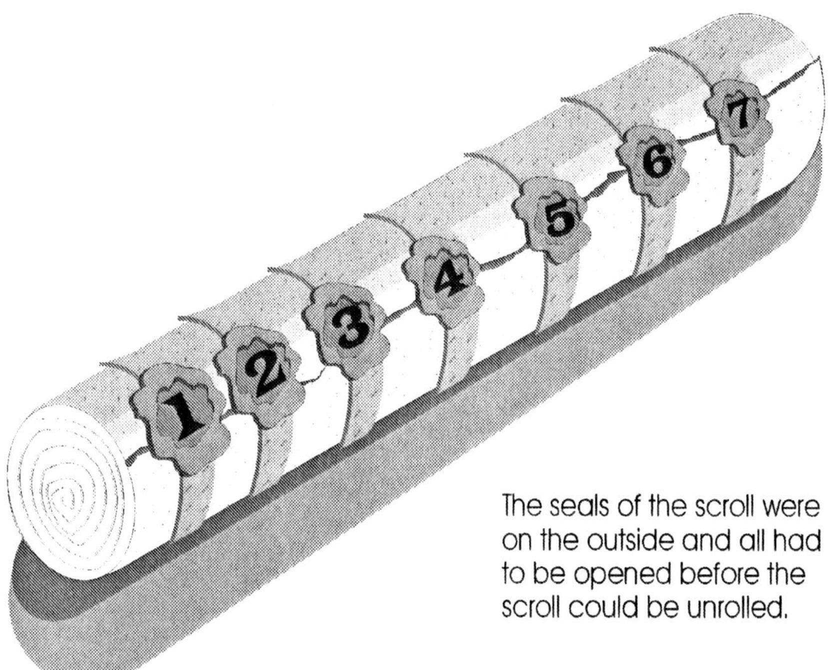

The seals of the scroll were on the outside and all had to be opened before the scroll could be unrolled.

The scene in heaven now shifts as John begins to weep bitterly because there was no one who was worthy to meet the conditions for opening, or even looking at, this scroll. In the midst of his weeping one of the elders indicates that Jesus, who is described as "the lion of the tribe of Judah, the Root of David," is worthy to open the scroll. Jesus is portrayed in these terms, because they describe His right to be the Messiah. As predicted in Scripture, Messiah would be from the tribe of Judah, as well as a descendant of King David (Genesis 49:10). It is common biblical knowledge that Jesus met these credentials. As John looks he does not see a Lion, but instead a Lamb as though it had been slain. The elder tells John that Jesus "has prevailed" and can therefore open the scroll. Jesus appearing as a Lamb who has been slain points to His victory over sin and death. Because He alone has conquered sin, He is allowed to open the scroll and reveal its awesome contents. This Lamb is also stated to have seven horns. In the Old Testament the horn is often symbolic of ruler-ship and kingly authority. Since they are seven in number, they indicate the perfect fullness of the power of Christ. Again, John sees the seven eyes that are the seven spirits sent into all the earth. This helps to convey the absolute omniscience of Christ. There is nothing that escapes His sight.[8]

esus comes before the throne and takes the scroll out of the hand of father. Because God's final plan for the ages is about to unfold, there rejoicing seen in heaven and on the earth. First, we see the four living es and the 24 elders break into what is called a "new song." There are ma... who point to this song as proving that the elders are redeemed believers, because in this song they include themselves. Since at one point they sing "And have redeemed **us** to God by your blood," many feel that this is a clear indication that they are numbered among the redeemed and thus they are resurrected saints. There are two major problems with this line of reasoning. First, the Greek translation of this passage is based on "an acceptance of an incorrect textual variant that includes the first person pronoun "us" in the song about redemption."[9] Second, and probably the most glaring difficulty, is that in verse eight, the four living creatures are also said to join in the singing of this song.[10] Now it is agreed upon by almost every biblical scholar that the four living creatures are not human, but part of God's angelic creation. If this is the case, it is not very likely that they would include themselves in a song that specifically affirms God's redeeming of "them" by His blood, making "them" kings and priests. Since the living creatures are not part of redeemed mankind, they would be singing along inaccurately. It is then obvious from this that the first person pronoun "us" should be correctly translated as "them" as well as "we" being translated "they," as is the case with the Greek of the Majority Text.

Following the song of the elders and the Seraphim, John sees and hears an innumerable multitude of angels also singing a hymn of praise to Jesus. As I pointed out before, John is very specific with numbers. When he says "24" he means just that. When he says "multitudes" then that is what he sees, as well as what he means. Revelation is very understandable if one follows it in this simple manner.

Finally, every other living creature in creation sings praise to Christ. As Paul declares, in the book of Romans, the very creation is groaning in expectation for the revealing of the redeemed and of the sons of God (Romans 8:19-22). This song is sung in the expectation of the imminence of this occurrence. Soon, the scroll will be opened and its contents revealed. The whole creation, since the fall of Adam, has waited for this moment. Now the Savior of the universe, Jesus Christ, will begin establishing His kingdom. Before all this can happen, the seals on the outside of the scroll must be broken. Nothing concerning the Day of the Lord, or the Day of the Wrath of the Lamb can start until this is accomplished.

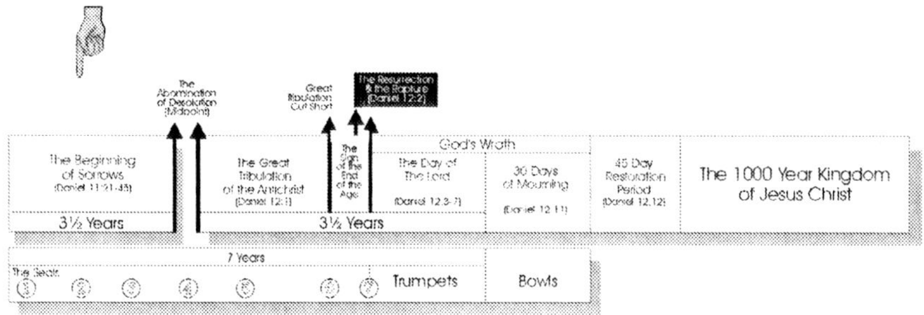

6

THE SEVENTIETH WEEK BEGINS

PROCEEDING INTO REVELATION chapter six, the parallel accounts of these same events that are given in Matthew 24 and Revelation chapters 12-14 also will be discussed. The one point that will remain consistent throughout our journey is that the book of Revelation is basically chronological in its presentation of the Seventieth Week. As I outlined previously, the seventh seal reveals the seven trumpets, and the seventh trumpet reveals the seven bowls. In certain portions of the text, the Apostle John returns to previous chapters and explains some aspects of God's judgment in greater detail. For example, in Revelation chapters 12, 13 and 14 John goes through the entire spiritual history of Israel to show the final outcome of God's redemptive plan for the Jewish people. In doing so, John describes in greater detail events, which have already taken place in the chronology Revelation, while this time revealing the outcome that they had on Israel. Also in Revelation chapter 18, John describes, with great specificity, the destruction of Babylon, which had previously taken place in the seventh bowl judgment of Revelation chapter 16. In these instances, the context of these "parenthetic" chapters will give light as to their relation to Revelation's overall chronology. As these passages are addressed, I will not twist them to fit a proposed Seventieth Week scenario. Rather, I will allow the words of John himself to reveal their proper placement. Also, where applicable, I will interject passages from other portions of Scripture that shed greater light on these symbolic and often times difficult scriptures. Hopefully, this will leave each reader with a greater understanding of the Apocalypse.

INTO THE SEVENTIETH WEEK

Revelation chapter 6 initiates the last seven-year period of God's dealing with the nation of Israel. As announced by the angel in Daniel 9:24, this last week of the seventy weeks is to:

> . . . finish the transgression, To make an end of sins, To make reconciliation for iniquity, To bring in everlasting righteousness, To seal up vision and prophecy, And to anoint the Most Holy (Daniel 9:24)

It is my firm belief that with the opening of the first seal, God's time clock for Israel again begins ticking. This is apparent for a couple of reasons. First, the context dictates that the next chapters of Revelation take place at a time after God's time of dealing with the Gentiles has almost been completed, and the redemption of national Israel is about to begin. Jesus, during the opening of the seven seals, will begin to bring the church age to a close, while also setting up the events that will bring Israel to repentance. The era of the church age is said to end when the "fullness of the Gentiles" has come (Romans 11:25).

Often there is confusion between what Jesus refers to as "the times of the Gentiles" (Luke 21:24), and Paul's "the fullness of the Gentiles" (Romans 11:25). The "fullness of the Gentiles" refers to the number of Gentile Christians that will put their faith in Christ before God is to spiritually restore national Israel. This is an amount, which only God knows, and once it has been reached the church will be gathered to Jesus. The "times of the Gentiles," however, is a reference back to the book of Daniel in which Daniel was given a vision of the Gentile empires that would rule the Jewish people until the return of Messiah. The "times of the Gentiles" began with the Babylonian captivity and will end when Jesus destroys the ten-nation kingdom of the Antichrist (Daniel 2:31-45).

The second reason why the Seventieth Week is inaugurated with the opening of the seals is because the rise of Antichrist is next presented. It is revealed in the book of Daniel that the Seventieth Week begins when the Antichrist "confirms" a seven-year treaty with Israel and her surrounding neighbors (Daniel 9:27). In the language that Daniel employs in his text, it is interesting to note that the Antichrist is said to "confirm" or enforce this treaty. It may very well be that a document for peace will already be in existence, and the Antichrist will be the one who is able to make all sides submit to its provisions.

Many pre-tribulation rapture theorists argue that in order for God to start working directly with Israel again, the church must be taken off the earth, or raptured. I accepted the same position for many years until I contemplated its implications in light of history. Even though, in this present dispensation, God is working specifically with the Gentiles, He still has fulfilled many prophetic promises to the Jewish people. For example, God dealt with the nation of Israel in 70 A.D. when their land was destroyed and they were scattered into all nations, as was predicted by the prophets and Jesus Christ (Deuteronomy 28:64-68 & Luke 21:24). This prophecy was fulfilled during the church age. In our own time, we have witnessed the Second World War wherein Adolf Hitler slaughtered over six million Jews. Because of this atrocity and the world's outcry, in May of 1948 the nation of Israel was restored to give the world's Jews a homeland. This restoration was also in specific fulfillment of Bible prophecy, as was previously discussed. Also in 1967, the world held its breath as the tiny Jewish nation was about to be attacked by its surrounding Arab neighbors. Against insurmountable odds, Israel was victorious in routing the Arabs and regaining the city of Jerusalem, thereby setting the stage for the beginning of the Seventieth Week. Also, before our very eyes, we are witnessing the ongoing stages of Middle East peace negotiations that may be the precursor to the treaty that the Antichrist will "confirm." Not a day goes by in which Israel, or Jerusalem, or uprisings along the West Bank, do not appear on the front pages of the daily newspapers. And where has the church been while all this has been occurring? It has been right here on earth going about its business of fulfilling the great commission to a lost and dying world. To adhere to the presumption that the church absolutely cannot be around while God begins to deal with national Israel is very weak in light of the amazing prophecies that have been fulfilled by God, concerning the Jewish people, while in the midst of the church age. There is nothing explicitly in Scripture, which declares that the church has to be removed from the earth in order for God to initiate the Seventieth Week. However, the church will be gone when the "fullness of the Gentiles" has come in, and The Day of the Lord begins. The Day of the Lord (also known as the End of the Age, or the Day of the Wrath of the Lamb) should not be confused with the Seventieth Week. To understand this point is absolutely essential for one to understand the correct timing of the rapture, along with the chronology of all other end-time prophecy.

The Day of the Lord is the time when God will bring the Jewish people to repentance, while also pouring out His judgments on the world and the kingdom of the Antichrist. I am emphatically convinced that the church of Jesus Christ will not be present during the Day of the Lord. Yet, the church will be present to witness the beginning, midpoint, and great tribulation of the Seventieth Week. As I stated before, while going through the book of Revelation, along with other scriptures, they, themselves, will indicate the exact chronology of these events.

THE OLIVET DISCOURSE

The interpretation of the seals of Revelation chapter six is fully explained by Jesus, Himself, in Matthew chapter 24. Since this is the case, there is no need for any speculation as to the correct interpretation of the seven seals. This important portion of Scripture is commonly referred to as the Olivet Discourse. The Olivet Discourse occurred right before Jesus was to be crucified.

It is crucial to understand that this particular dissertation took place upon the Mount of Olives. This is important, because many commentators confuse the Lord's pronouncement of the destruction of Jerusalem with His outline of the end of the age, given in the Olivet Discourse. The destruction of Jerusalem is predicted while Jesus is with His disciples and apostles in the temple area (Matthew 24:1-2; Mark 13:1-2; Luke 21:1-38). In the gospel of Luke, Jesus addresses in detail questions concerning the destruction of Jerusalem, while also mixing in details of His second coming. Luke is, in fact, the only gospel that records exactly what Jesus said to His followers in the temple area. After completing this teaching, Jesus leaves the temple area and goes to the Mount of Olives:

> And in the daytime He was teaching in the temple, but at night He went out and stayed on the mountain called Olivet (Luke 21:37)

It is what Jesus says while on the Mount of Olives that is recorded in Matthew 24:3-51 and Mark 13:3-37. This discourse on the Mount of Olives is not related to us by Doctor Luke in his gospel. In Luke, the Lord concentrates on more specifically the destruction of Jerusalem. In Matthew and Mark, Jesus only speaks of the events preceding His second coming. It must be kept in mind that Jesus is the one who speaks the words of the Olivet Discourse, and He is also the author of Revelation. Since this is so, one should see complete consistency in the chronology outlined. This is, of course, only if they are both referring to the same events.

Some Background

There has been much debate concerning exactly what audience Jesus was addressing in Matthew chapter 24. Many propose that the Lord was speaking only to the nation of Israel as it undergoes the great tribulation of Antichrist. This view does a serious injustice to the overall context of Matthew, as well as the context of the Olivet Discourse.

In order to understand the context, one needs to ask to whom was the gospel of Matthew written? The easiest answer is found at the end of Matthew's gospel, in which the final words of Jesus are recorded:

> Go therefore and make disciples of all the nations, baptizing them in the name of the Father and of the Son and of the Holy Spirit, teaching them to **observe all things that I have**

> **commanded you**; and lo I, am with you always, *even* to the end of the age. Amen (Matthew 28:19-20) {*Emphasis Mine*}

The apostles are told to teach new disciples to observe all the things that Jesus had commanded them. The only place where one finds the direct teachings and commandments of Jesus is within the gospel of Matthew, as well as the three other gospels. These gospels were not written merely for the nation of Israel, as some would have us believe, but they are written to every Christian believer whether they are Jew or Gentile. All disciples are commanded to observe the teachings of Christ in the Gospels, as well as the teachings in the epistles of the Apostle Paul. As Paul states:

> All Scripture *is* given by inspiration of God, and is profitable for doctrine, for reproof, for correction, for instruction in righteousness, that the man of God be complete, thoroughly equipped for every good work. (2 Timothy 3:16-17)

The resulting conclusion is that the gospel of Matthew was written to believers in Jesus Christ, whether they are Jew or Gentile. Since the overall context of the book of Matthew is geared toward believers, one must then look at the context of the Olivet Discourse, itself, and to whom Jesus was specifically speaking. This discourse takes place when, much to the dismay of His disciples, Jesus states that:

> . . . Do you not see all these things? Assuredly, I say to you, not one stone shall be left here upon another, that shall not be thrown down. (Matthew 24:2)

After this profound statement, Jesus departs from the temple and sits upon the Mount of Olives where He is pressed for further detail:

> . . . the disciples came to Him privately, saying, "Tell us, when will these things be? And what *will be* the sign of Your coming, and of the end of the age?" (Matthew 24:3)

From the context it is obvious that the Lord is addressing the questions of His disciples. In the gospel of Mark the disciples who questioned Jesus are mentioned by name:

> Now as He sat on the Mount of Olives opposite the temple, Peter, James, John, and Andrew asked Him privately, . . . (Mark 13:3)

What was spoken on the Mount of Olives was directed to, and is specifically relevant for, the disciples of Jesus Christ. These men were believers; therefore what Jesus is about to say to them is for those who believe in Him and not just for Jews in general. Sometimes it is argued that the Lord cannot be referring to the church, because it had not yet been revealed that there would even be a church. Yet, they ignore the fact that in Matthew chapter 16 Jesus specifically tells His apostles that there would be a church:

> And I say to you that you are Peter, and on this rock **I will build My church**, and the gates of Hades shall not prevail against it. (Matthew 16:18) {*Emphasis Mine*}

DISPENSATIONALISM GONE MAD

The above conclusions would seem to be very apparent for anyone who reads the gospel of Matthew at face value. The problems encountered are often because of a strict dispensational teaching that completely differentiates God's plan of salvation for the Jews, with God's plan of salvation for the Gentiles. It is critical to remember that Jew or Gentile, Old Testament or New, no one will be saved except through Jesus Christ. As the Old Testament Jews looked forward to the cross for salvation, so the New Testament church looks backwards to the cross for salvation. The Jewish believers before the church age were not in any way saved by keeping the law. This is clearly stated by the author of Hebrews:

> For *it is* not possible that the blood of bulls and goats could take away sins. (Hebrews 10:4)

He also states that the law, and its sacrificial system, was only a shadow of the things that would be fulfilled literally in the life of Jesus Christ (Hebrews 10:1). It is also evident, from the writings of Paul, that God has not called two separate peoples, but one people. Paul says that true Israel is made up of those who are the children of faith in Christ, not merely those who are born of Jewish descent:

> nor *are they* all children because they are the seed of Abraham; but, seed *"In Isaac your shall be called."* That is, those who are the children of the flesh, these *are* not the children of God; but the children of the promise are counted as the seed. (Romans 9:7-8)

Basically, only those who have faith in Christ are to be considered as being God's people. If one is born Jewish and rejects Christ, according to Paul, he is not considered to be part of God's people. This is the same for a Gentile who also rejects Christ. God has only provided one way of salvation and that is through the redemptive sacrifice of Jesus on the cross. In all of this, one must not forget that God does have a plan for the redemption of Israel as a nation. There are many that take what Paul said above, and decide that God is no longer concerned with national Israel. Paul vehemently denies this assertion:

> I SAY then, has God cast away His people? Certainly not! for I also am an Israelite, of the seed of Abraham, *of* the tribe of Benjamin. (Romans 11:1)

> For I do not desire, brethren, that you should be ignorant of this mystery, lest you should be wise in your own opinion, that hardening in part has happened to Israel until the fullness of Gentiles has come in. And so all Israel will be saved, as it is written: *"The deliverer will come out of Zion, and He will turn away ungodliness from Jacob; For this is My covenant with them, when I take away their sins."* (Romans 11:25-27)

God has chosen to work with different peoples during different ages: the Patriarchs before the Law, the Jewish people under the Law, the Gentiles under grace, and eventually the nation of Israel under grace. While God may focus on different groups, He is calling one specific group out of all these dispensations who have placed their faith in Jesus Christ. With this in mind, when reading Matthew chapter 24 one must understand that its text is primarily written to believers in Christ whether of Jewish or Gentile descent.

AN IMPORTANT PARABLE

In verse three of the Olivet Discourse the disciples ask Jesus to address two questions concerning His second coming:

> 1. When will these things be?
>
> 2. What will be the sign of your coming, and of the end of the age?

One must understand that the Jews associated the coming of Messiah with the Day of The Lord, or the End of the Age. The two were inseparable in the Jewish mindset. So the disciples were inquiring as to when Jesus would return for His faithful, overthrow the rule of the Gentiles, and set up the Messianic Kingdom. This is all precisely answered by Jesus. Before looking at the Lord's answer, there is a very important parable in Matthew chapter 13 that must be addressed. This parable is significant in that it gives one a clearer understanding of the words of Christ in the Olivet Discourse:

Another parable He put forth to them, saying: "The kingdom of heaven is like a man who sowed good seed in his field; but while the man slept, his enemy came and sowed tares among the wheat and went his way. But when the grain had sprouted and produced a crop, then the tares also appeared. So the servants of the owner came and said to him, 'Sir, did you not sow good seed in your field? How then does it have tares?' He said to them, 'An enemy has done this.' The servants said to him, 'Do you want us to go and gather them up?" But he said 'No, lest while you gather up the tares you also uproot the wheat with them. Let both grow together until the harvest, and at the time of the harvest I will say to the reapers, 'First gather together the tares and bind them in bundling to burn them, but gather the wheat into my barn.'" (Matthew 13:24-30)

Jesus then explains the meaning of this parable to His disciples:

He answered them saying to them: "He who sows the good seed is the Son of Man. The field is the world, the good seeds are the sons of the kingdom, but the tares are the sons of the wicked *one*. The enemy who sowed them is the devil, the harvest is the end of the age, and the reapers are angels. Therefore as the tares are gathered and burned in the fire, so it will be at the end of this age. The Son of Man will send out His angels, and they will gather out of His kingdom all things that offend, and those who practice lawlessness, and will cast them into the furnace of fire. There will be weeping and gnashing of teeth. Then the righteous will shine forth as the sun in the kingdom of their Father. He who has ears let him hear. (Matthew 13:37-43)

From this parable four important points are surmised:

1. The true believers are to be separated from the false believers (the wheat from the tares).

2. The true believers are to be gathered by Christ through His reapers, who are said to be His angels.

3. The false believers also will be gathered, and a fiery judgment, initiated by the reapers (angels), will burn them.

4. This harvest for both the true and the false disciples will occur at the end of the age, which is also known as the Day of the Lord.

This parable presents a good background as to what exactly is occurring in Revelation, and the Olivet Discourse. In this passage, Jesus identifies the key players, as well as what their specific roles are during the end of the age.

A WORD ABOUT THE COMING OF JESUS

When the disciples asked Jesus the second question, "what is the sign of Your coming?" Matthew uses an interesting Greek word for "coming": Parousia. "Parousia" is a special word that carries in its meaning the idea of a lasting presence. Vines states:

> "When used of the return of Christ, at the Rapture of the Church, it signifies, not merely His momentary coming for His saints, but His presence with them from that moment until His revelation and manifestation to the world."[1]

In his critical Greek lexicon, E.W. Bullinger defines "Parousia" as denoting "a coming which includes the idea of a permanent dwelling, from that coming onwards."[2] The "Parousia" of Jesus is then a reference to an overall event that encompasses the gathering of the elect, the Day of the Lord, and the destruction of the Antichrist at the battle of Armageddon. "Parousia" does not carry with it the meaning of moving from one place to the next. While there will be a number of times in which Jesus is to make an appearance in the earthly realm, there is only one "Parousia" or "coming." The other arrivals are to be within the overall event of the "Parousia," or second coming of Jesus. It is important to understand that the disciples were asking when the "Parousia" event would commence, with the Day of the Lord, or the end of the age immediately following. As the text of Revelation unfolds, it will be obvious that the Day of the Lord is a period when the entire world will be cognizant of the Lord's presence or "Parousia."

THE BREAKING OF THE FIRST SEAL

With the answers to the questions of the disciples in Matthew 24, along with the definitions given by Christ in the parable of the wheat and tares, it will be understood more clearly what is occurring as the seals of Revelation chapter six are broken.

> **Now I saw when the Lamb opened one of the seals; and I heard one of the four living creatures saying with a voice like thunder, "Come and see" And I looked, and behold, a white horse. And he who sat on it had a bow; and a crown was given to him, and he went out conquering and to conquer.** (Revelation 6:1-2)

> And Jesus answered and said to them: "Take heed that no one deceives you. For many will come in My name, saying 'I am the Christ' and will deceive many." (Matthew 24:4-5)

The Lord Jesus has just broken the first of the seven seals. It is crucial to remember that the scroll announcing the "Day of The Lord," cannot be opened until all seven seals are broken. Each of these seals represents a certain condition that must be met. When all these conditions have been met, then God's wrath will begin. What we are seeing at this point in the text is that God is bringing about the conditions that will precede the return of Jesus Christ. Each of these conditions is shown to John to be initiated by a living creature. The living creatures were the Seraphim before the throne of God. Their role at this point is to begin a separation of the true, from the false disciples of Jesus. When they are fully separated, the true believers will be gathered to Christ by His angels (reapers), and brought purified before His throne (barn). The false disciples will then be judged (burned) by God's angels (reapers), when the Day of the Lord begins.

According to the explanation given by the Lord, the Seventieth Week begins with the opening of the first seal. At that point, we are informed that there will then arise many false christs, who will cause many to be deceived. Foremost of these false christs, will be the Antichrist who will confirm a seven year treaty with the nation of Israel. His rise to power will be discussed in the next chapter. The next batch of false christs will be false disciples who will attempt to deceive the true believers in Jesus. The Apostle Paul states that preceding the return of Christ for the church, there will be a great falling away, or a great apostasy (2 Thessalonians 2:3). This is exactly what the Lord is outlining. Jesus warns that these false disciples will deceive many. I thoroughly believe that this deception is going to be so absolutely amazing that unless one knows exactly what Jesus has revealed about this time, one could possibly be deceived by the lie of the Antichrist. Many in their congregations have been taught that they will not see the Antichrist or his great tribulation, but that they will be taken off the earth preceding this time. What will occur when these believers suddenly realize that the church is in the midst of the Seventieth Week? Some will absolutely refuse to believe it, like the dead church of Sardis. Others will be scrambling to find church leaders who have answers as to why the rapture did not occur. It is at this moment, when the church is in a horrific panic that these incredible false prophets will arise. They will perform amazing miracles and lead thousands astray into the very clutches of the Antichrist. We must remember, from the Lord's letters to the seven churches, that the body of Christ entering the Seventieth Week will be full of bad teaching, false doctrine, and false prophets. Christ, in the seven letters, commanded to these believers that they are to overcome and persevere through this period. Many will argue that I am being an alarmist or that I am writing this to scare people. It should scare people, because if we have correctly followed the text of Revelation and Matthew, the rapture has not yet been said to occur. And according to Jesus, His disciples are soon to face a choice that will reveal how true their faith in Christ is.

THE SECOND SEAL

> **When He opened the second seal, I heard the second living creature saying, "Come and see." And another horse, fiery red, went out, and it was granted to the one who sat on it to take peace from the earth, and that people should kill one another; and there was given to him a great sword.** (Revelation 6:3-4)

> And you will hear of wars and rumors of wars. See that you are not troubled; for all *these things* must come to pass, but the end is not yet. (Matthew 24:6)

Contrary to what many in the church may have been taught, both Revelation and Jesus teach that the rise of Antichrist, after the signing of the treaty, will not be peaceful. The prophet Daniel states that after the covenant is made he (the Antichrist) "shall act deceitfully and shall become strong with a small number of people" (Daniel 11:23). As this man begins to consolidate his forces, he shall attack Syria and Egypt and eventually march into the Holy Land (Daniel 11:30-45). This period will become an intense time of national and political uprising. These wars and rumors of wars will continue until the midpoint, or the first three and a half years of the Seventieth Week are completed. At the midpoint, the Antichrist will demand and obtain the allegiance of ten kings or kingdoms, along with the rest of the world. The Antichrist will prove to the world that his military strength is unmatched and unbeatable. Daniel informs us that the Antichrist will be given an army to oppose the Jewish nation, bringing Israel to its knees (Daniel 8:12). The Antichrist will be one of the most incredible military strategists the world has ever known. He alone will control the lands that surround the entire Mediterranean basin.

Concerning these "wars and rumors of wars," Jesus tells His disciples that these things must occur or "come to pass," but the end of the age, or Day of the Lord is still to come (Matthew 24:6). By this we are to understand that what occurs in the second seal does not take place within the Day of the Lord, but rather is a condition that precedes it.

THE THIRD SEAL

When He opened the third seal, I heard the third living creature say, "Come and see." And I looked, and behold, a black horse, and he who sat on it had a pair of scales in his hand. And I heard a voice in the midst of the four living creatures saying, "A quart of wheat for a denarius, and three quarts of barley for a denarius; and do not harm the oil and the wine." (Revelation 6:5-6)

For nation will rise against nation, and kingdom against kingdom, And there will be famines, pestilences, and earthquakes in various places. All these things *are* the beginning of sorrows (Matthew 24:7-8)

Thrown now into the mix of false christs and wars, is a tremendous economic depression. This depression is shown to result in widespread famine and pestilence. The voice in the midst of the living creatures announces that a quart of wheat, and three quarts of barley, may be purchased for a denarius. A denarius, in the time of the Apostle John, was equivalent to a day's wages. So during this period it will take an entire day's wages to buy a quart of wheat, which was in that time the daily ration of a slave.[3] It is extremely possible that the Antichrist's invasion of the Middle East will give rise to this great worldwide economic and financial crisis. The Antichrist, in the book of Daniel, is stated to eventually take control over much of the world's economy: "He shall have power over the treasures of gold and silver . . ." (Daniel 11:43). The world has already witnessed that whenever there are problems in the oil rich Middle East, the entire global economy can be affected. When Iraq invaded the tiny nation of Kuwait, the world's stock markets made a sudden and devastating downturn. The same type of events will occur as the Antichrist makes his unsurpassed political and military moves in the Middle East.

History has shown that when there is serious economic depression and famine, people will look to any leader who can bring about a quick solution. This was the exact scenario that led to the rise of Nazi Germany. The worldwide Great Depression created a moment in history where the German people would accept anyone to lead them; no matter what the cost. This was the impetus for a previous type of antichrist to ascend to power: Adolf Hitler. The very same situation, only much more severe and intense, will be the force behind the events that see the world accept the Antichrist as the globe's great messiah. It will be at this critical moment in history when he will attempt his move toward world domination. Up until this point, the Antichrist will only be known for his incredible negotiation and confirmation of a peace treaty with Israel and her Arab neighbors.

GOD'S WRATH?

Jesus states two very important things to His disciples concerning the first three seals of Revelation chapter six:

1. "all *these things* must come to pass, but the end is not yet." (Matthew 24:6)

2. "All these *are* the beginning of sorrows." (Matthew 24:8)

According to Jesus, these first three conditions that must come to pass are the beginning of sorrows. The beginning "birth pains" would be a more accurate translation. This conveys the idea that the conditions created by the opening of the seals are part of the birthing process of the Day of the Lord. There are many scholars who feel that with the opening of the first seal the "Day of the Lord" or the "Day of God's wrath" begins. There are some simple reasons why this view cannot be correct:

1. These are only the seals that are upon the scroll. If the scroll itself contains the final wrath of God, then it stands to reason that this wrath cannot occur until the seals are broken and its contents revealed.

2. It is hard to believe that the world will see the proliferation of false christs, as well as the political and tactical rise of Antichrist, while God is pouring out His awesome judgments.

3. The Lord, Himself, defines what these seals are and tells us they are not the "Day of the Lord," but rather only the "beginning of sorrows" or birth pains. It is common knowledge that birth pains result in birth. In like manner, the seals are a prerequisite to the birth of God's wrath.

Others will contend that since Jesus is in control of these events, (because He is opening the seals), then it follows that they must be His judgments. I will concede that God is in control of everything, and often times He allows certain situations to happen to judge men. But just because Jesus is the initiator of a sequence of events, does it necessarily follow that it is His wrath? For example, it can be argued, and has been by many, that the great flooding in the Midwest in the summer of 1993 was a judgment of God upon our nation. There are some that would disagree with that assessment. This is because it is not really clear as to whether or not it was a direct judgment from God. Flooding happens all the time; is it always God's judgment? False disciples, wars, famine, and pestilence's are also common occurrences. What I am trying to get across is that when the Day of God's Wrath arrives, there will be absolutely no dispute as to whether the events are a common occurrence or a direct judgment from God Almighty. God's judgments will be so miraculous, widespread, and supernatural that the conditions preceding them will pale in comparison.

THE TIMING OF THESE EVENTS

With the end of the third seal, Jesus in the Olivet Discourse has brought us right up to the midpoint of the Seventieth Week. We are to understand that the first three and one half years will bring false christs, wars, pestilences, famines, an economic misery. With the next seal Jesus will describe the great tribulation of the Antichrist (Matthew 24:9-13), and then define it within its proper chronology as to when it is to begin (Matthew 24:15). In Matthew 24:15 the Lord states that the great tribulation will begin when the "abomination of desolation" occurs. The "abomination of desolation" comes about when the Antichrist marches his forces into the temple in Jerusalem. He stops the daily sacrifice and declares to the world that he is God (2 Thessalonians 2:3-4). Jesus reveals that this is the abomination that Daniel the prophet spoke of. In Daniel, we are then given the exact moment in the Seventieth Week that this event will occur:

> Then he (Antichrist) shall confirm a covenant with many for one week; But in the middle of the week He shall bring an end to sacrifice and offering. And on the wing of abominations shall be one who makes desolate, Even until the consummation, which is determined, Is poured out on the desolate. (Daniel 9:27)

From this passage it is apparent that after three and one half biblical years, or 1260 days from the beginning of the Seventieth Week, the Antichrist will commit the "abomination of desolation." Then the great tribulation of the Antichrist against: first, the nation of Israel, and second, the Christian believers will be unleashed. Before taking a look at the fourth seal and the great tribulation, it would be advantageous to have some background about the despot who will launch the greatest persecution since the Holocaust: The Antichrist.

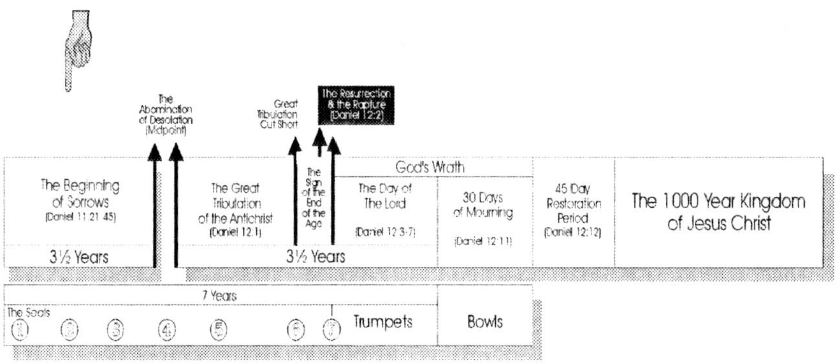

7
THE RISE OF ANTICHRIST

THERE IS NO FIGURE more interesting and enigmatic in all of end-time Bible prophecy than that of the Antichrist. Over the past two thousand years there have been scores of scholars who have tried in vain to identify this man. Prominent historical figures from Nero to Hitler have been named as the evil one. In this process there has been a great deal of inaccurate and unscriptural information given about where this leader will come from and who he may possibly be.

The Antichrist is referred to by many different names throughout all of Scripture. As the late A.W. Pink, a leading authority of the Antichrist, wrote:

> Isaiah mentions him: first as the "Assyrian," "the Rod" of God's anger (10:5); then as "the Wicked" (11:4); then as the "King of Babylon" (14:11-20 and cf 30:31-33); and also as the "spoiler"-Destroyer of the Gentiles" (4:7); the "Enemy," the "Cruel One" and "the Wicked" (30:14 and 23) Ezekiel refers to him as the "Profane and Wicked Prince of Israel" (21:25), and again under the figure of the "Prince of Tyre" (28:2-10), and also as "the chief Prince of Meshech and Tubal" (38:2). Daniel gives a full delineation of his character and furnishes a complete outline of his career. . . ..[1]

Without exception, the best place in all of Scripture to understand the Antichrist's rise to power is found within the pages of the book of Daniel. To the prophet Daniel is revealed many secrets about what this leader will do and where he arises from. Much of what you will now read will differ from what you may have previously heard about the Antichrist. This is because I am of the strong opinion that everything one needs to know about the Antichrist is revealed in Scripture. One does not need to look at world events to try and gain insight on who this man may be. This is because the Bible clearly details his rise to power. The events leading to his ascension must then fit the biblical scenario. One should not take what is currently being witnessed in world history and try and make it fit into God's chronology. There are many problems in using that type of approach. The most prominent of them, is that one tends to bend the meaning of Scripture to make it fit with what is currently happening. In doing so, recent world events are used to interpret Scripture when predictive prophecy should, itself, dictate what events are to occur. The Pharisees, during the time of Christ, were guilty of this very same approach. Although they knew that there would be a suffering Messiah, as well as a conquering Messiah, they refused to accept Jesus as the suffering Messiah. This was because they based the fulfillment of the Messianic prophecies solely on those that spoke of His second advent. They made the mistake of interpreting these scriptures in light of the events of their time in history.

They assumed that Jesus was going to destroy the Roman Empire and restore the greatness of Israel, as the prophets had predicted. The events of their time, in effect, blinded them to seeing Jesus as a redeeming Messiah. So although recent world events indicate that we are approaching the return of Jesus, they must not be used to interfere with the prophetic chronology that is clearly outlined in Scripture. In fact, not one event becomes significant until the Seventieth Week begins. With this important concept in mind let us solve the puzzle of this last world leader.

FOUR GREAT EMPIRES

In the second chapter of Daniel, the prophet interprets a dream that God had given to King Nebuchadnezzar of Babylon. It is important to understand that the nation of Israel had been conquered by Babylon in 606 B.C. as a result of the judgment of God. When Israel was led into captivity what is known as the "times of the Gentiles" began. Although Israel has been in possession of her land twice since the rule of Babylon, she has never been in full control. It has always been the Gentile world, which has held control of tiny Israel in one form or another. Nebuchadnezzar was given a dream in which God revealed all the empires that, during the "times of the Gentiles," would rule and persecute Israel. This vision took the form of a great statue that was made up of gold, silver, bronze, iron, and clay. Nebuchadnezzar was then shown the final ending of the "times of the Gentiles," when Jesus would set up

His eternal kingdom. He was very troubled by this dream and had the Hebrew prophet Daniel give its interpretation:

> This *is* the dream. Now we will tell the interpretation of it before the king. You, O king, *are* a king of kings. For the God of heaven has given you a kingdom, power, strength, and glory; and wherever the children of men dwell, or the beasts of the field and the birds of heaven, He has given *them* into your hand, and has made you ruler over all- you are this head of gold. But after you shall arise another kingdom inferior to yours; then another, a third kingdom of bronze, **which shall rule over all the earth**. And the fourth kingdom shall be as strong as iron, inasmuch as iron breaks in pieces and shatters all *things*; and like iron that crushes, *that kingdom* will break in pieces and crush all others. Whereas you saw the feet and toes, partly of potter's clay and partly of iron, the kingdom shall be divided; yet the strength of the iron shall be in it, just as you saw the iron mixed with ceramic clay. And *as* the toes of the feet *were* partly iron and partly of clay, *so* the kingdom shall be partly strong and partly fragile. As you say the iron mixed with ceramic clay, they will mingle with the seed of men; but they will not adhere to one another, just as iron does not mix with clay. And in the days of these kings the God of heaven will set up a kingdom which shall never be destroyed; and the kingdom shall not be left to other people; it shall break in pieces and consume all these kingdoms, and it shall stand forever. Inasmuch as you saw the stone was cut out of the mountain without hands, and that it broke in pieces the iron, the bronze, the clay, the silver, and the gold- the great God has made known to the king what will come to pass after this. The dream is certain and its interpretation sure. (Daniel 2:36-45) {*Emphasis Mine*}

Daniel gives an amazing interpretation to what seems to be a very puzzling dream. Fortunately, we have the benefit of history to understand exactly what empires Daniel's interpretation was referring to. One must keep in mind that these empires are only mentioned because of their relation to the nation of Israel. They are empires that, from Babylon onwards, would persecute God's chosen people while they were in the land of Israel. There are many other Gentile kingdoms that have also persecuted the Jews throughout world history, but it is only these four empires that God has specifically identified as being pertinent to understanding end-time events. We must not, as some do, enter secular history and pull out the Assyrian, Egyptian, Syrian, German or other empires which have not explicitly been given to us by God. When one does this, one's view of where the Antichrist is to arise becomes very subjective, along with being out of the scope of what God has revealed. I have read numerous authors who present other empires that have persecuted Israel, pinpointing them as the region where the Antichrist will come from. The problem is that there tends to be a large amount of disagreement among these scholars, making the solution to the origin of the Antichrist more muddled and problematic than it should be. God has presented us with a very specific portrait of this man in the book of Daniel. One should then not second-guess what God has already revealed. It is extremely crucial that one stays within the realm of what has already been disclosed in understanding the rise of the Antichrist, as well as all of end-time prophecy.

The first empire mentioned by Daniel was the Babylonian Empire. It is with king Nebuchadnezzar of Babylon that the "times of the Gentiles" were to begin. In approximately 606 B.C. the Babylonian Empire destroyed the temple of Solomon and led Israel into captivity for seventy years. This judgment was brought upon Israel for their failure to repent from idol worship and sexual immorality. The Babylonian Empire was a regal empire that was unequaled in the ancient world. This is why it is represented as being the head of gold.

The next empire spoken of, which is represented by the two arms of silver, is the Medo-Persian Empire. This empire was mightier than Babylon, as silver is stronger than gold. Yet, it was not as regal as its predecessor. This empire conquered Babylon, and its Persian king Cyrus eventually allowed the Jews to go forth and restore the city of Jerusalem and the temple. Amazingly, the prophet Isaiah predicted that a ruler named Cyrus would allow the Jews to return to Israel after their seventy years of servitude had ended:

> Who says of Cyrus, "*He is* My shepherd, and he shall perform all My pleasure, even saying to Jerusalem, 'You shall be built,' and to the temple, 'Your foundation shall be laid.'" (Isaiah 44:28)

This prophecy was penned years before Israel was ever taken into captivity. This reveals that God is very specific and detailed where prophecy is concerned. The Persian Empire commenced in approximately 536 B.C. and continued until it was succeeded by the next great empire.

The next empire, symbolized by the bronze, was the Grecian Empire that was ruled by Alexander The Great. Alexander destroyed the Medo-Persian kingdom and ruled the Grecian Empire for eight short years before dying, possibly of marsh fever, at the age of 33.[2] It is interesting to note that Daniel says that this empire of bronze "shall rule over all the earth." While the Greek Empire did have vast territories, it cannot be categorically stated that it ruled the entire earth. This is because after Alexander's death his kingdom was divided, with the respective rulers battling each other. Later, we will see that this statement by Daniel will take on great significance.

The fourth empire of iron is none other than the Roman Empire. As iron is the strongest and heaviest of the statue's metals, so Rome was the mightiest and most powerful of the Gentile empires. It destroyed and conquered all others before it, and it was under their jurisdiction that the Lord Jesus Christ was crucified. It is shown of this empire, as seen by the two legs, that it would eventually be divided. History reveals that the Roman Empire was divided into an eastern division, with Constatinople as its capital, as well as a western division, with Rome as its capital, in A.D. 364. According to the dream this empire would continue to exist in a very weak form up until the return of Christ. This is an indication that the people and nations of Rome would continue to exist, but not in a unified nature. Unlike the previous empires, Rome was never conquered; it just decayed from within. It has existed in one form or another since its demise, but it has never had the unified power that it once did. The Catholic Church tried to reunite it under the Holy Roman Empire. Napoleon and Adolph Hitler also tried. The European Union is another attempt to bring back the iron rule of Rome; it also will fail.

When the Antichrist unites ten kings (the ten toes) under his power the empire of Rome will revive itself. After this happens Christ will crush the rule of the ten kings, and set up His kingdom. Christ crushes the iron, clay, the silver, and the gold. This indicates that parts of all the former Gentile empires will be around in some form when Jesus returns. It is also important to note that Daniel states that the feet of the statue are made of clay mixed with iron, as well as the toes also consisting of the same composition. What does the clay represent? Many had proposed communism, but with the fall of the Soviet Union the clay is now said to symbolize democracy. The problem with accepting either of these views is that there are no scriptures supporting them. There is however, a more scriptural interpretation of what the clay may symbolize. I would like to suggest that it is most likely a reference to the nation of Israel. Both Jeremiah and Isaiah state that "clay" is one of God's symbols for Israel:

> Then the word of the Lord came to me, saying: "O house of Israel, can I not do with you as this potter?" says the Lord. "Look, as the clay is in the potter's hand, so *are* you in My hand, O house of Israel! (Jeremiah 18:5-6)
>
> But now, O Lord, You are our Father; We are the clay, and You our potter; And all we *are* the work of Your hand. (Isaiah 64:8)

Nebuchadnezzar's Statue (Times of the Gentiles)
Daniel 2:31-45

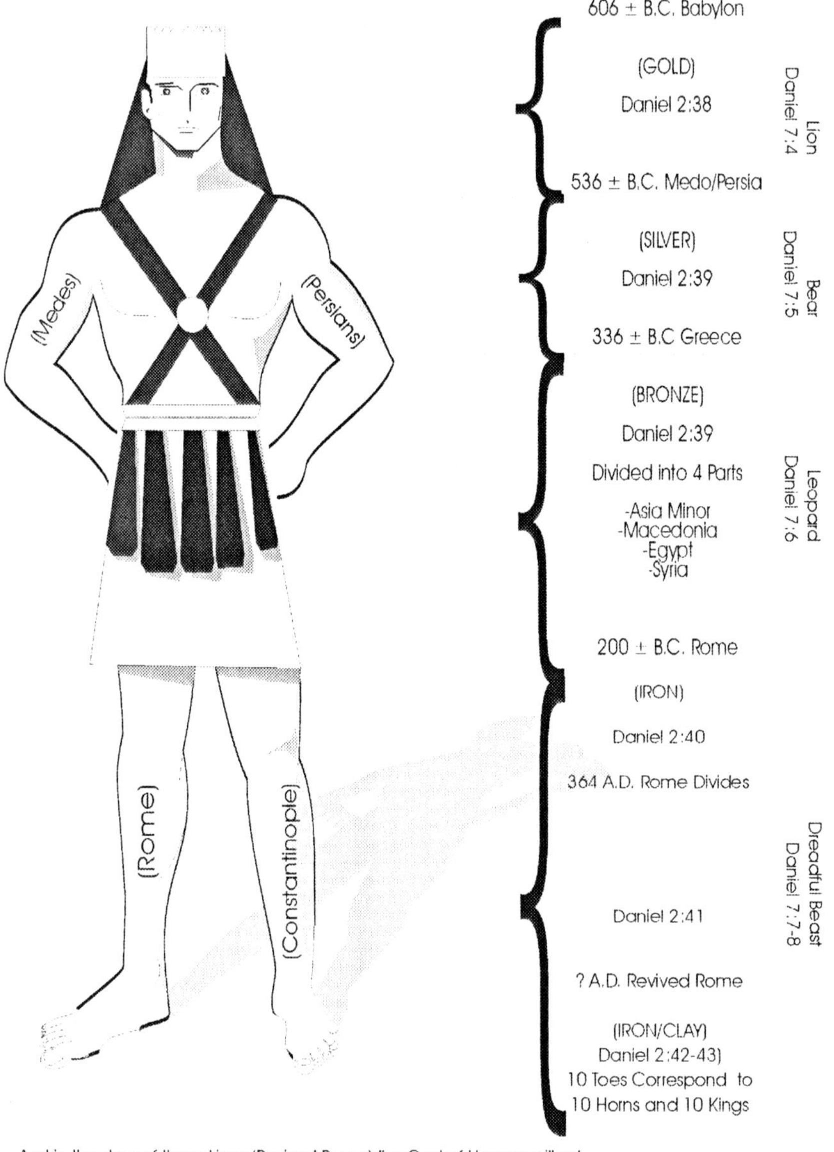

And in the days of these kings (Revived Rome) the God of Heaven will set up a kingdom which shall never be destroyed; and the kingdom shall not be left to other people; it shall break in pieces and consume all these kingdoms, and it shall stand forever - Daniel 2:44

The breakdown in downward continuity from the legs to the feet, as well as the feet's mixture of iron and clay, is a perfect portrayal of the beginning and ending of the Seventieth Week.[3] At the beginning of this seven year period the Antichrist will enforce a treaty between the Gentile powers and the nation of Israel (Daniel 9:27). In fact, Daniel discloses that the "clay" (Israel) is to mingle with the "seed of men" (the Gentile nations), "but they will not adhere to one another, just as iron does not mix with clay." (Daniel 2:43). The Seventieth Week will begin with an alliance of Jewish and Gentile powers, and culminate with the persecution of Israel by the ten nation Gentile kingdom that is led by the Antichrist. There is a very intriguing passage in the book of Habukkuk, which may speak of the Antichrist's initial deceptive alliance with the "clay" of Israel: [4]

> Indeed, because he transgresses by wine, *He is* a proud man, And he does not stay at home. Because he enlarges his desires as hell, And he *is* like death, and cannot be satisfied, He gathers to himself all nations And heaps up for himself all peoples. Shall not all these take up a proverb against him, And a taunting riddle against him, and say, "Woe to him who increases what is not his-how long?" And to him who loads himself with **many pledges** (thick clay)? (Habakkuk 2:5-6) {*Emphasis Mine*}

Although translated as "many pledges" in the New King James Version, the Hebrew word used, "Abtiyt," also carries the meaning of "thick clay."[5] Both meanings are relevant, for through a "pledge" or covenant the Antichrist will align himself with "thick clay" or Israel. In verse eight of Habukkuk chapter two, it is pronounced that the remnant of those he has allied himself with, will eventually be his undoing.

FOUR GREAT BEASTS

Many years later, after his interpretation of the Nebuchadnezzar's dream, Daniel himself is given a vision of these four great Empires. The last vision revealed how a Gentile ruler viewed these empires: as a magnificent statue. It is now disclosed as to how God views them: as great beasts:

> Daniel spoke saying, "I saw in my vision by night, and behold, the four winds of heaven were stirring up the Great Sea. And four great beasts came up from the sea, each different from the other. The first *was* like a lion, and had eagle's wings. I watched till its wings were plucked of; and it was lifted up from the earth and made to stand on two feet like a man, and a man's heart was given to it. And suddenly

> another beast, a second, like a bear. It was raised up on one side, and had three ribs in its mouth between its teeth. And they said thus to it: 'arise, devour much flesh!' After this I looked, and there was another, like a leopard, which had on its back four wings of a bird. The beast also had four heads, and dominion was given to it. After this I saw in the night visions, and behold, a fourth beast, dreadful and terrible, exceedingly strong. It had huge iron teeth; it was devouring, breaking in pieces, and trampling the residue with its feet. It was different from all the beasts that *were* before it, and it had ten horns. (Daniel 7:2-8)

As Daniel, in his vision, stands by the great sea or Mediterranean, he sees four great beasts come up from its waters. These four beasts correspond exactly to the four empires that Nebuchadnezzar saw in the statue. The first, which is like a lion with eagle's wings, correlates with the head of gold, which Daniel revealed was representative of king Nebuchadnezzar, as well as the Babylonian empire. We are told that this lion's wings were plucked; it was then given a heart and made to stand like a man. This is a reference to God's judgment upon Nebuchadnezzar where he became insane and his hair grew like feathers, and nails like birds claws (Daniel 4:33). When Nebuchadnezzar finally realized that God was the one who was ultimately in control of the Babylonian Empire, his sanity was restored. Nebuchadnezzar no longer saw himself as a god, so a man's heart was given to him.

The second beast, that of a bear, correlates with the silver of the great statue. The silver was said to symbolize the Medo-Persian Empire. The bear has one side higher than the other, as the Persians held a greater portion of this empire's power. The three ribs in the bear's jaws correspond with the three areas conquered by this empire: Lydia, Babylon, and Egypt.[6]

Next, corresponding to the bronze empire of Greece, Daniel sees a leopard, which has four wings as well as four heads. The four wings represent the swiftness with which the Greek Empire gained its territories. The four heads typify its division into four regions, after the death of its first ruler: Alexander the Great. It is crucial to note that Daniel says of the leopard with four heads that "dominion was given to it." The other beasts will later be stated to have had their dominion taken away. Yet, one of the heads of the leopard will later be seen playing an important role, as dominion is again given to it.

The final beast that Daniel sees complements the iron portion of the statue, which symbolized the Roman Empire. This empire is said to be exceedingly strong as it stamps out and destroys the former empires. This beast is also said to have ten horns, which are the same as the ten toes of Nebuchadnezzar's statue. What Daniel is shown in his vision, correlates exactly with what Nebuchadnezzar was also shown. This reveals how amazingly consistent God's word is.

Here then is what is to be understood concerning these beasts:

1. Babylon in God's eyes is like a lion, and it has one head.

2. Medo-Persia is like a bear, and it also has one head.

3. Greece is like a leopard, and it is said to have four heads.

4. Rome is an indescribable beast, and it is said to have one head and ten horns.

If one were to combine all the features of these beasts into one great beast it would create a beast that has seven heads: Babylon one, Medo-Persia one, Greece four, Rome one. This beast also would have ten horns, along with features pertaining to a lion, a bear, and a leopard. Amazingly, this is exactly what the Apostle John sees when he is given a view of the rise of the Antichrist during the midpoint of the Seventieth Week. While, like Daniel, on the shores of the Mediterranean John writes:

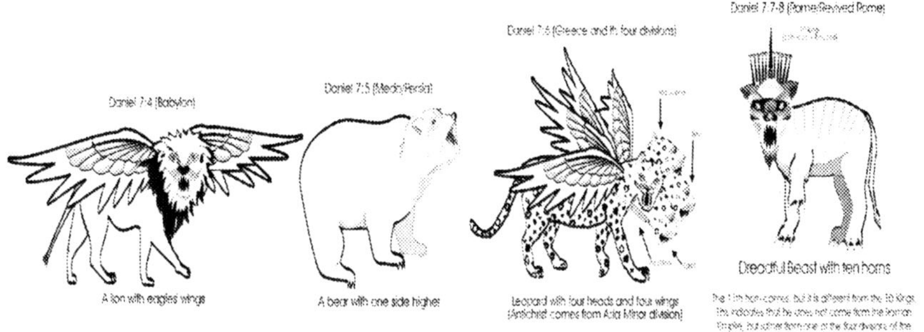

The Four Gentile Empires seen successively by Daniel
They correspond with the four empires seen by Nebuchadnezzar

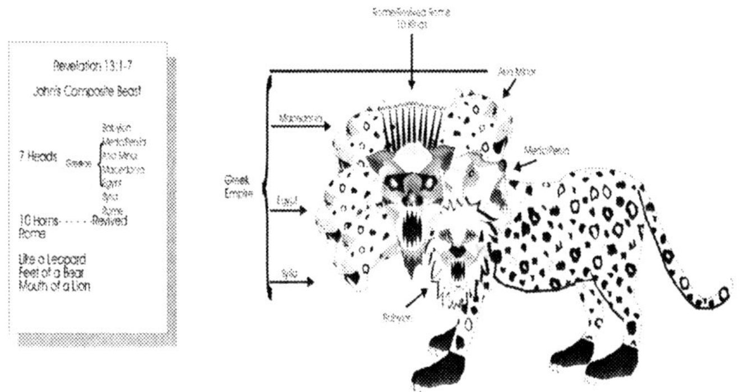

> Then I stood on the sand of the sea. And I saw a beast rising up out of the sea, having **seven heads** and **ten horns**, and on his horns ten crowns, and on his heads a blasphemous name. Now the beast which I saw was like a **leopard**, his feet were like *the feet of* a **bear**, and his mouth was like the mouth of a **lion**. And the dragon gave him his power, his throne, and great authority. (Revelation 13:1-2) {*Emphasis Mine*}

Both John and Daniel are describing the exact same creature, but John is describing as a composite what Daniel saw as being successive. This is because John is describing the beast in its final form when the Antichrist takes control of the ten kings of the revived Roman Empire. Understanding this will unlock the keys of where the Antichrist will arise from. It is right after the vision of these beasts that the Antichrist is introduced in the book of Daniel. Daniel was considering the ten horns of the fourth beast, which symbolized the revived Roman empire, when he saw a "little horn" come up among them, and overthrow three of the ten horns, or kings (Daniel 7:8). Daniel relates that this horn had the eyes of a man and it was speaking pompous words. Daniel was grieved in his spirit, and he wanted to know more about this last world empire with ten horns, and about the "little horn": the Antichrist (Daniel 7:19-20). It was also seen by Daniel that this "little horn" was making war against the saints, and prevailing against them (Daniel 7:21). Finally, an angel reveals more about the Antichrist:

> Thus he said: "The fourth beast shall be A fourth kingdom on earth, Which shall be different from all *other* kingdoms, And shall devour the whole earth, Trample it and break it in pieces, The ten horns *are* ten kings *Who* shall arise from this kingdom. And another shall arise after them; He will be different from the first *ones*, And shall subdue three kings. He shall speak *pompous* words against the Most High, Shall persecute the saints of the Most High, And shall intend to change times and law. Then the saints shall be given into his hands For a time and times and half a time. (Daniel 7:23-25)

Greater details are now given, concerning the Antichrist. First, there will arise ten kings out of the old Roman Empire who will form a coalition. Then will arise the Antichrist; he will be different from them and will take over the rule of three of the first ten kings. It is stated that he is different from the first ten kings, because he will not arise from the Roman Empire, as will be revealed in Daniel chapter eight. This Antichrist will be given "a time and times and a half a time (3 1/2 years)" to persecute and prevail over the saints of God. However, this time allotment will be cut short by God as the heavenly courts are convened and the Antichrist's power is broken (Daniel 7:26). Daniel was still perplexed about this "little horn," so God shed even more light on him.

THE RAM AND THE GOAT

Daniel later, had another vision concerning this "little horn" in which he saw a ram with two horns crash into a goat that had one notable horn (Daniel 8:1-8). The ram was cast down and trampled by the goat, and the goat grew very great. In the midst of its greatness, the goat's notable horn was broken and replaced with four smaller horns. It was from out of one of these smaller horns that the Antichrist, the "little horn," came from:

> And out of one of them (the four notable horns) came a little horn which grew exceedingly great toward the south, toward the east, and toward the Glorious *Land.* And it grew up to the host of heaven; and cast down *some* of the host and *some* of the stars to the ground, and trampled. He even exalted *himself* as high as the Prince of the Host; and by him the daily *sacrifices* were taken away, and the place of the sanctuary was cast down. Because of transgression, an army was given over *to the horn* to oppose the daily *sacrifices*; and he cast truth down to the ground. He did all this and prospered. (Daniel 8:9-12)

This "little horn" has all the markings of the Antichrist; he is said to trample down the host of heaven (saints). He exalts himself a high as the Prince of the Saints: Jesus Christ. He commits the "abomination of desolation" by taking away the daily sacrifices. He is also said to have an army, and that he would cast down truth and prosper. Scores of commentators will argue that this passage is speaking of a Syrian despot known as Antiochus Epiphanes, and not the Antichrist. This view is clearly inaccurate. To dismiss these verses as merely concerning Antiochus Epiphanes will never allow a proper understanding of the Antichrist's origin. Although Antiochus did desecrate the Jewish temple, he was only a type of the Antichrist. It is clearly stated by Jesus that the desecration of the sanctuary, spoken of by Daniel the prophet, was still future (Matthew 24:15). It had not yet occurred in Jewish history, or at least until the time of Christ. So although a type of the Antichrist, the exploits of Antiochus should not be read into these passages. Daniel's concern was not for some minor figure that persecuted the Jews during the Greek empire. Daniel's desire was to know more about the "little horn" he had seen in his previous vision. Finally, in case there was any question in Daniel's mind as to whether this was the "little horn" he had seen previously, he is told specifically to: ". . . Understand son of man, that the vision refers to the time of the end."(Daniel 8:17). Again, immediately before the vision was interpreted, he was told

"Look, I am making known to you what shall happen in the latter time of the indignation (great tribulation) for at the appointed time the end shall be."(Daniel 8:19). The angel stresses twice that what Daniel saw, was to occur in the last days, or the day preceding the kingdom of Messiah. This information seals the fact that the passage must be referring to the Antichrist. To argue otherwise calls into question what God's word has specifically stated to us.

Daniel is next given the interpretation:

> The ram which you saw, having the two horns-*they are* the kings of Media and Persia. And the male goat is the kingdom of Greece. The large Horn that *is* between its eyes *is* the first king. As for the broken *horn* and the four that stood up in its place, four kingdoms shall arise out of that nation, but not with its power. **And In the latter time of their kingdom**, When the transgressors have reached their fullness, A king shall arise, Having fierce features, Who understands sinister schemes. His power shall be mighty, but not by his own power; He shall destroy fearfully, And shall prosper and thrive; He shall destroy the mighty, and *also* the holy people. Through his cunning He shall cause deceit to prosper under his hand; And he shall magnify *himself* in his heart. He shall destroy many in *their* prosperity. He shall even rise against the Prince of princes; But he shall be broken without *human* hand. (Daniel 8:20-25) {*Emphasis Mine*}

The angel reveals that the goat represents the empire of Greece that will destroy the kingdom of Medo-Persia. The large horn between its eyes is the first king; this was Alexander the Great. The first horn was broken when Alexander died, and four other horns come up in its place. In history, after the death of Alexander, four of his generals divided up the empire into four provinces (remember the leopard representing Greece had four heads): Cassander took Macedonia, Lysimachus took Asia Minor (Turkey), Seleucus took Syria, and Ptolemy took Egypt.[7] It is out of one of these four areas that it is said that the Antichrist will arise. This will happen in the "latter time" of these four kingdoms (Daniel 8:23). For the third time the angel stresses to Daniel that these passages refer to the end times. It was stated previously of the "little horn" that he was to be different from the ten horns. This is because he arises from one of the provinces of the Greek empire, and not from the Roman Empire, as do the ten horns. Understanding this allows many scriptures in Daniel to make sense. For instance, in chapter eleven, Daniel presents the entire history of the provinces of the Greek kingdom after Alexander's death (11:3-4). Daniel relates this detailed history until he reaches the arrival of the Antichrist. It has always puzzled me as to why Grecian history, with the battles of Syria and Egypt, is presented with great specificity in Daniel chapter eleven. When one realizes that the Antichrist will arise from one of these four provinces, "in the latter time of their kingdom."(Daniel 8:23), it all becomes crystal clear.

WHICH PROVINCE?

The search for the origin of this evil ruler has now been narrowed down to one of four possible areas: Syria, Egypt, Macedonia, and Asia Minor. In the reading Daniel chapter eleven, one is able to eliminate two of these four provinces. Predominately, chapter eleven concerns itself with wars between the King of the South (Egypt) and the King of the North (Syria). Remember these kingdoms are presented in their directional relation to Israel. Egypt is south of Israel, while Syria is directly north. In verse 40 it is revealed that the Antichrist is attacked by the king of the South (Egypt), as well as the King of the North (Syria). Since both these provinces are attacking him, they can both be ruled out as being the land from which he will arise. We are then left with Macedonia or Asia Minor as the remaining possibilities. In order to determine which of these two is the correct area, an important portion of the book of Ezekiel must be examined.

In Ezekiel chapter 38 we are presented with a portrait of the Antichrist's invasion of Israel. He is referred to as being "Gog" the Prince of Rosh, Meshech, and Tubal. There have been many believers who have been told that "Rosh" is clearly a reference to Russia, "Meshech" to Moscow, and "Tubal" to the Russian city of Tobolsk. So what Ezekiel is really picturing is a Russian invasion of Israel. This story has been told so many times that most commentators write about its accuracy without even researching to verify its truthfulness. I have thoroughly researched the matter, and to identify "Gog" as being some leader from Russia is absolutely incorrect. One thing that commentators stress to prove this presumption is to point to the fact that this invasion is said to come from the north, and Russia is directly north of Israel. But, just because an army is said to come from the north, it does not necessarily follow that it must be Russia. As evidence of this, I point to the book of Jeremiah where the prophet states that Babylon will destroy Jerusalem and that they will come from the north (Jeremiah 4:6). Wait a second! Anyone knows that Babylon, or modern Iraq, is directly east of Israel. Jeremiah must have been having a bad day. The solution to this contradiction lies in the existence in the Middle East of what is known as the "Fertile Crescent." As prophecy writer Tim Dailey states:

> The biblical world is sometimes referred to as "the fertile crescent" a curved swath of arable land that follows the Tigris and Euphrates Rivers to Northern Syria and then down throughout the promised land.[8]

The Fertile Crescent in the Middle East

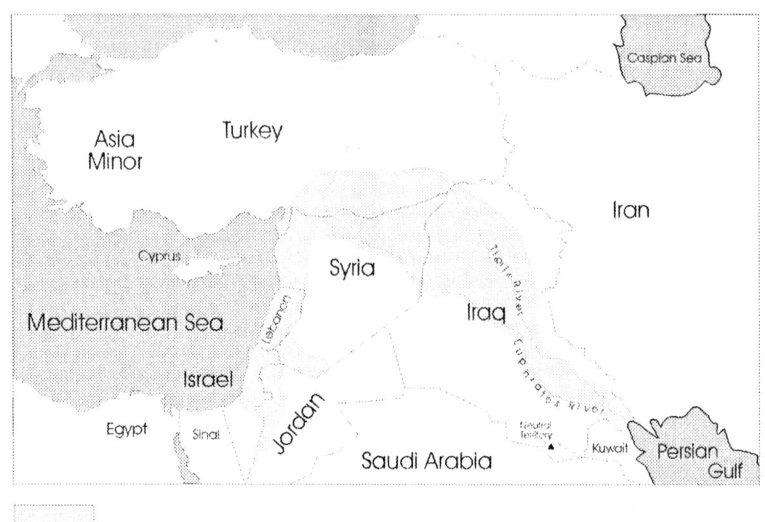

Fertile Area

Travelers and armies would go around the desert wastelands by traveling through this Fertile Crescent. So in order to invade the Holy Land, they would follow this crescent down through Syria and into Israel. This was the precise route that Babylon took. Even though they were from the east, they ended up invading from the north. It will be no different for the Antichrist; his army will invade through the Fertile Crescent and come down on Israel from the north. It is also argued that the Hebrew word used in the text of Ezekiel for "north" means "far north." Russia is therefore, the only war power to the far north of Israel. They fail to address the fact the Ezekiel states that the "house of Togamarth from the far north" also will take part in this invasion. All scholars agree that the land that the house of Togamarth inhabited was within the region of what is today known as Armenia. A quick look at any world atlas will show that the region of Armenia, which is to the "far north" of Israel, is fairly far south from Russia.[9]

Since the Antichrist is said to be the ruler of the land of Meshech and Tubal, if we can establish where these regions are located his origin can then be known. So where exactly are Rosh, Meshech, and Tubal located? According to the Holman Bible Dictionary, "Rosh" is best understood as:

> Personal name meaning "head" or "chief." Seventh son of Benjamin (Genesis 46:21) . . . ..[10]

"Rosh" should more accurately be translated as the word "chief." Ezekiel 38:2 should then read Gog of the land of Magog the "chief" (Rosh) prince of Meschech and Tubal. In fact, the New American Standard Bible a the King James Version both translate it this way. There is some speculatio that "Rosh" may refer to an Assyrian King named "Rashu," but his kingdom was located in the modern areas of northern Iran and Iraq; not Russia.[11] The term "Magog" is merely a Hebrew construction that means "place of Gog." Magog was also a descendent of Noah (Genesis 10:2).

The location of Meshech and Tubal are no real mystery either. If one obtains any modern Bible atlas or Bible dictionary there is no dispute to where Meschech and Tubal were located.[12] This is because there have been many monumental discoveries in Assyrian cuneiform texts that have led to the proper identification of these regions.

Location of Meshech and Tubal in Asia Minor

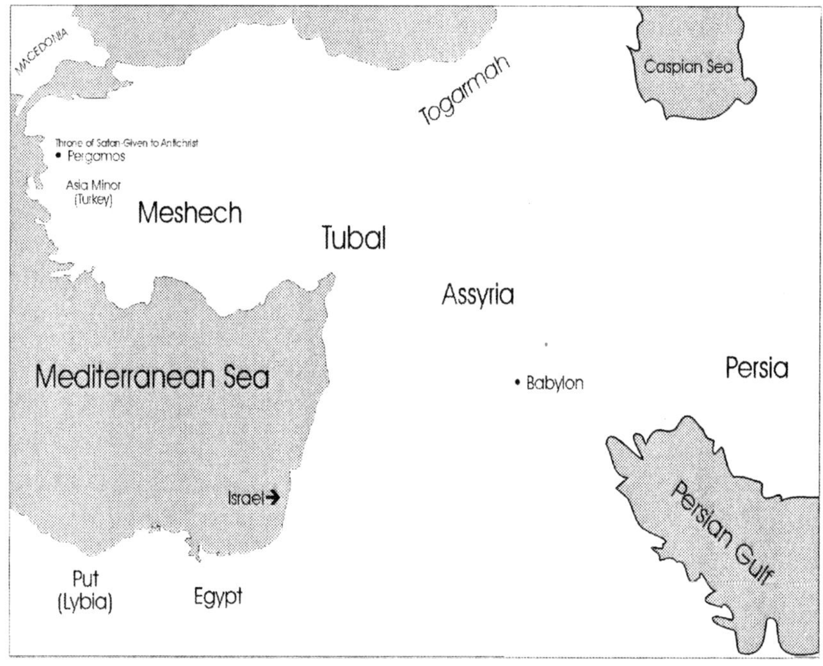

According to the Holman Bible Dictionary:

> MESHECH a people of **Asia Minor** (Gen10:2, 1Chron 1:5), Known for trading in copper vessels (Ezekiel 27:13), frequently associated with Tubal (Ezekiel 32:26; 38:2-3; 39:1). **This Meshech is identical to the Assyrian Mushki and the Greek Moschoi.**[13]

> TUBAL a son of Jepheth (Gen 10:2; 1Chron 1:5) and ancestor of a people, known for their metalworking ability, likely of Cappadonia or Cicilia in **Asia Minor** (Isa. 66:19; Ezek 27:13; 32:26; 38:2-3; 39:1)[14]

Author George Roux, in his definitive book on ancient Iraq, also mentions the location of Tubal:

> Starting from the north, we find in the heart of the Taurus Mountains about twelve city states forming the confederation of Tabal (the Tubal of the Bible) and along the Upper Euphrates, the kingdom of Kummanu with Milid (modern Malaysia) for capital city.[15]

The Taurus Mountains are located in the area known as Asia Minor. The people of Meshech and Tubal are well documented in Assyrian cuneiform texts as being located in central and eastern Anatolia (Asia Minor). [16] Even author Hal Lindsey, who is one of the biggest promoters of the Russian invasion theory, tenaciously quotes scholar R.H. Alexander who admits that:

> The Mushki (Meshech) eventually migrated northward and apparently gave their name to Moscow, and Tubal to the Tibereni and Tobolsk, but this tradition is not free from controversy.[17]

The tradition is not free from controversy because there is absolutely no archeological or historical basis for it. In fact, Lindsey quotes Alexander after he spends two pages showing that the peoples of Meshech and Tubal are from the area of Asia Minor. Basically, there is very solid historical and archeological evidence that shows that these people were from the area known as Asia Minor, or modern day Turkey.

THE PUZZLE SOLVED

These passages from Ezekiel solve the last piece of the Antichrist puzzle by eliminating the province of Macedonia. This establishes Asia Minor as the province of Greece from where the Antichrist will arise. Is it any wonder that the book of Revelation is addressed to seven churches in the province of Asia Minor? Or that the church of Pergamos, within Asia Minor, is said to reside where Satan's throne is (Revelation 2:13). Revelation 13:2 states that Satan will give the Antichrist his throne. If our Lord has told us that the throne of Satan is in Pergamos of Asia Minor, it stands to reason that this will be the place where the Antichrist would arise and ascend to power. Jesus addressed these churches, because this would be the very area that would witness the initial rise to power, as well as the incredible deception of the Antichrist.

The solution to understanding this world leader's ascension to power has been in taking what God has revealed at face value. I have tried to keep my interpretation completely within the confines of God's word. As this important Asia Minor piece fits in, all the other passages that are concerned with the Antichrist also fit into place. His rise from Asia Minor is in complete agreement with every other biblical passage concerning his origin. In fact, this solves every seeming contradiction that is encountered when studying the Antichrist. With this understanding of the Antichrist, our focus will again be shifted back to the book of Revelation as the midpoint of Daniel's Seventieth Week is addressed.

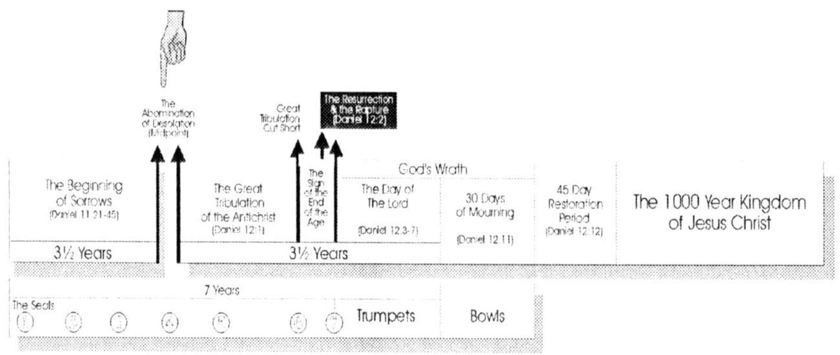

8
THE MIDPOINT

FROM THE MIDPOINT of the Seventieth Week and forward, is the portion of Christ's Second Advent that Bible prophecy predominately deals with. Very few details are given about the first three and one half years. Once the "abomination of desolation" is committed by the Antichrist, the details of the last three and a half years become quite extensive. There are three time frames given by God that define the last three and a half years: "time and times and half a time," "forty-two months," and "one thousand two hundred sixty days." These terms, without exception, always refer to the last half of the Seventieth Week. It is this last half of the seven-year period that is unveiled as the fourth seal is broken. There are an incredible amount of events that occur at the moment the Antichrist sits in the Jewish temple and declares to the world that the he is God. Through these events, the world will be forced to worship him as God, or face death.

To fully understand what is happening, it would be best to have some additional background on the Antichrist. It has previously been outlined that he will be a man that confirms a treaty with Israel, and he will come from an area known as Asia Minor, or modern day Turkey. In Revelation chapter 17, John is given a look at the spiritual forces that help bring the Antichrist to power. This portion of Scripture details the period preceding the midpoint of the Seventieth Week. This is one of those "parenthetic" chapters that help to give greater detail on what is occurring within the chronology of the events of Revelation. I am discussing this vital chapter at this moment for three reasons:

1. Its events take place at a point where the Antichrist has not been revealed, as such, and he has not yet taken power (Revelation 17:8)

2. The ten horns (kings) do not have crowns and are also said not to, at this moment, have received their kingdom (Revelation 17:12). Also, they have not yet pledged their authority to the Antichrist (Revelation 17:13).

3. The ten horns (kings) are also stated to have not yet put to an end the false religion that precedes the Antichrist's rise (Revelation 17:16).

What is contained in chapter 17 then, are details right before and up until the midpoint of the Seventieth Week.

THE FACE OF BABYLON

> **Then one of the seven angels who had the seven bowls came and talked with me saying to me, saying to me, "Come, I will show you the judgment of the great harlot who sits on many waters, with whom the kings of the earth committed fornication, and the inhabitants of the earth were made drunk with the wine of her fornication." So he carried me away in the Spirit into the wilderness. And I saw a woman sitting on a scarlet beast *which was* full of names of blasphemy, having seven heads and ten horns. The woman was arrayed in purple and scarlet, and adorned with gold and precious stones and pearls, having in her hand a golden cup full of abominations and the filthiness of her fornication. And on her forehead a name was written: MYSTERY, BABYLON THE GREAT, THE MOTHER OF HARLOTS AND OF THE ABOMINATIONS OF THE EARTH. And I saw the woman, drunk with the blood of the martyrs of Jesus. And when I saw her, I marveled with great amazement.** (Revelation 17:1-6)

One of the angels gives John an incredible look behind the scenes of what occurs in the spirit world. John sees a "harlot" who sits upon many waters. Later, we are informed that these waters represent "peoples, multitudes, nations, and tongues" (Revelation 17:15). There are two women presented within the book of Revelation. The first is the true woman that is made up of God's elect. The second is the false woman that is made up of those who have refused to believe in God's way of salvation, but have chosen Satan's way. John is told that the kings of the earth have committed fornication with the false woman, or "harlot." Since this vision is spiritual in its nature, the angel is referring to spiritual fornication. This means that the kings of the earth have committed spiritual fornication by following gods other than the true God Almighty. This woman is said to be supported by a scarlet beast with seven heads and ten horns. Physically, this beast takes shape as the final kingdom of the Antichrist. Spiritually, the force that propels the Antichrist, and carries the woman, is Satan himself. The seven heads represent the seven spiritual prince demons who ruled over the Gentile empires that persecuted the nation of Israel, since the time of Babylon. In the book of Daniel, we are given greater insight into these princes who are the spiritual forces that ruled these empires:

> Then he said, "Do you know why I have come to you? And now I must return to fight with the prince of Persia; and when I have gone forth, indeed the prince of Greece will come." (Daniel 10:20)

The angel speaking to Daniel reveals that as each one of these princes are defeated in the spirit realm; the physical empire itself loses its dominion. When the demonic ruler overseeing the Medo-Persian Empire was defeated, Alexander the Great conquered Medo-Persia and the Grecian empire was empowered. In the western mind-set one often views physically what is happening, forgetting the spiritual force behind the occurrence. It is vital to comprehend both the physical manifestation and the spiritual forces behind what is being presented in Revelation chapter 17. The two should not be separated or an incomplete picture will emerge.

This harlot is said to be the "mother of all harlots and of the abominations of the earth." She does not merely represent one branch, but all branches of false religion. It is from her womb in which all the false religions of the world have arisen, and it has been Satan who has been the force behind them. She is referred to as "Babylon the Great," because it is from the Babylon of Nimrod's time from which all false religions started.[1] False religion began when Nimrod, a type of Antichrist, incited the world to consolidate their power and build a tower that would reach to heaven (Genesis 11:1-9). This structure was most likely a Ziggurat, which was used for astrological purposes in the worship of the heavens. Babylon was the city of Nimrod and was founded in rebellion against God. It was the seat of idolatry in which man attempted to become like God. The mentality of Babylon's past will see its culmination in the Antichrist, who will again incite the world to unite behind him against God Almighty. There are many false religious systems, some greater than others, but they are all the offspring of the original Babylonian idolatry. It will be this false religious system that will bring about a great deception that Jesus stated from which many false christ's would arise (Matthew 24:24). John discloses that the "harlot" is drunk with the blood of the saints and the martyrs of Jesus. Throughout history there have been many true disciples who have been martyred by those who belong to these false religions. Likewise, there will be numerous believers, during the great tribulation, who also will be killed for not bowing down to the Antichrist.

THE SPIRITUAL RISE OF THE ANTICHRIST

> **But the angel said to me, "Why did you marvel? I will tell you the mystery of the woman and of the beast that carries her, which has seven heads and ten horns. The beast that you saw was, and is not, and will ascend out of the bottomless pit and go to perdition. And those who dwell on the earth will marvel, whose names are not written in the Book of Life from the foundation of the world, when they see the beast that was, and is not, and yet is. Here *is* the mind that has wisdom: The seven heads are seven mountains on which the woman sits. There are also seven kings. Five have fallen, one is, *and* the other has not yet come. And when he comes, he must continue a short time. And the beast that was, and is not, is himself also the eighth, and is of the seven, and is going to perdition. And the ten horns which you saw are ten kings who have received no kingdom as of yet, but they receive authority for one hour as kings with the beast. These are of one mind, and they will give their power and authority to the beast. These will make war with the Lamb, and the Lamb will overcome them, for He is Lord of lords and King of kings; and those *who are* with Him *are* called, chosen, and faithful. And he said to me, "The waters which you saw, where the harlot sits, are peoples, multitudes, nations, and tongues. And the ten horns which you saw on the beast, these will hate the harlot, make her desolate and naked, eat her flesh and burn her with fire. For God has put it into their hearts to fulfill His purpose, to be of one mind, and to give their kingdom to the beast, until the words of God are fulfilled. And the woman which you saw is that great city that reigns over the kings of the earth.** (Revelation 17:7-18)

We are now presented with incredible information that the Antichrist will be a personage whom God allows to come forth from the bottomless pit. It is said that he "was, and is not, and yet is." Similar phraseology is utilized by

Jesus, when speaking in terms of His own death and resurrection: "I am he who lives, and was dead, and behold I am alive forevermore."(Revelation 1:18). John also sees Jesus as a "Lamb as though it had been slain" (Revelation 5:6). The exact same wording is used of the Antichrist when John sees him at the midpoint in Revelation chapter 13. John states that one of the seven heads, which represents the Antichrist, was "as if it had been mortally wounded." (Revelation 13:3). The term used for both "mortally wounded" and "slain" is the Greek word Sphazo, which means to slay, particularly in terms of a sacrifice.[2] It seems that the Antichrist will be a false representation of what the true Christ accomplished. Just as Jesus was the Son of God who died in His obedience to God, and rose again, the Antichrist also will, in a special way, be the son of Satan who died in obedience to Satan, and will rise again. I would like to stress that I am in no way insinuating a belief in reincarnation. The Antichrist will not be reincarnated, but will be resuscitated as Lazarus was when the Lord brought him back from the dead (John 11:1-44). When it is understood that the Antichrist is a dead man come back to life, it is said the whole world will marvel. Some believe that the Antichrist will be assassinated at the midpoint of the Seventieth Week, and then rise from the dead. I do not see anything explicit in Scripture that shows that he will be assassinated. Rather, at the midpoint, the Antichrist will be revealed to the world as to who he really is. It is somewhat ironic that the same scholars that propose the great assassination tale would have concerns with the scenario I have just outlined. In both scenarios we are confronted with a man who will rise from the dead. Whether it occurs within three days or three thousand years of his death, it still involves a supernatural miracle that God allows Satan to perform. So in either case, the Antichrist will perhaps be an individual upon whom a false resurrection is performed. It is at the moment where he reveals his true self, that he commands all humanity to worship him. Who this man is, I can only speculate. Some suggest Judas, since he was the only one ever called the "son of perdition" (John 17:12).[3] The Lord Jesus also referred to him as being a "devil" (John 6:70). He was also the only man ever said to be taken over by Satan, himself (Luke 22:3). He died in service to his father Satan by hanging himself on a tree (Matthew 27:5). Jesus died in obedience to His father by being crucified upon a tree. Jesus ascended into heaven, while of Judas it is said that he went to his own place (Acts 1:25). It is also interesting that Psalm 55 which speaks of Judas' betrayal says:

> For *it is* not an enemy *who* reproaches me; then I could bear it. Nor *is it* one *who* hates me who has magnified *himself* against me; then I could hide from him. But *it was* you, a man my equal, my companion and my acquaintance. We took sweet counsel together, *and* walked to the house of God in the throng. (Psalm 55:12-14)
>
> He has put forth his hands against those who were at peace with him; he has broken his covenant. *The words* of his

> mouth were smoother than butter, but war *was* in his heart;
> his words were softer than oil, Yet they *were* drawn swords.
> (Psalm 55:20-21)

Is it possible that this Antichrist who breaks his treaty with Israel is a resuscitated Judas Iscariot? Again this is only speculation; the Bible does not explicitly say who this man will be. It will only be at the midpoint where he will be revealed.

John is next told that the seven heads of the scarlet beast are seven mountains. Immediately, there are those who say that this is a clear reference to the Seven Hills of Rome. There are two problems with this assumption: one, hills are not mountains and mountains are not hills, and two, John is specifically told that the seven mountains are also seven kings, or kingdoms. This makes more sense, because mountains in Scripture are often used to represent kings or kingdoms. For example, in Daniel 2:35, Christ and His kingdom are said to become "a great mountain that filled the whole earth." The understanding of this passage calls for wisdom, not worldly wisdom, but biblical wisdom. This means that we must employ what has already been learned from the prophetic scriptures, in order to understand what is occurring within the text. The seven heads are seven mountains, or kingdoms upon which the harlot sits. So these are seven empires that had the Babylonian type religion as its power source. Of these seven kings, five are said to have fallen. The seven heads or kings are the same seven that were given to us by Daniel: Babylon, one head; Medo-Persia, one head; Greece, four heads (Egypt, Syria, Macedonia, and Asia Minor); and Rome, one head. The five that have fallen or have had their dominion take away (Daniel 7:12) are: Babylon, Medo-Persia, Egypt, Syria, and Macedonia. It is interesting to note that each one of these kingdoms had a Babylonian type of idolatry as its chief religion. One of the empires is said to still be in existence. This would be the Roman Empire which Daniel said would extend, as the legs of Nebuchadnezzar's statue extended, until the return of Christ. The empire that has not come and will continue a short time, of only forty-two months, is the revived Roman Empire, with the ten kings united by the Antichrist. This revived Roman Empire will not begin its existence as such until the midpoint of the Seventieth Week. This last empire is merely an extension of the seventh head, as the ten toes were an extension of the statue's feet (Daniel 2:41-45), as well as the ten horns being an extension of Daniel's fourth beast (Daniel 7:7). It should therefore, not be considered as being another head. John has now addressed six of the seven heads: Babylon, Medo-Persia, Egypt, Syria, Macedonia, and Rome, with its revived extension. The ruling demon princes of each of the first five regions have been defeated and have fallen. The demon prince of the Roman Empire has not fallen and will become mighty again when the ten kings of his empire give their authority to the Antichrist. John then discusses who the final head of the seven-headed beast is. John reveals that the final head is ruled by the Beast or the Antichrist. He is said to be the eighth king, but ruler over one of the seven heads, which again has been restored to world dominion (Remember Daniel said the kingdom of Greece would one day rule over all the earth in Daniel 2:39). The only remaining head that I have not yet listed is the Asia Minor division of Greece. This is where the throne of Antichrist is said to reside, as well as where I had previously concluded that the Antichrist would arise (Revelation 2:13). This is the head from which he will rule. The first demon prince of Asia Minor was defeated, and became a fallen head when the empire of Rome emerged. During the Seventieth Week, a prince will be let out of the bottomless pit to restore the dominion of Asia Minor. He is the eighth of these princes or kings, and is also none other than the Antichrist. This then reveals the supernatural nature of the Antichrist. While a man physically, he will command the same authority as a demon prince spiritually. What can then be concluded from these passages is that the Antichrist will rule the ten-nation revived Roman Empire, but he will do so from the Asia Minor province of the Grecian empire. Recall that John describes only five of the seven heads as being fallen. This is because two of the heads: Asia Minor and Rome, with its revived extension, will both be in power during the Seventieth Week. What John has described is in exact correlation with what Daniel had outlined. They both complement each other perfectly with absolutely no contradictions.

The ten kings will give their authority to the beast and will destroy the harlot. This will happen at the midpoint where the Antichrist demands that he alone is to be worshipped. Because of this, he will allow no other forms of religion to exist. The false religions that have been propagated by Satan throughout history will come to an end. Satan will finally, himself, receive the world's worship through their adoration of his son the Antichrist. It is at this point where the church is called to be an overcomer, to persevere, and under no circumstance bow the knee to the Antichrist. This time of tremendous persecution begins with the fourth seal and is known as the great tribulation.

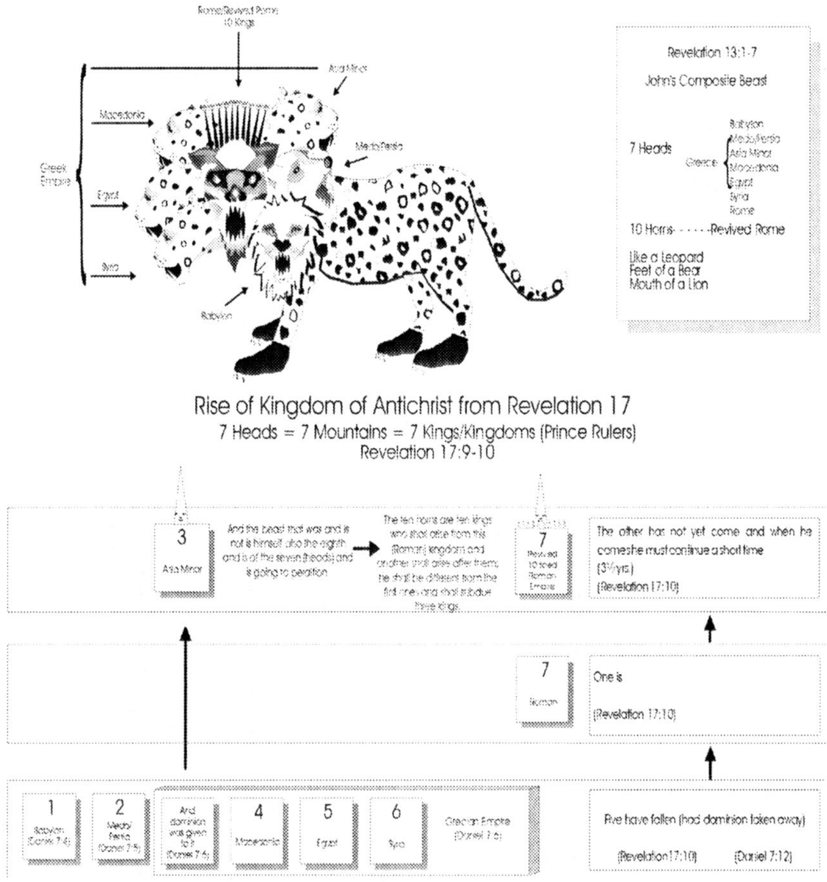

THE FOURTH SEAL (THE GREAT TRIBULATION)

When He opened the fourth seal, I heard the voice of the fourth living creature saying, "Come and see" And I looked, and behold, a pale horse. And the name of him who sat on it was Death, and Hades followed with him. And power was given to them over a fourth of the earth, to kill with sword, with hunger, with death, and by the beasts of the earth. (Revelation 6:7-8)

Then they will **deliver you up to tribulation** and kill you, and you will be hated by all nations for My name's sake. And then many will be offended, will betray one another,

> and will hate one another. Then many false prophets will rise up and deceive many. And because lawlessness will abound, the love of many will grow cold. But he who endures to the end shall be saved. And this gospel of the kingdom will be preached in all the world as a witness to all nations, and then the end will come. (Matthew 24:9-14) {*Emphasis Mine*}

As the fourth seal is unloosed, a pale horse rides out with a rider named Death, and Hades is following close behind. This is a picture of the Antichrist as he begins his persecution first, of the nation of Israel, and second, of the church of Jesus Christ. Our Lord stated that He was the resurrection and the life (John 11:25). The Antichrist is spoken of as being Death and Hades (hell). The treaty that Israel agrees to with him is called their treaty with death, or their treaty with hell (Isaiah 28:15). The rider on the horse has been granted authority over one fourth of the earth. This one fourth most likely composes those who are of the church, as well as those of national Israel. Modern figures show that Christianity composes approximately 25 percent of the world's population. It is this 25 percent that will be given into his hands for the last three and a half years.[4] In order to understand why this great persecution begins at this point, one must look at Revelation chapters twelve and thirteen. These chapters are written, in the context of Revelation, after the Seventieth week has ended and national Israel has accepted their Messiah as being Jesus. God is now preparing to pour His bowl of judgments on the kingdom of the Antichrist. Before this happens, John is given an overall spiritual view of what has previously taken place in the history of Israel and the church. John is, in a sense, given an instant replay of the battle of the ages between God and Satan. He is shown how each of God's people has come through this incredible time of testing. Essentially, these verses give us greater detail into the events of the great tribulation. Let's begin with chapter twelve.

> **Now a great sign appeared in heaven: a woman clothed with the sun, with the moon under her feet, and on her head a garland of twelve stars. Then being with child, she cried out in labor and in pain to give birth. And another sign appeared in heaven: behold, a great, fiery red dragon having seven heads and ten horns, and seven diadems on his heads. His tail drew a third of the stars of heaven and threw them to earth. And the dragon stood before the woman who was ready to give birth, to devour her Child as soon as it was born. And she bore a male Child who was to rule all nations with a rod of iron. And her Child was caught up to God and to His throne. Then the woman fled into the wilderness, where she has a place prepared by God, that they should feed her there one thousand two hundred and sixty days.** (Revelation 12:1-6)

The woman seen here is a spiritual picture of true Israel, as opposed to the harlot who was representative of false believers. The symbols of the sun, moon, and the stars point us back to Joseph's dream in Genesis 37:9. This was where young Joseph dreamed that his eleven brothers, who were the Patriarchs of the twelve tribes, would bow down before him. These symbols have always been associated with national Israel. They are used here so that we understand that this woman represents Israel. Israel is also referred to as a woman in Isaiah 54:1.

We are next shown Satan represented as a dragon having seven heads and ten horns. The seven heads have diadems (crowns) upon them, revealing that they are the prince demon rulers, through whose empires Satan persecuted the nation of Israel. It is important to note that the ten horns are addressed independently, as an extension of one of the seven heads. This correlates with what John detailed in Revelation chapter 17.

We know that this is Satan, because in Revelation 12:9 he is referred to as "that serpent of old, called the Devil and Satan." The third of the stars that he draws with him to the earth are the angels that have chosen to follow him. Angels are often spoken of as being stars in the Old Testament (Job 38:7). This dragon is said to be standing before the woman ready to devour her child as soon as it is born. This shows that Satan was the spiritual force behind the Gentile empires that tried to subjugate and annihilate the nation of Israel. His ultimate goal through them was to kill Jesus Christ, the "Child" who would eventually rule all nations. Initially, he tried to do this when Jesus was born, by having King Herod kill all the babies who were two years old and under (Matthew 2:16). God was able to warn Joseph, the father of Jesus, who then brought Him safely to Egypt. Satan was finally able to have Jesus crucified, but it was to his own demise. Little did he realize that he had not only sealed his own doom, but had allowed Jesus to redeem mankind. Because of the sinless nature of Jesus Christ, the grave was not able to hold Him. He was resurrected and caught up into heaven. John is then told that the women (true Israel) fled into the wilderness for 1260 days. We will see shortly that Satan will launch his final bid to destroy God's people: first, on the nation of Israel, and second, upon the church. There will then be those of national Israel who will escape the wrath of Satan. They will, later, become the first to accept Jesus as their Messiah.

> **And war broke out in heaven: Michael and his angels fought against the dragon; and the dragon and his angels fought, but they did not prevail, nor was a place found for them in heaven any longer. So the great dragon was cast out, that serpent of old, called the Devil and Satan, who deceives the whole world; he was cast to the earth, and his angels were cast out with him. Then I heard a loud voice saying in heaven, "Now salvation, and strength, and the kingdom of our God, and the power of His Christ have come, for the accuser of our brethren,**

> **who accused them before our God day and night, has been cast down. And they overcame him by the blood of the Lamb and by the word of their testimony, and they did not love their lives to the death. Therefore rejoice, O heavens, and you who dwell in them! Woe to the inhabitants of the earth and the sea! For the devil has come down to you, having great wrath, because he knows that he has a short time."** (Revelation 12:7-12)

Witnessed within these verses, is an incredible war in heaven between Satan and the Archangel Michael. It is a commonly held belief that Satan resides in hell, but this is not what is taught in Scripture. In the book of Job, when asked by God where he had been, Satan answered "From going to and fro on the earth, and from walking back and forth on it."(Job 1:7). From the writings of Job, as well as the prophet Zechariah, it is evident that Satan has access to heaven. He often goes there to accuse believers before God. This is what he did with the high priest Joshua in the book of Zechariah:

> Then he showed me Joshua the high priest standing before the Angel of the Lord, and Satan standing at his right hand to oppose him. And the Lord said to Satan, "The Lord rebuke you, Satan! The Lord who has chosen Jerusalem rebuke you! *Is* this not a brand plucked from the fire?" (Zechariah 3:1-2)

Satan is constantly accusing God's righteous saints of improprieties. At the midpoint of the Seventieth Week, God will have had enough, and Satan will be kicked out of heaven by Michael and his angels. Michael is an important figure, for in Daniel he is said to be the restrainer for the people of Israel:

> But I will tell you what is noted in the Scripture of Truth. (No one **upholds** me against these, except Michael your prince. Also in the first year of Darius the Mede, I, *even* I, stood up to confirm and strengthen him.) (Daniel 10:21-11:1) {*Emphais Mine*}

The Hebrew term used for "upholds" is the word "Chazak," which means to bind or restrain.[5] It is Michael's role to watch over the nation of Israel and to restrain the demonic princes. It is only at the midpoint where he will stop his restraint and allow Satan to freely vent his final fury on the nation of Israel. This is allowed in order to bring them to national repentance. This final period is also addressed by Daniel:

> At that time Michael shall **stand up**, The great prince **who stands *watch*** over the sons of your people; And there shall be a time of trouble, Such as never was since there was a

nation, *Even* to that time. And at that time your people shall be delivered, Every one who is found written in the book. (Daniel 12:1) {*Emphasis Mine*}

After Satan is cast to earth it is said that Michael "shall stand up". This literally means to arise and stand still, or to cease.[6] It is at the moment that Michael ceases to guard over Israel, that the fourth seal is broken and the great tribulation begins. We are told in Revelation 12:12 that the devil has come down having great wrath because he has a very short time. In verses 13 through 17, we are given a picture of what he will do once on earth:

> **Now when the Dragon saw that he had been cast to earth, he persecuted the woman who gave birth to the male *Child.* But the woman was given two wings of a great eagle, that she might fly into the wilderness to her place, where she is nourished for a time and times and half a time, from the presence of the serpent. So the serpent spewed water out of his mouth like a flood after the woman, that he might cause her to be carried away by the flood. But the earth helped the woman, and the earth opened its mouth and swallowed up the flood which the dragon had spewed out of his mouth. And the dragon was enraged with the woman, and he went to make war with the rest of her offspring, who keep the commandments of God and have the testimony of Jesus Christ.** (Revelation 12:13-17)

Satan is absolutely incensed that he has been kicked out of heaven, and his final doom is imminent. He first launches his attack against the "woman," or nation of Israel. Israel is then said to flee to a place prepared for her and dwell there for "a time and times and half a time," or 1260 days (Revelation 12:6 12:14). Since this period is referring to the last three and a half years of the Seventieth Week, it can be concluded that these parenthetic passages speak for themselves as to where they are to be put in the overall context of Revelation. It is believed that the faithful remnant of Israel, most likely the 144,000, flee to a city known as Petra. Petra is situated within mountains, and the heights of its sides are 200-1000 feet.[7] It has one narrow entrance, and from a tactical standpoint it is virtually impregnable.[8] It is located in Edom (Jordan) which is one of the areas that is said to escape control of the Antichrist (Daniel 11:41). This is because God will prepare this city for the 144,000 to take refuge in during the tribulation of Antichrist.

Because he is unable to destroy the Jews who escape, Satan then launches the second prong of his attack against the rest of the woman's offspring: those "Who keep the commandments of God and have the testimony of Jesus Christ" (Revelation 12:17). Consistently, this term has always referred to Christians throughout Revelation. Further confirmation that the Church will be attacked is given by Jesus in the Olivet Discourse:

> Then they will deliver you up to tribulation, and kill you, and you will be hated by all nations for My name's sake. (Matthew 24:9)

Remember, in context, Jesus was talking to His disciples. He says that they, and not only the nation of Israel, will be delivered up to tribulation. His disciples will be hated for His name's sake. Therefore, only those who have the "testimony of Jesus Christ" will be given up to this persecution. We are informed in Revelation twelve verse 11 that:

> . . . they overcame him by the blood of the Lamb and the word of their testimony, and they did not love their lives to the death. (Revelation 12:11)

In the letters to the seven churches, the assemblies were told over and over again to overcome and to persevere. There will be many false believers and prophets that will rise up and attempt to deceive the true believer. These false brethren will begin to betray and hate the true disciples of Jesus (Matthew 24:10). It will truly be a time where God will separate the "wheat" from the "tares."

There are many more things that go on during the midpoint which will be discussed in the next chapter. As we move forward, we should look for extreme consistency in all of the scriptures relating to this period. Also, there should be absolutely no contradictions. This is what we have established thus far about the midpoint:

1. At the midpoint Satan is thrown out of heaven.

2. Michael "stands aside" and no longer restrains Satan from attacking Israel.

3. Satan empowers the Antichrist to break the treaty, commit the "abomination of desolation," and launch the first prong of his attack against the nation of Israel.

4. The faithful Jews in Israel will escape Satan, and flee to Petra in Edom.

5. Satan will be infuriated and allow his servant, the Antichrist, to launch his next attack against the church.

6. It will be a time of trouble for Israel and the church that has never been seen nor ever will be seen again.

With these points in mind let us move on.

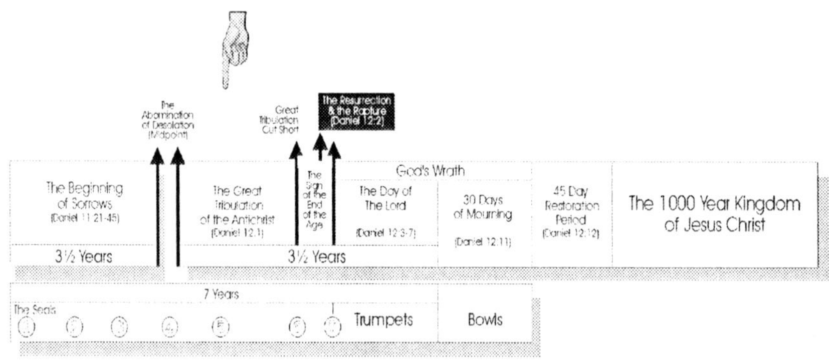

9
THE GREAT TRIBULATION

WHILE MOVING FORWARD into the tribulation scenario, it should be stressed that we are still in the period of the fourth seal of Revelation. We have just been shown the whole set up of these events in the spiritual realm. John will now reveal what the results are on planet earth.

Jesus has just told His disciples in Matthew 24:9-14, that they would be handed up to tribulation and be killed for His name's sake. In the following verses, He then answers the first question the disciples put forth, as to "when will these things be?"(Matthew 24:3). Jesus gives them a specific event to look for that will be the tell-tale sign that the great tribulation of Antichrist has begun. What He next reveals to them should continue to be absolutely consistent with the six points I outlined at the end of chapter ten. The Lord's words also should completely parallel what has been revealed by the prophets, as well as the book of Revelation:

> Therefore when you see the "*abomination of desolation*," spoken of by Daniel the prophet, standing in the holy place (whoever reads, let him understand) (Matthew 24:15)

THE ABOMINATION OF DESOLATION

Jesus reveals that the "abomination of desolation" is the signal that the time of trouble for the church and Israel is to begin. Matthew adds, that whoever reads these verses "let him understand." What Matthew states is important, because it implies that this text is written only to those who have spiritual understanding, as well as those who are going to read the book of Matthew. This shows again, that these passages are not written merely for the unbelieving nation of Israel, but to the believers in Christ at the time these events unfold. When Jesus mentions the "abomination of desolation" in Matthew 24, He speaks of this event as still being future. Although there may have been types of the "abomination of desolation" in Israel's past, they cannot be seen as fulfilling what Daniel had spoken of. This is because Jesus tells His disciples that it will be this event which will initiate the great tribulation, which up until that moment in time had not yet occurred. The prophet Daniel refers to the "abomination of desolation" in three crucial passages:

> He (Antichrist) even exalted *himself* as high as the Prince of the host; and by him the daily *sacrifices* were taken away, and the place of His sanctuary was cast down. Because of transgression, an army was given over *to the horn* to oppose the daily *sacrifices*; and he cast down truth to the ground. He did all this and prospered. (Daniel 8:11-12)

> Then he (Antichrist) shall confirm a covenant with many for one week; But in the middle of the week He shall bring an end to sacrifice and offering. And on the wing of abominations shall be the one who makes desolate, Even until the consummation, which is determined, is poured out on the desolate. (Daniel 9:27)

> And forces shall be mustered by him (Antichrist), and they shall defile the sanctuary fortress; then they shall take away the daily *sacrifices*, and place *there* the abomination of desolation. (Daniel 11:31)

From our prior look at Revelation chapter 12, it was understood that Satan would be cast out of heaven and have only 3 1/2 years to vent his fury upon the children of God. We also know that Michael, at that moment, ends his restraint that protects the nation of Israel. Satan then empowers the Antichrist to break the seven-year treaty that began the Seventieth Week. In the text of Daniel it is revealed that the Antichrist will be given an army, will enter the Holy Land, and then invade Jerusalem (Daniel 8:11-12). This invasion by the Antichrist is mentioned in Ezekiel chapter 38. Gog (a name for the Antichrist) is said to invade the Holy Land at a time when Israel is dwelling peacefully. This is due to the fact that they have signed a covenant with the Antichrist. Daniel states that in the middle of this seven year period, the Antichrist will break the covenant and invade Israel (Daniel 9:27). It is this initial invasion, into the land of Israel, that is pictured in Ezekiel chapter 38. Later, after the Day of the Lord begins, the Antichrist will bring his armies to the mountains of Israel where he will be destroyed by Jesus at the battle of Armageddon (Ezekiel 39). One must not confuse these two battles. The first, when he invades the entire land of Israel, occurs in Ezekiel chapter 38. The second, which takes place near the mountains of Israel, is spoken of in Ezekiel chapter 39.

With his massive army, said to be made up of troops from Persia (Iran), Ethiopia (Sudan), Libya, Gomer (central Turkey), and the house of Togarmah (Armenia and areas along the Euphrates), he will march into Jerusalem heading toward the temple mount. The Antichrist will enter into a structure where the Jewish sacrifices are being carried out. This structure may initially be a temporary tent-like structure, like the tabernacle of the time of Moses. The term in the Greek, used for "temple," also can mean a tabernacle or shrine type of structure.[1] Once the Jews have permission to use the temple mount for sacrifices, they may erect a temporary structure while constructing the permanent temple. It is quite amazing to see that the preparations are currently underway for the reinstatement of the Jewish sacrificial system.

The Ministry and Career of... Jesus Christ	The Ministry and Career of... the Antichrist
Jesus is called the Christ (Matt. 16:16)	The other is called the Antichrist (1 John 4:3)
Jesus came from Heaven (John 3:13)	Antichrist comes from bottomless pit (Rev. 11:7)
Jesus was a Man of Sorrows (Isa. 53:3)	Antichrist is a man of Sin (2 Thess. 2:3)
Jesus was the Son of God (John 1:34)	Antichrist is called the Son of Perdition (2 Thess. 2:3)
Jesus was the seed of the woman (Gen. 3:15)	Antichrist is the seed of the Serpent (Gen 3:15)
Jesus is called the truth (John 14:6)	Antichrist is called the Lie (John 8:44)
Jesus was the Lamb of God (Isa. 53:7)	Antichrist is the Beast of Satan (Rev. 11:7)
Jesus was the Holy One (Mark 1:24)	Antichrist is the Lawless One (2Thess. 2:8)
Jesus came in His Father's Name (John 5:43)	Antichrist comes in his own name (John 5:43)
Jesus humbled Himself (Phi. 2:8)	Antichrist exalts himself (2 Thess. 2:4)
Jesus was despised (Isa. 53:3)	Antichrist admired (Rev. 13:3-4)
Jesus was the Good Shepherd (John 10:4-15)	Antichrist is the worthless Shephard (Zech. 11:16-17)
Jesus came to do the Fathers will (John 6:38)	Antichrist came to do his own will (Daniel 11:36)
Jesus "The Mystery of Godliness"	Antichrist "The Mystery of Iniquity"
is God manifest in the flesh (1Tim. 3:16)	is Satan manifest in the flesh (2 Thess. 2:7)
Jesus cleansed the Temple (John 2:14-16)	Antichrist desecrates the Temple (Matt. 24:15)
Jesus was energized by the Holy Spirit (Luke 4:14)	Antichrist is energized by Satan (Rev. 13:4)
Jesus was slain for the people (John 11:51)	Antichrist slays the people (Isa. 14:20)
*Jesus was recalled into heaven (Acts 1:11)	Antichrist is thrown into the Lake of Fire (Rev. 19:20)

emple Institute in Israel has already prepared many of the ceremonial ıents that will be used in the rebuilt temple.[2] How the nation of Israel wııı ʋe allowed to rebuild this structure can only be speculated upon. Perhaps peace talks will lead to a dividing of east and west Jerusalem. With the western half going to the nation of Israel, and the eastern portion given to the Arabs. Because of this concession, Israel may be allowed to rebuild their temple. It is possible that the Antichrist, himself, will be the one who will enforces this agreement. I must stress that this is only speculation. Scripture is not specific as to how this is to occur; it only states that it will occur. The Apostle Paul provides believers with additional details into what is to take place when the Antichrist enters the rebuilt Jewish temple:

> Let no one deceive you by any means; for *that Day will not come* unless the falling away comes first, and the man of sin is revealed, the son of perdition, who opposes and exalts himself above all that is called God or that is worshipped, so that he sits as God in the temple of God, showing himself that he is God. (2 Thessalonians 2:3-4)

The Antichrist will declare to the world that he alone is to be worshipped. It is at this moment that the ten kings of the revived Roman Empire will give their allegiance to the Antichrist. This is also the point that they put to an end "Babylon the Great," the false religion that has deceived the kings of the earth. This is because the Antichrist, now empowered by the fallen Satan, will accept no more false religions; the mask has come off. Satan has always wanted to be worshipped, and has been indirectly, through false religions. He will now be directly worshipped through the Antichrist. Paul goes on to say that this unveiling of the Antichrist cannot begin until the restrainer has been removed:

> And now you know what is restraining, that he may be revealed in his own time. For the mystery of lawlessness is already at work; only He who now restrains *will do so* until He is taken out of the way. And then the lawless one will be revealed, whom the Lord will consume with the breath of His mouth and destroy with the brightness of His coming (2 Thessalonians 2:6-8)

We see from this passage that the restrainer must first be taken out of the way, or cease his restraint. Once this occurs, the Antichrist will be revealed for whom he really is, and the great tribulation will unfold. This is also confirmed by Daniel:

> At that time Michael shall stand up, The great prince who stands *watch* over the sons of your people; And there shall be a time of trouble, Such as never was since there was a

nation, *Even* to that time. And at that time your people shall be delivered, Every one who is found written in the book. (Daniel 12:1)

At the midpoint Michael is to "stand up," or stand aside and cease his restraint. I should at this point address the fact that there is some debate as to the exact identity of the "restrainer." There are two alternate views, which propose that Paul is referring either directly to the church, or to the Holy Spirit who works indirectly through the church. From Paul's text I believe that the church itself can be immediately ruled out. This is because Paul refers to the restrainer as being a "He." This seems to indicate that it is a single entity who is holding the restraint of the Antichrist. If Paul were referring to the church as being this entity, he would have more accurately referred to the restrainer as being a "she," since the church is the bride of Christ (Ephesians 5:30-32 & 2 Corinthians 11:2).

It is somewhat more conceivable that the restrainer could be the Holy Spirit. It is highly likely that it is the Spirit of God who restrains against the unveiling of the Antichrist. Personally, as evidenced previously, I am more inclined to lean toward the Archangel Michael as being the restrainer. This is because Paul's text in second Thessalonians 2:3-4 deals specifically with the "abomination of desolation" where the Antichrist reveals, within the Jewish temple, that he is now to be worshipped as God. This event is to occur precisely at the midpoint of the Seventieth Week. It is stated in two critical biblical passages, that Michael is to play a unique and important role at the midpoint of the Seventieth Week (Daniel 12:1 & Revelation 12:7-12). I feel that scripturally there is a stronger basis to conclude that Michael is indeed the restrainer of the Antichrist. Despite these facts, many Pre-tribulation rapture theorists will push the belief that the restrainer absolutely must be the Holy Spirit. To conclude that the restrainer is the Holy Spirit would, as they argue, prove that the church will be gathered off the earth before the Seventieth Week begins.

Their reasoning goes along these lines:

1. The restrainer is the Holy Spirit.

2. The Holy Spirit's presence on earth is expressed through the church.

3. When the Holy Spirit stops His restraint and is taken out of the way, then the church will also be taken out of the way.

4. Therefore, since Paul states that the restrainer will be removed immediately before the Antichrist is revealed, the church must be gathered off the earth before the great tribulation of the Antichrist begins.

This argument seems logical, but it is flawed in a number of important areas:

1. Just because the restrainer is stated to have ceased His restraint, or to have been taken out of the way, does not imply that He is no longer present upon the earth. For example, if the United States ceased its role as a defender and protector of Israel it would not necessarily follow that the United States is no longer present or in existence. It would merely mean that the United States is no longer in an active role of defending that nation. To assume more is occurring in this passage than the cessation of the restrainer's active role of restraint, merely reads too much into Paul's text.

2. When put into the context of second Thessalonians this argument, once again, crumbles. This is because, in effect, Paul would be contradicting the sequence of events outlined in the verses that immediately precede the restrainer passage. In second Thessalonians 2:3-4 Paul states that there would first be a great falling away, next the revealing of the Antichrist in the temple, and then the day of the church's gathering would occur. If the restrainer passage is referring to the gathering of the church, the sequence would be the removal, or gathering, of the church first, and then the revealing of the Antichrist in the temple. Paul would thus be blatantly contradicting the sequence of events he initially outlined. Paul is either seriously confused, or the gathering of the church is not what is being referred to in the restrainer passage.

3. Finally, if one were to concede somehow that the restrainer passage was referring to the gathering of believers and then the revealing of the Antichrist, it would put the gathering well into the Seventieth Week. This is because Paul defines the Antichrist's revealing as being when he sits in the Jewish temple and declares that he is God. It is an inescapable fact that this is to occur at the midpoint of the Seventieth Week. Paul's text seems to imply that the revealing of the Antichrist immediately follows the removal of the restrainer. If the church is also removed at this moment, it would put its removal at the midpoint of the Seventieth Week and not before it begins, as Pre-tribulationist's propose. In fact, for them to argue that the removal of the church is what is being implied in the

restrainer passage, is extremely damaging to the Pre-tribulationist viewpoint!

In any event, now that all restraint has been removed, we should now see the Antichrist launch his first attack against Israel, and next against the church, as was outlined in Revelation chapter 12. Again, we focus on the words of Christ in the Olivet Discourse:

> Then let those who are in Judea flee to the mountains. Let him who is on the housetop not come down to take anything out of his house. And let him who is in the field not go back to get his clothes. But woe to those who are pregnant and to those with nursing babies in those days! And pray that your flight may not be in the winter or on the Sabbath. For then there will be great tribulation such as has not been since the beginning of the world until this time, no, nor ever shall be. And unless those days were shortened no flesh would be saved; but for the elect's sake those days will be shortened. Then if anyone says to you "look, here is the Christ!" or "There!" do not believe *it*. For false prophets will arise and show great signs and wonders, so as to deceive, if possible, even the elect. See that I have told you beforehand. Therefore if they say to you, "Look, He is in the desert!" do not go out; or "Look, *He is* in the inner rooms!" do not believe *it*. (Matthew 24:16-26)

Jesus echoes exactly what the other scriptures have said. He lets His disciples know that if they are in Jerusalem when the "abomination of desolation" occurs, they must drop everything and get out. This will be the first stage of the Antichrist's attack, and it will unleash persecution that will make the holocaust look like child's play. Jesus is not talking specifically to the nation of Israel, but only those who have read and understood what has been written. All believers, Jewish or Gentile, are told to get out of Jerusalem. It is likely that at this time the 144,000 will realize that Israel has made a treaty with "death," and they will make their escape to Petra. Most in Israel will bow allegiance to the Antichrist, while others will choose to defend Jerusalem to no avail. It is disclosed, by Daniel, that the Antichrist shall come in rage against the holy covenant and do great damage (Daniel 11:30).

THE PHYSICAL RISE OF THE ANTICHRIST

Revelation chapter 13 reveals a portrait of the Antichrist as he takes world control and begins his persecution of God's elect. Keep in mind that these verses in Revelation chapter 13 are written immediately after Satan has been kicked out of heaven by Michael. They too follow the exact sequence of events just outlined by Paul, and our Lord.

> **Then I stood on the sand of the sea. And I saw a beast rising up out of the sea, having seven heads and ten horns, and on his horns ten crowns, and on his heads a blasphemous name. Now the beast which I saw was like a leopard, his feet were like *the feet* of a bear, and his mouth like the mouth of a lion. And the dragon gave him his power, his throne, and great authority. I saw one of his heads as if it had been mortally wounded, and his deadly wound was healed. And all the world marveled and followed the beast. So they worshipped the dragon who gave authority to the beast; and they worshipped the beast, saying, "Who *is* like the beast? Who is able to make war with him?" And he was given a mouth speaking great things and blasphemies, and he was allowed to continue for forty-two months. Then he opened his mouth in blasphemy against God, to blaspheme His name, His tabernacle, and those who dwell in heaven. And it was granted him to make war with the saints and to overcome them. And authority was given him over every tribe, tongue, and nation. And all who dwell on the earth will worship him, whose names have not been written in the Book of Life of the Lamb slain from the foundation of the world. If anyone has an ear let him hear. He who leads into captivity shall go into captivity; he who kills with the sword must be killed with the sword. Here is the patience and the faith of the saints.**
> (Revelation 13:1-10)

John here is describing as a composite the same four beasts that Daniel saw (Daniel 7:1-8). In this particular passage, John is describing them in their final form, under the absolute authority of the Antichrist and Satan. Pictured then, in this description, is the physical manifestation of the spiritual forces that were detailed in Revelation chapter 17. The ten horns are said to have ten crowns, this indicates that the ten kings have now given their authority to the beast and rule as kings under his direction. This is exactly what the angel told John would occur, in Revelation 17:12. John also reveals that one of the seven heads looked as if it were wounded or slain. This confirms that the Antichrist is an eighth king, but rules from one of the seven heads (Revelation 17:11). A good way to understand this would be to think of the seven heads as seven houses with seven owners. The seven owners would be the demon princes who ruled the Gentile empires that the seven heads represent (Daniel 10:20). Say one the owner's dies, and a new owner buys one of the seven houses. He would be an eighth owner, but there would still be only seven houses. There would not be eight houses. In the same sense, we are to understand that the seven heads are seven kingdoms (houses), and they are also seven kings (owners). One of the former kings (owners) was defeated and, hence his head was slain. The Antichrist is to be the eighth king (owner), and rules from one of the seven kingdoms (houses). This was determined to be the Asia Minor head, from the four-headed empire of Greece. The revival of the head of this beast is twofold. In the physical, it takes the form of the resurrection to life of the Antichrist. In the spiritual, it involves the installation of a new demonic prince who will revive the rule of the fallen Asia Minor head, and restore its dominion. The Antichrist, himself, is the embodiment of a demonic prince and a human being, the seed of Satan so to speak (Genesis 3:15). John also relates that this beast was like a leopard, indicating that the Grecian empire would be the most prominent part of this last world kingdom. Since, at this point, the Antichrist is revealed for whom he really is, as outlined by the Apostle Paul (2 Thessalonians 2:3), it is said that the whole world will marvel at the beast and worship the dragon, or Satan. The Antichrist is now given authority to continue for 42 months. This passage now times itself as occurring at the midpoint of the Seventieth Week. The Antichrist is said to persecute God's people for "a time and times and half a time" which is 3 1/2 years, or 42 biblical months. From this, we are to understand that at the exact moment when Satan is kicked out of heaven, he will empower the Antichrist, and will attempt to destroy God's people. Through the Antichrist, Satan is given authority over believers for 42 months. It is stated that he will make war with the saints and overcome them (Revelation 13:7). These persecuted saints are "those who are the offspring of Israel and have the testimony of Jesus" (Revelation 12:17). Daniel agrees completely with John on this scenario:

> He shall speak *pompous* words against the Most High, Shall persecute the saints of the Most High, And shall intend to change times and law. Then the saints shall be given into his hand for a time and times and half a time. (Daniel 7:25)

> Those who do wickedly against the covenant he shall corrupt with flattery; but the people who know their God shall be strong and carry out *great exploits*. And those of the people who understand shall instruct many; yet *for many* days they shall fall by the sword, and flame, by captivity and plundering. Now when they fall, they shall be aided with a little help; but many shall join with them by intrigue. And *some* of those of understanding shall fall, to refine them, purge *them*, and make *them* white, *until* the time of the end; because it is still for the appointed time. (Daniel 11:32-35)

In the Olivet Discourse, Jesus said that His disciples would be handed up to tribulation, and they would be hated by all nations for His name's sake

(Matthew 24:9). This will be a period of time when many will be martyred for identifying with Jesus. Only those who are truly His will overcome. It is vital to remember that the letters to the seven churches were written to warn believers of this time. Jesus also declared that His disciples must not heed the words of the false teachers and preachers, but persevere and follow Him. In Revelation chapter 13, John sees that all those who dwell on the earth will worship Satan and the Antichrist. The term "earth dwellers" always refers to unbelievers. This is because believers are not of this world (John 15:19). Next, we are told by John that "**If anyone has an ear, let him hear**" (Revelation 13:9). Where have these words been seen before, and to whom do they relate to? Seven times this phrase was used in reference to the congregations of the seven churches in Asia Minor.

This phrase becomes extremely important, because it is employed as a reminder to those believers who will now enter the great tribulation. This phrase, as we have seen, consistently applies to the churches of Revelation. Yet, most scholars do not feel that the church will be upon the earth at this moment. I have some news for them, our Lord knew that His disciples would be there, and He has John tell them "if anyone has an ear, let him hear," because "Here is the patience and the faith of the saints" (Revelation 13:10). Jesus, in this passage, is proclaiming to His church that if they could understand and comprehend what the Spirit said to the seven churches, then they had better apply it, because the time has now come. This is the moment when the false disciples will show their true colors, and the true disciples may lose their lives for following Jesus.

In Matthew chapter 24, Jesus said that false prophets would arise and show great signs and wonders. Their power will be so absolutely amazing that, if it were possible, event the "elect," or His true disciples, could be deceived. I do not believe we have any idea how unbelievable these miracles may very well be. Many in the church today are lulled by phony faith healers and those who employ imaginative spiritual gimmicks to obtain money. Imagine what will happen to the church when a man arrives with all the authority and power that Satan has to offer. This man then announces to the church that he is the second coming, and has the absolute power to back up his claims. History already provides us with the answer. The Christian church in Germany was lulled to sleep by Adolf Hitler, and even supported his rise to power.[3] These very same believers looked the other way when the Holocaust began. There was a faithful remnant, but the vast majority was captured by the absolute satanic magnetism of Hitler. God help us when the Antichrist arrives on the scene, because many will deny Christ, and others will be slaughtered, not even knowing what hit them.

THE FALSE PROPHET

Continuing in Chapter 13 we are given a glimpse of what is to occur next.

> **Then I saw another beast coming up out of the earth, and he had two horns like a lamb and spoke like a dragon. And He exercises all the authority of the first beast in his presence, and causes the earth and those who dwell in it to worship the first beast, whose deadly wound was healed. He performs great signs, so that he even makes fire come down from heaven on the earth in the sight of men. And he deceives those who dwell on the earth by those signs which he was granted to do in the sight of the beast, telling those who dwell on the earth to make an image to the beast who was wounded by the sword and lived. He was granted *power* to give breath to the image of the beast, that the image of the beast should both speak and cause as many as would not worship the image of the beast to be killed. And he causes all, both small and great, rich and poor, free and slave, to receive a mark on their right hand or foreheads, and that no one may but or sell except one who has the mark or the name of the beast, or the number of his name. Here is wisdom. Let him who has understanding calculate the number of the beast, for it is the number of a man: His number *is* 666.** (Revelation 13:11-18)

This second beast will be the head honcho of all the false prophets who will arrive on the scene. He has two horns like a lamb, symbolizing his false identification with the true Lamb of God, Jesus Christ. This false prophet will be an apostate of the highest caliber. The fact that he speaks like a dragon indicates that his very words will be straight from Satan himself. He will perform miracles of biblical proportions, and will cause the world to worship the Antichrist. He will also tell the world to make images to the beast (Antichrist); these images that they are to create will be given breath (spirit), and the ability to speak. The images will, most likely, be little idols that people will wear, which will be inhabited by the angels who were cast out of heaven with Satan (Revelation 12:9).[4] Anyone who does not worship these images, or idols, will be killed. This may sound a little far fetched, but, then again, so does the ability of one to cause fire to come out of heaven (Revelation 13:13). This whole period of the Seventieth Week will be an unparalleled time, the likes of which will never again be duplicated. On top of all this, the false prophet will cause all ruled by the Antichrist to have a mark placed on their right hand or forehead. This will either be a mark, the name of the beast, or the number of his name. No one will be able to buy or sell anything unless they have bowed allegiance to the Antichrist and are physically identified as one of his. Through this method the Antichrist will obtain control over the entire economy of the Middle East, as well as the world. This economy will be regulated through the rebuilt city of Babylon (Revelation 18). Babylon will then become the trade center of the entire world. Whether the mark of the Antichrist will be a UPC code that will be read during a purchase, or a tattoo that must be shown when purchasing, I cannot say for sure. It is not wise to look at current trends toward a cash-less society and begin to identify them as being the system that will initiate the mark of the beast. It must be recalled that with the opening of the second and third seals, the world will suffer large-scale wars along with the crash of its economic system. So any trends we are now seeing may not have any significance at the middle of the Seventieth Week.

John is next informed that the number of the beast is the number of a man, and this number is 666. In Scripture the number six is often used to symbolize fallen man. Seven is the number of completeness, and six falls one short of seven. Man has fallen short of perfection since Adam's sin. Since the number of God is seven, the number of the Holy Trinity would be 777. The Antichrist is claiming to be god, so the number of his unholy trinity would be 666.

These passages in chapter 13 paint an incredible picture of what will happen to believers when the rider on the fourth horse uses his power over the fourth of the earth, or the saints. He will kill with the sword, and with hunger, because believers will not be able to buy or sell if they do not take his mark. He also will kill by the beasts of the earth (Revelation 6:8). This may be a reference to the little images of the beast that will be inhabited and controlled by the fallen angels. These demonic idols will spot believers, and if they do not worship the image they will be killed. The "great tribulation" are the only words that are appropriate in describing this period of human history.

GOD'S FEARFUL WARNINGS

God will not leave the world without a witness of His gospel during the great tribulation. As I address Revelation chapter 14, (the last of these parenthetic chapters that deals with the midpoint, during the fourth seal) God's final warnings to the earth will be seen. Jesus told His followers that the gospel would be preached to all the world; then the end, or the "end of the age" would come (Matthew 24:14). This demonstrates that the Day of the Lord cannot begin until the gospel is preached to the entire world. This evangelism will never be accomplished by the church, as most believe. Although many will be saved through the disciples witness during the great tribulation, God has an even more efficient way of proclaiming the gospel. His foolproof method is revealed in Revelation chapter 14:

Then I saw another angel flying in the midst of heaven, having the everlasting gospel to preach to those who dwell on the earth-- to every nation, tribe, tongue, and people-- saying with a loud voice, "Fear God and give glory to Him, for the hour of His judgment has come; and worship Him who made heaven and earth, the sea and springs of water." And another angel followed, saying, "Babylon is fallen, is fallen, that great city, because she has made all nations drink of the wine of the wrath of her fornication." Then a third angel followed them, saying with a loud voice, "If anyone worships the beast and his image, and receives *his* mark on his forehead or on his hand, he himself shall also drink of the wine of the wrath of God, which is poured out in full strength into the cup of His indignation. And he shall be tormented with fire and brimstone in the presence of the holy angels and in the presence of the Lamb. And the smoke of their torment ascends forever and ever; and they have no rest day or night, who worship the beast and his image, and whoever receives the mark of his name." Here is the patience of the saints; here *are* those who keep the commandments of God and the faith of Jesus. Then I heard a voice from heaven saying to me, "Write: 'Blessed *are* the dead who die in the Lord from now on.'" "Yes," says the Spirit, "that they may rest from their labors, and their works follow them." (Revelation 14:6-13)

I have not, at this point, included the first five verses of chapter 14. This is because they should really be read as part of chapter 13, since there is no paragraph break in the Greek text until Revelation 14:6. In Revelation chapters 12 and 13, John has outlined the entire spiritual history of the nation of Israel. At the beginning of Revelation chapter 14 he then shows the 144,000 who are the first of national Israel to believe in Jesus Christ as Messiah. He is thus contrasting those who are sealed with the name of God, with those who are sealed with the name of the Antichrist.

It must be understood when reading these parenthetic verses, that they are written in the period after the seventh trumpet of God's wrath is blown, which ends the Seventieth Week. Since Israel has concluded the Seventieth Week, John gives a brief spiritual overview of how the salvation of national Israel came to be. Basically, John is giving greater details on how these events unfolded from the midpoint of the Seventieth Week to its conclusion. After writing about the first of national Israel to be saved, John, in Revelation 14:6, goes back to the midpoint to show the destiny of the church, as well as of those who follow the Antichrist.

We first are shown an angel who has the everlasting gospel that will be preached to everyone on planet earth. This will fulfill what Jesus stated about the gospel being preached to the world before the Day of the Lord occurs (Matthew 24:14). I am convinced that this will be a literal angel who, at the midpoint, will travel the entire earth proclaiming the everlasting gospel. I do not believe it will be a satellite beaming down Christian television, as some suppose. Many argue that the "everlasting gospel" is not the same as the "gospel of the kingdom" that Jesus spoke of. They believe that these are two completely different gospels. As Christians we know that there is only one gospel; the good news that Jesus paid for the sins of the world and rose from the dead. This was the gospel of the Old Testament unrevealed, and the gospel of the New Testament revealed. God has never changed His plan of salvation, for it was determined before the foundation of the earth. Besides, Paul tells believers in the book of Galatians that if an angel from heaven comes preaching any other gospel, he is to be accursed (Galatians 1:8). This angel should then be preaching a gospel consistent with the word of God. His gospel will present truth in the midst of the greatest spiritual deception ever perpetrated upon humanity. It will be a true witness to counteract the deceptive witness of the Antichrist and the False Prophet. Angels have always wanted to play an active role in God's redemptive plan (1 Peter 1:12), now they will have their chance to participate. This first angel will warn the world that the moment of God's judgment is almost upon them. The world is also warned that they are not to worship the Antichrist, but rather they are to worship the true God who created the things that are in the earth. This preaching will begin at the midpoint and culminate when the Day of the Lord begins.

The next angel, who immediately follows the first angel, announces the destruction of the false religion "Babylon The Great." The angel uses the phrase "Is fallen" twice, to stress that there will be two falls of Babylon. First destroyed, is the false religious system. This occurs at the midpoint of the Seventieth Week. The second to be judged is the city of Babylon which is destroyed at the seventh bowl judgment of God. What we then have in view in this particular passage is the destruction of the false religious system. It is apparent that the false religious system is being referred to, because:

1. The angel is making his announcement in a period before the wrath of God has actually hit. Since this is the case, the bowl judgment that destroys the city of Babylon cannot at this point occur.

2. We were told previously that the ten kings would give their allegiance to the Antichrist at the midpoint, and in turn they would destroy "Babylon The Great" the false religion that has deceived the world (Revelation 17:16-17).

Therefore, since the judgment of God has not yet taken place in the context of these verses, the angel's announcement must come sometime after the midpoint, but before the Day of the Lord. Since the angel informed John that the ten kings give their authority to the Antichrist at the midpoint, it is highly likely that the destruction of the harlot Babylonian religion is what is being announced by the second angel.

The third angel God sends forth warns the world not to take the mark of the beast. The world is told that whoever worships the beast and receives his mark, will taste of the wrath of God. Again, from the text it can be demonstrated that these angels are making their announcements sometime during the tribulation of Antichrist, but before the wrath of God has come upon those who have received the mark and worshipped the beast. Because of these warnings, God will accept no excuses for anyone who takes the mark of the Antichrist. One either chooses to serve Satan or God; there will be no middle choice. Those that choose the Antichrist will be hit so severely with God's furious wrath that it will make their heads spin. They are also informed that they will spend eternity separated from God in the lake of fire. The consequences of taking the mark of the beast will be both severe and final. In verse 12 of Revelation chapter 14, John encourages the saints to persevere. Those who do not bow down to the Antichrist are said to be "those who keep the commandments of God and the faith of Jesus." These are the "wheat" among the "tares." It will not, during this persecution, matter if you have "a personal relationship with Jesus" or have "accepted Him as your Savior." What is relevant is whether or not you take the mark of the beast. If you take the mark it is a sign that you are indeed a false disciple. Those who persevere and do not receive the mark may die, but they will be blessed of God. This will be a time when believers must overcome by the blood of the Lamb, and love not their lives to the death (Revelation 12:11). Through the message of these three angels God will make clear to the world the gospel of Jesus, as well as the consequences for refusing to put their faith in Him. Along with these angels, God also will provide an incredible witness to the unbelieving nation of Israel.

THE TWO WITNESSES

> **Then I was given a reed like a measuring rod. And the angel stood, saying, "Rise and measure the temple of God, the altar, and those who worship there. But leave out the court which is outside the temple, and do not measure it, for it has been given to the Gentiles. And they will tread the holy city underfoot *for* forty-two months. And I will give *power* to my two witnesses, and they will prophecy one thousand two hundred and sixty days, clothed in sackcloth. These are the two olive trees and the two lampstands standing before the God of the earth. And if anyone wants them, fire proceeds from their mouth and devours their enemies. And if anyone wants**

> **to harm them, he must be killed in this manner. These have power to shut heaven, so that no rain falls in the days of their prophecy; and they have power over waters to turn them to blood, and to strike the earth with all plagues, as often as they desire. Now when they finish their testimony, the beast that ascends out of the bottomless pit will make war against them, overcome them, and kill them.** (Revelation 11:1-7)

In Revelation chapter 11 which is written in context, after the sixth trumpet judgment, John is shown two men who will witness Jesus as Messiah to the nation of Israel. John presents the background of the beginning of their ministry up until their deaths at the end of the Seventieth Week, which precedes the blowing of the seventh trumpet judgment. John is told to measure the temple of God which is in the city of Jerusalem. He is also told to leave out measuring the outer court, which shall be trampled by the Gentiles for 42 months. This parenthetic passage now times itself, because it is known that the Antichrist defiles the outer court and the sanctuary at the midpoint of the Seventieth Week (Daniel 11:31). It is also known that the Antichrist will lead an invasion of Gentile forces into Jerusalem at the same time. What John then writes concerning these two witnesses, occurs during the last half of the Seventieth Week. The witnesses are said to be given power from God, and they will prophesy for 1260 days, or 42 months. Although contrary to the context of this passage of Scripture, there are those who insist that these two start their ministry at the beginning of the seven-year period. However, this is inconsistent with other scriptures that also speak about these witnesses. In fact, the prophet Malachi gives the identity of one of these two men, as well as the timing of his arrival.

BEHOLD I SEND YOU ELIJAH

It was a commonly held Jewish belief that the prophet Elijah would return to earth before the arrival of Messiah. To this day, at Passover, it is customary to leave an open seat and place setting for the prophet Elijah.[5] Elijah never died but was taken bodily into heaven by God (II Kings 2). Because of this, it was believed that he would return bodily to proclaim the coming of the Messiah.[6] The apostles also knew of this belief and questioned the Lord about it:

> And His disciples asked Him, saying, "Why then do the scribes say that Elijah must come first?" Then Jesus answered and said to them, **"Elijah is truly coming first and will restore all things**. But I say to you that Elijah has come already, and they did not know him but did to him

> whatever they wished. Likewise the Son of Man is also about to suffer at their hands." Then the disciples understood that He spoke to them of John the Baptist. (Matthew 17:10-13) {*Emphasis Mine*}

Jesus does not rebuke the disciples for their inaccuracy, but confirms that Elijah would indeed come first and restore all things before His return. Jesus then informs them that if they could comprehend it, John the Baptist was in a special way Elijah who was to come. If Israel had not rejected Jesus as their Messiah, John's ministry would have fulfilled the scriptures that spoke of the coming of Elijah. Since the Jews killed John, and did not accept Jesus, God will, at a future moment in time, send Elijah to give Israel a second chance. In the book of Malachi we are told when Elijah will be sent and what his ministry will be:

> Behold, I will send you Elijah the prophet Before the coming great and dreadful day of the Lord. And He will turn the hearts of the fathers to the children, And the hearts of the children to their fathers, Lest I come and strike the earth with a curse. (Malachi 4:5-6)

It is very important that we understand that Elijah will be sent "**before**" the Day of the Lord begins. Now there are many who teach that the Day of the Lord begins with the opening of the first of the seven seals of Revelation. Since the first seal begins the last seven-year period, the above reasoning would mean that Elijah would have to appear 1260 days before the Seventieth Week begins. This would not only be illogical, but in complete disagreement with prophetic Scripture. This is because John is specifically told that these two witnesses will preach sometime during the seven-year period, and not before or after.

During this time, they are given the ability to do incredible miracles and will eventually be killed by the Antichrist. The events of their ministry must then occur during a time after the Antichrist has revealed his true colors and has begun the great tribulation. It then becomes inescapable that these two witnesses, Elijah and possibly Moses, must appear at the midpoint of the Seventieth Week. I lean toward Moses as being the second of the two witnesses, because the miracles performed by the second witness are very much like the ones that Moses performed. It is also revealed by Jude that Satan and the Archangel Michael had a dispute over who would control his deceased body (Jude 1:9). This may have implications that Satan knew God would resuscitate the body of Moses during the last half of the Seventieth Week. I use the term resuscitate because Moses, if one of the witnesses, will be killed by the Antichrist. He will be like Lazarus who was called forth from his tomb, but eventually died again (John 11:1-44). Finally, Moses was seen atop the Mount of Transfiguration, with Elijah, speaking with Jesus (Matthew 17:1-9). This is probably one of the strongest evidences that Moses will be the second of the two witnesses. Whatever the case, they will appear at the midpoint, preach for 1260 days, and then be killed by the Antichrist at the end of the Seventieth Week. This then allows Elijah and Moses to appear before the "coming great and dreadful Day of the Lord," which does not occur until the great tribulation is cut short by God. As we will soon see the Day of the Lord begins sometime after the midpoint, but before the end of the Seventieth Week. It then follows that the seven seals cannot possibly be God's wrath, because Elijah is to be sent before the wrath of God begins. The two witnesses are sent to bring Israel to the realization that Jesus was their Messiah, before He returns to pour out His vengeance upon the unbelieving nation of Israel, as well as the unbelieving Gentile world. It will, most likely, be through their testimony that the rest of Israel that does not flee to the wilderness will come to be saved.

God will make the choices very clear to the world, when the fourth seal is opened and the great tribulation of Antichrist begins. Yet with all this, they still will not believe God, and will be caught unaware when the great Day of the Lord begins. There will even be those who bear the name of Jesus Christ who will refuse to believe that the Day of the Lord is upon them. There will be no mistaking it, because there will be an incredible sign in heaven signaling that the end has arrived.

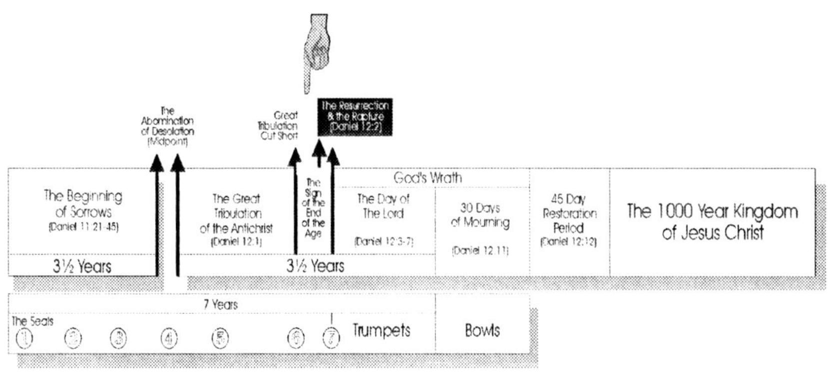

10
THE GREAT SIGN OF THE END

PRESENTLY, IN THE PROGRESSION OF EVENTS outlined in Revelation and the Olivet Discourse, we are in the period known as the great tribulation of Antichrist. This tribulation began with the unloosening of the fourth seal of Revelation. The Antichrist has committed the "abomination of desolation" and is attempting to wipe out every believer on planet earth. Viewed also were Revelation chapters: eleven, twelve, thirteen, fourteen, and seventeen, which revealed greater details of the events that are to occur during this period. Jesus has warned His disciples that this would be such an intense time of persecution, that if God did not shorten the great tribulation none of His disciples would survive (Matthew 24:22).

THE FIFTH SEAL

As the fifth seal of Revelation is broken, John is shown the results of this great persecution:

> **When He opened the fifth seal, I saw under the altar the souls of those who had been slain for the word of God and for the testimony which they held. And they cried with a loud voice, saying, "How long, O Lord, holy and true until You judge and avenge our blood on those who**

> **dwell on the earth?" And a white robe was given to each of them; and it was said to them that they should rest a little while longer, until both *the number* of their fellow servants and their brethren, who would be killed as they *were*, was completed.** (Revelation 6:9-11)

John is shown the souls of those who had been slain for their belief in the word of God. This group most likely represents the martyred of all the ages, as well as those who have undergone the great tribulation of Antichrist. It is important to note that these martyrs are said to be "souls" who are "under" the altar of God. They have not at this point received their resurrection bodies. The martyrs are told that they will not receive their resurrection bodies until the rest of their brethren are also slain for their testimony. The final martyrs who are to die for their testimony, will be the two witnesses who are killed by the Antichrist at the end of the Seventieth Week. Once Jesus has destroyed the Antichrist, He will then give these martyred believers their resurrection bodies. The martyrs of the ages are said to be given a special resurrection, because of dying for their faith in Christ. The author of Hebrews speaks of this special resurrection of the Lord's martyrs:

> "Women received their dead raised to life again. **And others were tortured, not accepting deliverance, that they might obtain a better resurrection**. (Hebrews 11:35) {*Emphasis Mine*}

Those who have been tortured and killed for their faith in Christ, will be part of a special resurrection at the beginning of Christ's rule on earth (Revelation 20:4). They also will be given special status in the Lord's government, because of their martyrdom.

It is crucial to note in this text that the martyrs are crying out to God asking Him when He will finally pour out His wrath on "those who dwell on the earth." Throughout Revelation the term "earth dwellers" is always applied to unbelievers. Their home is this world, for their father is Satan the ruler of the world. If the first four seals are the beginning of God's judgment, as many contend, then the scholars are much smarter than the martyrs. According to the text, the martyrs had absolutely no clue that the first four seals were God's judgment. In fact, they are pleading with God for Him to finally begin the Day of the Lord. In this instance, I have to believe that the martyrs are not confused, but comprehend exactly what is happening. They understand that the seals are only conditions that are to precede God's judgment, and are not to be confused with His direct wrath. The great tribulation is a persecution by the hand of the Antichrist and Satan; not of God. God does not persecute His own disciples. He will allow persecution, but He is not the one initiating it. As seen in the book of Job, as well as the rest of Scripture, it is Satan that persecutes the righteous (Job 1&2). I stated previously, that I find it hard to believe that the Antichrist will have a heyday destroying God's people at the same moment that God is pouring out the "wrath" of the seal judgments upon the earth. However, God's wrath will begin shortly and the martyrs are aware that it is extremely close.

THE GREAT AND TERRIBLE DAY OF THE LORD

In the text of Matthew chapter 24, the Lord told His disciples that unless the days of the great tribulation were shortened, none of His disciples would survive (Matthew 24:22). The Antichrist would literally attempt to annihilate every single breathing Christian. Jesus states that it is only for the "elects sake" that the days will be shortened. The "elect" being referred to are those who have placed their faith in Christ, either Jew or Gentile. Paul refers only to those who have faith in Christ as being the elect; not merely to those who are born of Hebrew descent:

> What then? Israel has not obtained what it seeks; but the elect have obtained it, and the rest were hardened. (Romans 11:7)
>
> But it is not that the word of God has taken no effect. For they *are* not all Israel who *are* of Israel, nor *are they* all children because they are the seed of Abraham; but, "*In Issac your seed shall be called.*" That is, those who are the children of the flesh, these *are* not the children of God; but the children of the promise are counted as the seed. (Romans 9:6-8)

Even if one concedes that the "elect" of this passage are Israel, by following Paul's logic it becomes inescapable that the "elect" must be believers in Christ:

> 1. Lets suppose that Israel is the "elect" of Matthew 24:22.
>
> 2. Paul states that only those that are of faith are to be numbered with Israel. (Romans 9:6-8)
>
> 3. Israel is then made up of all believers, Jew or Gentile, who have placed their faith in Christ and not merely those of Hebrew descent. (Romans 11:7)

> 4. The conclusion becomes inescapable that the term "elect" is always a reference to faithful believers in any given dispensation.

So only for the sake of the disciples of Jesus, will the great tribulation will be shortened. One absolutely must not confuse the great tribulation period with the Seventieth Week. The Seventieth Week will not be shortened for it has been decreed to last the entire seven years. The Seventieth Week has been decreed upon the unbelieving nation of Israel to bring them to final repentance and belief in Jesus. The great tribulation, on the other hand, is a period that begins at the midpoint where Satan, through the Antichrist, will attempt to thwart God's final plan for Israel and the church. This period will separate the true believer from the false. It is this persecution that will be cut short when the Day of the Lord begins, and not the Seventieth Week. The prophet Daniel is shown this very occurrence:

> I was watching; and the same horn (Antichrist) was making war against the saints, and prevailing against them, until the Ancient of Days came, and a judgment was made *in favor* of the saints of the Most High, and the time came for the saints to possess the kingdom. (Daniel 7:21-22)

Although the Antichrist is given authority over the saints for three and a half years, God will cut this period short. The term that Jesus uses for "shortened" (Matthew 24:22) is the Greek word Koloboo, which literally means to "amputate".[1] So although the saints or elect are given into the hands of the Antichrist for three and one half years, God will sovereignly choose to amputate the amount of time allotted to him.[2] This amputation will occur when Jesus comes to gather His elect at the rapture, and initiate the wrath of God. This scenario is also confirmed by the Apostle Paul in His second letter to the Thessalonians:

> And then the lawless one (Antichrist) will be revealed, whom the Lord will consume with the breath of His mouth and **destroy** with the brightness of His **coming**. (2 Thessalonians 2:8) {*Emphasis Mine*}

Paul states that at the "coming," or Parousia of Christ, the Antichrist will be "destroyed." Paul employs the Greek term "Katargeo" for "destroy." This word means to render inactive, or reduce to inactivity the works of the lawless one.[3] In other words, when Jesus comes to gather the elect and initiate the Day of the Lord, the great persecution of the Antichrist will be rendered inactive. Later, at the end of the Day of the Lord, Jesus will "consume" the Antichrist at Armageddon. Believers are not to know the day or the hour that this "amputation" or shortening of the great tribulation will occur; they are just told to persevere until Jesus returns.

THE SIGN OF THE COMING OF JESUS

In the Olivet Discourse Jesus states that there will be the employment of incredible deception in an attempt to get believers out of hiding, but they are warned by Jesus not to move until the great sign of the end of the age is revealed. It is at this moment that Jesus answers the disciple's second question: "What will be the sign of your coming and the end of the age:"

> For as lightning comes from the east and flashes to the west, so also will the coming of the Son of Man be. For wherever the carcass is, there the eagles will be gathered. (Matthew 24:27-28)

Jesus reveals that the sign of His coming will be an incredible flash of light that will blaze across the globe from east to west. It will be the return of the Shekinah glory of God back to earth. Jesus then tells His disciples that the sign of His coming will immediately follow the sign of the end of the age, or the Day of the Lord. He then relates the proper procession of these events:

> Immediately after the tribulation of those days the sun will be darkened, and the moon will not give its light; the stars will fall from heaven, and the powers of the heavens will be shaken. Then the sign of the Son of Man will appear in heaven, and then all the tribes of the earth will mourn, and they will see the Son of Man coming on the clouds of heaven with power and great glory. (Matthew 24:29-30)

From this passage we are to understand that:

1. The sign that the end of the age, or the Day of the Lord is about to begin, involves the darkening of the sun, moon, and stars.

2. This sign will immediately follow the great tribulation, not the Seventieth Week. It will in fact signal the amputation or shortening of the great tribulation of Antichrist.

3. After the sign of the sun, moon, and stars, the sign of the coming of the Son of Man will appear; which Jesus previously detailed (Matthew 24:27-28).

4. The people of the earth will realize that the Day of the Lord has actually come and they will mourn because of the impending doom.

THE SIXTH SEAL

What our Lord has just outlined to His disciples should be exactly what occurs at the opening of the sixth seal of Revelation. Jesus has followed every seal so far, and the sixth seal should be no different. Let's take a look at the opening of the sixth seal in the book of Revelation:

> **I looked when He opened the sixth seal, and behold, there was a great earthquake; and the sun became black as sackcloth of hair, and the moon became like blood. And the stars of heaven fell to the earth, as a fig tree drops its late figs when it is shaken by a mighty wing. Then the sky receded as a scroll when it is rolled up, and every mountain and island was moved out of its place. And the kings of the earth, the great men, the rich men, the commanders, the mighty men, every slave and every free man, hid themselves in the caves and in the rocks of the mountains, and said to the mountains and rocks, "Fall on us and hide us from the face of Him who sits on the throne and from the wrath of the Lamb! For the great day of His wrath has come, and who is able to stand?"** (Revelation 6:12-17)

It is absolutely amazing that the very same events now occur in Revelation that was outlined by Jesus in the Olivet Discourse. The sign of the sun, moon, and stars occurs immediately after the fourth and fifth seals, which had previously revealed the events of the tribulation of Antichrist. This same sign cuts off the great tribulation and shows the unbelieving world that the Day of the Lord is upon them. The sign of the sun, moon, and stars is not some sort of nuclear explosion as many propose. If God wanted John to describe a nuclear war He would have had him done so more specifically. It must be remembered that Jesus, not John, is the author of the Revelation. Although John may not have understood what a nuclear war was, Jesus would have. The fact remains that this is a supernatural sign in the heavens that will be given by God to warn the world that His wrath has come. The Old Testament gives numerous references to this great sign in the heavens.

The Lord states in Genesis that He created the sun, moon, and stars to be for "Signs and seasons, and for days and years" (Genesis 1:14). This great sign will appear immediately before the Day of the Lord begins, as seen also by these Old Testament passages:

> Behold, the day of the Lord comes, Cruel, with both wrath and fierce anger, To lay the land desolate; And He will destroy its sinners from it. For the stars of heaven and their constellations Will not give their light; The sun will be

> darkened in its going forth, And the moon will not cause its light to shine. I will punish the world for *its* evil, And the wicked for their iniquity; I will halt the arrogance of the proud, And will lay low the haughtiness of the terrible. I will make mortal more rare than fine gold, A man more than the golden wedge of Ophir. Therefore I will shake the heavens, And the earth will move out of her place, In the wrath of the Lord of Hosts And in the day of His fierce anger. (Isaiah 13:9-13)

> And I will show wonders in the heavens and in the earth: Blood and fire and pillars of smoke. The sun shall be turned into darkness, And the moon into blood, Before the coming of the great and terrible day of the Lord. And it shall come to pass *That* whoever calls upon the name of the Lord Shall be saved. For in Mount Zion and in Jerusalem there shall be deliverance, As the Lord has said, Among the remnant whom the Lord calls. (Joel 2:30-32)

In both of these passages it is apparent that this sign occurs right before the Day of God's wrath. It can then be easily concluded from Isaiah, Joel, Matthew, and Revelation that the Day of the Lord will not begin until sometime after the midpoint but, before the end of the Seventieth Week.

The sixth Seal in Revelation reveals that the "Great Day of His wrath has come." This again demonstrates, beyond a reasonable doubt, that the first five seals have absolutely nothing to do with the wrath of God. For the Christians in hiding, this sign will be the indication that Jesus is to return and take them off the earth before the wrath of God begins.

THE RETURN OF JESUS CHRIST

Moments after God turns off the lights of the sun, moon, and stars, the illumination and glory of the return of Christ will blast over the face of the entire earth. It will be so spectacular and amazing that there will not be anyone in the entire world who will miss it. It is at this time that those of the nation of Israel who have trusted in the Antichrist as messiah will realize their grave error:

> Behold, He is coming with clouds, and every eye will see Him, **and they *also* who pierced Him**. And all the tribes of the earth will mourn because of Him. Even so, Amen. (Revelation 1:7) {*Emphasis Mine*}

In order to solve an enigma one must often move outside of their regular thought process and view things from a different perspective. In the same sense, in order to understand Revelation one must remove his or herself out from their preconceived theological boundaries, and take the word of God at face value. There are those who have theological problems with believing that Jesus returns at the sixth seal. This is because it is commonly taught that Jesus does not return to earth visibly until chapter 19 of Revelation, immediately before the battle of Armageddon. To resolve this major discrepancy, scholars interpret the sixth seal as being Christ's return at Armageddon. The problem with this view is that the sixth seal has absolutely nothing to do with the battle of Armageddon. There still remain seven trumpets, as well as the seven bowls of God's wrath, before Armageddon can take place. Besides, if Jesus returns only in Revelation chapter 19, what is He doing on Mount Zion with the 144,000 in chapter 14 of the Apocalypse? The problem lies in theological beliefs, rather than in Scripture itself. There is nothing explicitly in the Bible that states that Jesus has to make His first appearance to the world at Armageddon. In fact, it is believed by most of evangelical Christianity that Jesus will return halfway to the Earth to take away His disciples in a "secret rapture." So it is considered orthodox to believe Jesus comes halfway to earth in secret, but almost heretical to propose that He returns halfway in glory and in power and in full view of the world. There is not a single passage in all of Scripture which declares that Jesus returns for His church in secret. This is merely a theological fallacy created by those who cannot accept an open majestic return of Jesus for His church. Revelation declares that Jesus will return and every eye will see Him. The entire earth will then understand that He is the one behind the fury that is about to ensue. We need to believe the word of God, that Jesus will return at the sixth seal cutting short the great tribulation, as well as the rule of Antichrist. This is the revealing of the Day of the Lord. It is solely the Lord's moment and no one will be magnified other than Him. There will no longer be any confusion as whether what is occurring upon the earth is a natural disaster or a supernatural judgment from God above. Men will literally hide in caves to escape the wrath of God. Remember the world has been told by the angels and the two witnesses, that if they take the mark of the beast they will be destroyed. The world now realizes that God really meant what He said. There will be no escape from the awesome destruction of God. In Luke we are told that men will literally die of the fear that will come upon the earth when Christ is revealed (Luke 21:26). Men, who have chosen to believe only in the love of God, while forgetting His holiness and His justness, will be in for a tremendous surprise. The false believers who were among the seven representative churches of Asia Minor will now realize their error, but it will be too late. The doom of everyone who has followed and worshipped the Antichrist has been sealed. In Isaiah we are told that men will throw away the little idols that they made into the image of the beast. This is because they will now realize that they have worshipped one who is not really the "god" he claimed to be:

> They shall go into the holes of the rocks, And into the caves of the earth, From the terror of the Lord And the glory of His majesty, When he arises to shake the earth mightily. In that day a man will cast away his idols of silver And his idols of gold, Which they made, *each* for himself to worship, To the moles and bats, To go into the clefts of the rocks, And into the crags of the rugged rocks, From the terror of the Lord And the glory of His majesty, When He arises to shake the earth mightily. (Isaiah 2:19-21)

Before this great wrath is poured out, Jesus must take His church. For His disciples are not to undergo the wrath of God. In the gospel of Luke believers are assured that:

> Now when these things begin to happen, look up and lift your heads, because your redemption draws near. (Luke 21:28)

It is at this very moment that the event which the body of Christ has desired and dreamed for takes place. This unique occurrence is the "blessed hope" of the church: the Rapture.

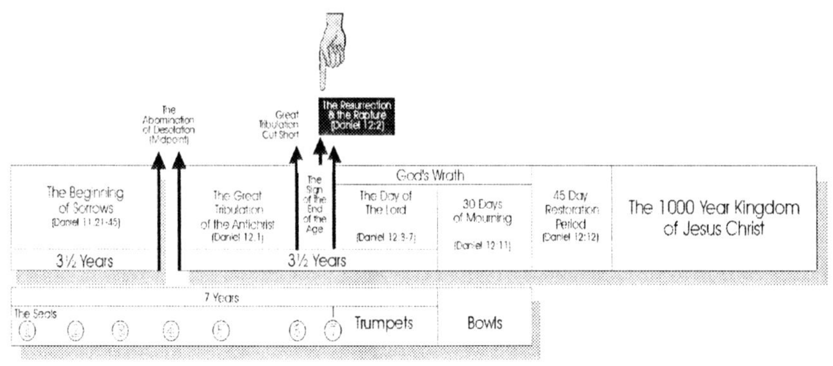

11
THE RESURRECTION AND THE RAPTURE

THE RAPTURE OF THE CHURCH has been one of the most abused, debated and misunderstood doctrines of Scripture. There are many teachers who have decided that they know the exact date of this event and have led many in the church into utter confusion. In fact, there have been so many spurious predictions that the rapture would occur, that some in the church have begun to doubt if Jesus will ever return for His elect. These believers have become like those spoken of by the Apostle Peter:

> Knowing this first: that scoffers will come in the last days, walking according to their own lusts, and saying, "Where is the promise of His coming? For since the fathers fell asleep, all things continue as *they were* from the beginning of creation." (2 Peter 3:3-4)

This dangerous trend toward indifference to the second coming of Christ, has led believers to focus more on their lives on earth, than in the hope of the resurrection. There are now many movements within the church that believe that Jesus will only return when Christianity converts the world to Christ. Unfortunately, the book of Revelation speaks quite to the contrary. The state of the church and the world will become worse and worse as we reach the second advent of Jesus Christ. The church, as evidenced in the Lord's letters to the assemblies of Asia Minor, will become weaker, because of the false teachings that have crept in. The world, in turn, will become more hateful of the handful of genuine Christians who will choose to stand on the word of God in defiance of the world's system. This will culminate in the period of the great tribulation.

Because of this, it is extremely critical that the church is keenly aware of the approximate timing of the rapture. It is important to note that Jesus emphatically declares that no one will be able to know the exact day or the hour of His return for the church (Matthew 24:36). Yet, believers are commanded to look for and recognize the signs that will announce that His return is imminent. Christ's disciples are warned not to be caught unaware as this day approaches. While specific times are often given in God's dealing with the nation of Israel, they are never given in reference to Christ's return for the church. It has been this hope, for the return of Jesus that has allowed previous believers to undergo and persevere through tremendous persecution. It will be this very same hope that will propel believers to be overcomers during the great tribulation of Antichrist.

THE BLESSED HOPE

What exactly is the rapture? The word rapture does not actually appear in Scripture. The term comes from the Latin word "rapere" which means "to be caught up." It was originally used in the Latin Vulgate version of the Bible and has become a term that has survived the centuries. The rapture, or "catching up," will occur when Jesus returns to earth, before the Day of the Lord, to gather His believers before the wrath of God begins. Believers must not confuse the rapture with the resurrection. The rapture was a "mystery" that was revealed by the Apostle Paul:

> **Behold, I tell you a mystery**: We shall not all sleep, but we shall all be changed in a moment, in the twinkling of an eye, at the last trumpet. For the trumpet will sound, and the dead will be raised incorruptible, and we shall be changed. For this corruptible must put on incorruption, and this mortal *must* put on immortality. (1 Corinthians 15:51-53) {*Emphasis Mine*}

The resurrection itself was not the mystery Paul spoke of. The resurrection, in fact, is spoken of many times in the Old Testament and was a common belief in the nation of Israel. There were certain groups, such as the Sadducees, that did not believe in a resurrection (Matthew 22:23-28), but for the most part this was a widely held belief. The mystery spoken of by Paul is that not all believers would experience physical death (sleep). Rather, the believers who are alive at the time the resurrection occurs will have their bodies instantly changed into immortal ones that will never die. This is, again, confirmed by Paul in 1 Thessalonians:

> For if we believe that Jesus died and rose again, even so God will bring with Him those who sleep in Jesus. For we say this to you by the word of the Lord, that we who are alive *and* remain until the coming of the Lord will by no means precede those who are asleep. For the Lord Himself will descend from heaven with a shout, with the voice of an archangel, and with the trumpet of God. And the dead in Christ will rise first. Then we who are alive *and* remain shall be caught up together with them in the clouds to meet the Lord in the air. And thus we shall always be with the Lord. Therefore comfort one another with these words. (1 Thessalonians 4:14-18)

> From Paul's words the following can be assessed:
>
> 1. There will be a group of living believers who will witness the return of Jesus and be given resurrection bodies without seeing death.
>
> 2. The resurrection of those who have already died in Christ will occur first and immediately following will be the rapture of the living believers.
>
> 3. The Lord himself will descend; there will then be a shout of the archangel, and a great trumpet will be blown. All believers, both dead and alive, will then be gathered to Christ.

What has been revealed by Paul is that when the resurrection of the dead occurs, the rapture will immediately follow. From this it can concluded that anytime the resurrection is presented in either the Old or New Testament, the rapture must also be implied as occurring.

In the text of Revelation it is apparent that believers will undergo the great tribulation of Antichrist. The return of Christ for His elect will then occur sometime after the midpoint but before the end of the Seventieth Week. There are many who argue that the Pre-wrath Rapture (the idea that the church will see the great tribulation and be raptured out as the Day of the Lord begins) is a recent belief. Actually, the Pre-wrath perspective is not new, because it has always been proclaimed clearly in Scripture. Unfortunately, our theological hang-ups have blinded us to clearly understanding this perspective. In the same way, many argued that Luther's preaching of justification by faith alone, was also a new belief. Yet, it was in Scripture for centuries, along with being the doctrine of the early church. God opened Luther's eyes and thus began the

Protestant Reformation. In a similar manner, the belief that the church would undergo the great tribulation of Antichrist is also not a new revelation. It was the solid conviction of virtually every early church father, until the fourth century. This began to change when men, such as Origen and Augustine, began to allegorize Scripture. There is a collection of documents, known as the writings of the Ante-Nicene Fathers, which contain the beliefs of many of the church fathers. These writings which preceded the council of Nicea in the fourth century clearly detail the eschatological perspective of many of the leaders of the early church. Some of these men were disciples of the Apostles, and their teaching often reflects what the Apostles had taught them. As I have sifted through these early church writings, I found almost without exception, the belief that the church would undergo the persecution of Antichrist and then be taken out before the wrath of God began. I am citing the below captioned quotes from some of these writings, in order to show the views these writers held. Obviously, these quote's are not to be regarded as highly as Scripture, but they do convey what the early disciples understood and believed about end-time prophecy:

> Watch for your lifes sake. Let not your lamps be quenched, nor your loins be unloosed; but be ye ready, for you know not the hour in which our Lord cometh. But often shall ye come together, seeking things which are befitting your souls: for the whole time of your faith will not profit you, if ye be made not perfect in the last time. For in the last days false prophets and corrupters shall be multiplied, and the sheep shall be turned in to wolves, and love shall be turned into hate; for when lawlessness increaseth, they shall hate and persecute and betray one another, and then shall appear the world deceiver as Son of God, and shall do signs and wonders, and the earth shall be delivered into his hands, and he shall do iniquitous things which have never yet come to pass since the beginning. Then shall the creation of men come into the fire of trial, and many shall be made to stumble and shall perish; but they that endure in their faith shall be saved from under the curse itself. And then shall appear the signs of truth; first, the sign of an outspreading in heaven; then the sign of a sound of a trumpet; and third, the resurrection of the dead; yet not of all, but as it is said: The Lord shall come and all His saints with Him. Then shall the world see the Lord coming upon the clouds of heaven. (The Didache or Teachings of the Twelve Apostles) [1]

What becomes apparent from the above text is that the early believers followed exactly what was outlined by Jesus in the Olivet Discourse. The disciple is first warned that he must be prepared for the return of the Lord. False prophets will arise, and then Antichrist will be revealed. There will next appear the sign of the opening of heaven (the sign of the Son of Man), with the blowing of the trumpet and the resurrection of the dead. This document puts the resurrection, hence the rapture, after the appearance of the Antichrist and the sign of the Son of Man. This is in complete agreement with what Jesus stated in the Olivet Discourse.

Other church fathers had this to say concerning the church and the great tribulation:

> That the beast Antichrist with his false prophet may wage war on the church of God. (Tertullian) [2]

> And they (the ten kings) shall lay Babylon waste, and burn her with fire, and shall give their kingdom to the beast and put the church to flight. (Irenaeus)[3]

> He shall come from heaven with glory, when the man of apostasy (Antichrist) who speaks strange things against the most High, shall venture to do unlawful deeds on the earth against us the Christians . . . (Justin Martyr)[4]

> Now concerning the tribulation of the persecution which is to fall upon the church from the adversary (Antichrist) . . . (Hippolytus)[5]

> That refers to the one thousand two hundred and threescore days (the half of the week) during which the tyrant is to reign and persecute the church which flees from city to city . . . (Hippolytus)[6]

As is evidenced above, it was the consistent belief of these early believers that the church would see the persecution of the Antichrist. In fact, when the early church was experiencing the persecution of Nero, it was believed that he was possibly the Antichrist. Many believed that he would be killed and rise from the dead; this was known as the Nero Redivivus Myth.[7] Why would the early Christians believe that Nero was the Antichrist if they had been explicitly taught by the Apostles that they would not be around to see his unveiling?

The whole problem with the rapture's timing seems to lie in the definition of exactly when God's wrath begins. Almost all conservative scholars agree that the church will not be on earth during the wrath of God, or the Day of the Lord. If one defines the entire seven year period as the Day of the Lord, then it stands to reason that the church will not be around for this period. The problem with this view is that Scripture consistently reveals that the Day of the Lord does not begin until after the sign of the sun, moon, stars, and the sign of the Son of Man, as detailed by Jesus, as well as the book of Revelation. Chronologically, these signs occur at the sixth seal, which is opened sometime after the midpoint of the Seventieth Week. The breaking of this sixth seal takes place in the midst of the great tribulation of Antichrist. This cuts the great tribulation short and announces the Day of the Lord. In order for our hermeneutic to remain consistent, then the church must remain on earth at least until the opening of the sixth seal of Revelation. If what I am proposing is correct, the same series of events should be presented in every scripture dealing with the resurrection or the rapture. We should then, consistently see that the gathering of the elect is to take place after the revealing of Antichrist, and after the sign of the sun, moon, and stars.

BACK TO OLIVET

Continuing in the Olivet Discourse, it must be remembered that, in context, Jesus has just described the great tribulation, the sign of the sun, moon, and stars, and the sign of the return of the Son of Man. Here is what the Lord states is to occur next:

> And He will send His angels with a great sound of a trumpet,
> and they will gather together His elect from the four winds,
> from one end of heaven to the other. (Matthew 24:31)

This verse can be referring to nothing else but the rapture of His disciples. It occurs right after the sign of the sun, moon, and stars and after the sign of the Son of Man. In the rapture passage in 1 Thessalonians 4:14-18 Paul had revealed the following:

1. The Lord would descend to earth.

2. There would be a shout of the voice of the archangel.

3. There would be the sound of a trumpet and believers, both living and dead, would be gathered to Jesus.

Also, in the parable of the wheat and the tares, Jesus revealed that the angels (the reapers) would gather the wheat, or the true disciples, into the barn (Heaven) at the "end of the age."

In Matthew 24:29 Jesus unveils the sign of the "end of the age." In agreement with His parable, angels now descend to earth, with the sound of a trumpet, to gather the elect from the four winds. The trumpet that is sounded is the trumpet of God which is also described in 1 Thessalonians 4:16 and 1 Corinthians 15:52. This trumpet is sounded by the Lord, Himself, after the sign of the Son of Man (His lightning flash of glory from east to west), as detailed by the prophet Zechariah:

> Then the Lord will be seen over them, And His arrow will go forth like lightning. The Lord God will blow the trumpet, And go with whirlwinds from the south. (Zechariah 9:14)

Who are these elect that are being gathered? Jesus has already disclosed that they are the "wheat," or His true disciples. Also, in Romans 11:7 the elect are defined as being both Jews and Gentiles who have put their faith in Jesus as Savior. In the context of Matthew chapter 24, Jesus has been addressing His disciples and what would befall them in the days preceding His return. It should be safe to conclude that it is these same believers that are being gathered by the angels as the Day of the Lord begins. There are many who shift the context of this verse as referring to the nation of Israel being gathered back their land. There are a couple of reasons why this view is obviously incorrect:

> 1. Never, at any point in Matthew chapter 24, does Jesus address national Israel. He always speaks in terms of the disciples or the elect. Even those who are told to flee Jerusalem, when the "abomination of desolation" occurs, are ones who have read and understood the words of the Lord in these passages hence, they are believers.
>
> 2. The elect are said to be gathered from the four winds. They are not said to be taken back to Israel or protected by the angels. To infer this reads into what the text actually states.
>
> 3. This verse employs the exact language that is used in terms of Christ's coming for His church at the resurrection: the descent of Jesus to the earth (Matthew 24:30), the sound of a trumpet, and the angels, or reapers, gathering the elect.
>
> 4. There is nothing in the Old Testament or New Testament that speaks of national Israel being gathered back to their nation by angels. Yet, as we have observed, there is Scripture that relates to angels gathering believers at the harvest of the "end of the age"

In order that His disciples completely understood what He was speaking about in these verses, Jesus next gives them a parable and two illustrations.

THE PARABLE OF THE FIG TREE

> Now learn this parable from the fig tree: When its branch has already become tender and puts forth leaves, you know that summer *is* near. So you also, when you see all these things, know that it is near, at the *very* doors. Assuredly, I say to you, this generation will by no means pass away till all these things are fulfilled. Heaven and earth will pass away, but My words will by no means pass away. (Matthew 24:32-35)

Many who write about this passage come up with a very convoluted interpretation. It is argued that the fig tree represents national Israel, and that this tree began budding when Israel became a nation in 1948. Since a generation in Scripture is forty years, then Jesus should have returned in 1988. Obviously, this rapture date has passed with no return of Jesus. The problem, again, is that too much is being read into the text. While it is true that Israel is often referred to, and is symbolized by the fig tree, it does not necessarily follow that every time a fig tree is used in Scripture that it is speaking of Israel. Remember when Jesus saw Nathaniel under the fig tree (John 1:48). Does this passage mean that Jesus saw Nathaniel under the nation of Israel? [8] The fig tree must not be taken to mean anything other than a fig tree unless the context demands otherwise.

So what is the point of this parable? Jesus is using a simple analogy to explain to His apostles how they could know that His coming for them was near. Just as they knew that summer was near when the fig trees put forth their leaves, they were also to understand that His second coming was near when they saw the signs that He had just outlined for them. Just as the budding of leaves is the sign of the imminence of summer, the signs that Jesus just spoke about, signal the imminence of His return. There have been many prophecies, proclaimed in Scripture that have taken literally hundreds or thousands of years to be fulfilled. But Jesus tells His disciples, that the generation that witnesses the beginning of these signs, will see all of them fulfilled within their lifetime (Matthew 24:34). This is precisely because these end-time prophecies will be fulfilled in a very short span of time: seven years.

THE ILLUSTRATION OF THE DAYS OF NOAH

> But of that day and hour no one knows, no, not even the angels of heaven but My Father only. But as the days of Noah *were*, so also will the coming of the Son of Man be.

> For as in the days before the flood, they were eating and drinking, marrying and giving in marriage, until the day that Noah entered the ark, and did not know until the flood came and took them all away, so also will the coming of the Son of Man be. Then two *men* will be in the field: one will be taken and the other left. Two *women will* be grinding at the mill: one will be taken and the other left. Watch therefore, for you do not know what hour your Lord is coming. But know this, that if the master of the house had known what hour the thief would come, he would have watched and not allowed his house to be broken into. Therefore you also be ready, for the Son of Man is coming at an hour when you do not expect *Him*. (Matthew 24:36-44)

Jesus now uses the illustration of Noah and the flood to really hit home exactly what He was speaking about in the entire Olivet Discourse. Our Lord states that no one will know the day of His return. He must, in context, be referring to His coming for His church, because Scripture explicitly states that Jesus will return to the nation of Israel at the end of the seven-year period. It will be very easy to calculate what day this will be once the seven-year treaty is signed or after the abomination of desolation occurs. However, Jesus is emphatic in revealing that no one will be able to compute the day that He will return for His church at the rapture. (*The main argument for the imminent return of Christ and a surprise super-secret rapture is based on the "no one knows the day or hour" verse in Matthew 24. Oddly pre-tribulationists equally argue, and quite passionately, that these very same passages in Mathew apply solely to National Israel and Christ's return at Armageddon. It seems to me that that one cannot have it both ways.*) Jesus likens His return to the days of Noah, when everyone went about their daily activities until Noah entered the ark and God poured out His judgment on the world. In the same way, before the second return of Jesus, the world will still be going about its daily business, until His elect are gathered out and the Day of God's wrath begins. To illustrate this point further, Jesus discloses that two will be in the field and one will be taken, and two will be grinding and one will be taken. The Scripture twisters immediately change the simple meaning intended by Jesus in this passage. They argue that this whole illustration refers to His return at Armageddon, and that the one taken is taken in judgment at Armageddon. The one left is spared to enter Christ's kingdom. There are some major flaws with this line of reasoning:

> 1. This particular event is said to occur at a day and hour which no one would know, and would catch the world, and possibly "believers", by surprise. The battle of Armageddon will catch no one by surprise. In fact, as we will later see, the Antichrist and his armies will be waiting to fight against

> Jesus at the battle of Armageddon. This is because they know the exact moment He will return.
>
> 2. The battle of Armageddon has not been addressed at all in the entire Olivet Discourse. Why then do commentators feel that they are free to believe that Armageddon is being implied in these verses?
>
> 3. The word used for "taken" in verses 40 and 41, is the Greek word Paralambano. Strong's Concordance defines Paralambano as "to receive near, i.e. associate with oneself".[9] Vines defines it as "to take to (or with) oneself." It does not mean to be judged, or taken in a negative sense.[10]

In looking more closely at the Greek word "Paralambano," it is interesting to note that Jesus uses this very same word when He speaks of His return for His disciples in John 14:1-3.[11]

> Let not your heart be troubled; you believe in God, believe also in Me. In My Fathers house there are many mansions; if *it were* not *so*, I would have told you. I go to prepare a place for you. And if I go to prepare a place for you, I will come again and **receive you to Myself**; that where I am, *there* you may be also. (John 14:1-3) {*Emphasis Mine*}

The words that read "receive you to Myself" are the translation of the term "Paralambano." By getting a clearer picture of the meaning of this word, we are to understand that "two will be in the field: one will be taken (received to Christ), and the other left" just as Noah was received into the boat, and the ungodly world left for destruction. Since Jesus has just spoken of the angels gathering His elect, it is very consistent with the context of this passage to interpret it as referring to His return for His church. Jesus warns His disciples to "keep watch," because the exact hour of His return is not known. However, the signs He outlined should give believers ample warning that it is imminent. If we recall, the letters to the seven churches indicated that some "believers" would not be prepared for the great tribulation, or the return of Jesus. In fact, to the church of Sardis, Jesus said He would come as a thief, and they would be caught completely by surprise (Revelation 3:3). Many scholars teach that the rapture of the church is signless, and it will occur without warning. If this is true, why does Jesus spend a full chapter in Matthew detailing the signs that would precede His coming for the elect? Simple logic demonstrates that if one is told to "watch" and "be ready" there must be something to watch for. The fact is, the entire Olivet Discourse contains the very events that the Lord's disciples should be watching for.

33

LLUSTRATION OF THE TWO ANTS

> ho then is a faithful and wise servant, whom his master made ruler over his household, to give them food in due season? Blessed is that servant whom his master when he comes, will find so doing. Assuredly, I say to you that he will make him ruler over all his goods. But if that evil servant says in his heart, "My master is delaying his coming," and begins to beat *his* fellow servants, and to eat and drink with the drunkards, the master of that servant will come on a day when he is not looking for *him* and at an hour that he is not aware of, and will cut him in two and appoint *him* his portion with the hypocrites. There shall be weeping and gnashing of teeth. (Matthew 24:45-51)

This final illustration in Matthew chapter 24 leaves no doubt that the entire discourse has been addressed to the Lord's servants or disciples, and not solely the nation of Israel. The servants who have been faithful, have persevered, and overcome the great persecution will be rewarded by Jesus. Those false servants who have not had genuine faith, but have turned from Christ and have beaten and persecuted His true servants, will have their portion with the rest of the unbelieving world, during the wrath of God. These are those who were never true disciples. As the Apostle John states:

> They went out from us, but they were never of us; for if they had been of us, they would have continued with us; but *they went out* that they might be made manifest, that none of them were of us. (1 John 2:19)

These unfaithful servants are the "tares" who will be left on earth when God's reapers gather the "wheat," or the true believers, into His barn. They are also those who were the false disciples amongst the seven churches.

It is at this point with which we conclude our study of the Olivet Discourse. Jesus does not give any further information concerning the Day of God's wrath, because that is not what the apostles were inquiring about. They just wanted to know what would be the sign of Christ's coming for His elect, as well as the sign that the Day of the Lord had begun. As we have seen, our Lord's answer correlates completely with every other passage we have studied thus far. We should then continue to see the timing of the rapture occurring after the great tribulation and the sign of the "end of the age," in all other related Scripture; especially in the book of Revelation. Before moving back to Revelation, it would be wise to see if there is the same consistency in the timing of the resurrection, within the Old Testament, as well as the writings of the Apostle Paul.

THE RESURRECTION IN THE OLD TESTAMENT

There are two main passages in the Old Testament that deal with the timing of the resurrection. Although the rapture is not mentioned in the pages of the Old Testament, it is understood, from the writings of Paul, that it is to occur immediately following the resurrection of the dead. The first passage that we will address is contained in the book of Isaiah:

> Your dead shall live; *Together with* my dead body they shall arise. Awake and sing, you who dwell in dust; For your dew *is like* the dew of herbs, And the earth shall cast out the dead. Come my people, enter your chambers, And shut your doors behind you; Hide yourself, as it were, for a little moment, Until the indignation is past. For behold, the Lord comes out of His place To punish the inhabitants of the earth for their iniquity; The earth will disclose her blood, And will no more cover her slain. (Isaiah 26:19-21)

This scripture, which is speaking of the resurrection, reveals that it is to occur before the Day of the Lord. Those who are resurrected are hidden in God's chambers until the "indignation" is past. This "indignation" is defined as being the day that "the Lord comes out of His place to punish the inhabitants of the earth for their iniquity." It is apparent, from this passage, that the resurrection, which includes the rapture, will take place before the wrath of God is poured out. This is in complete agreement with the Olivet Discourse which shows believers being gathered immediately at the unveiling of the Day of the Lord.

Another Old Testament passage, that concerns itself with the resurrection, is found in the book of Daniel:

> At that time Michael shall stand up, The great prince who stands *watch* over the sons of your people; And there shall be a time of trouble, Such as never was since there was a nation, *Even* to that time. And at that time your people shall be delivered, Every one who is found written in the book. And many of those who sleep in the dust of the earth shall awake, Some to everlasting life, Some to shame *and* everlasting contempt. Those who are wise shall shine like the brightness of the firmament, And those who turn many to righteousness Like the stars forever and ever. (Daniel 12:1-3)

This "time of trouble," described by Daniel, was defined by Jesus as being the great tribulation (Matthew 24:21). It is to begin at the midpoint of the Seventieth Week. Daniel discloses that at this time many of his people will be delivered. This is, most likely, speaking of the 144,000, and others of national Israel, who will flee to escape the wrath of the Antichrist. Next said to occur, is the resurrection of the righteous, and eventually, the resurrection for death of the unrighteous. What is important to understand is that again the resurrection is said to occur after the "time of trouble," or the great tribulation, has begun. If the rapture is to follow the resurrection, then it also cannot happen, according to Daniel, until after the great tribulation has commenced. This passage clearly gives the timing of the resurrection, and is, again, in agreement with the timing of the gathering of the elect given in the Olivet Discourse.

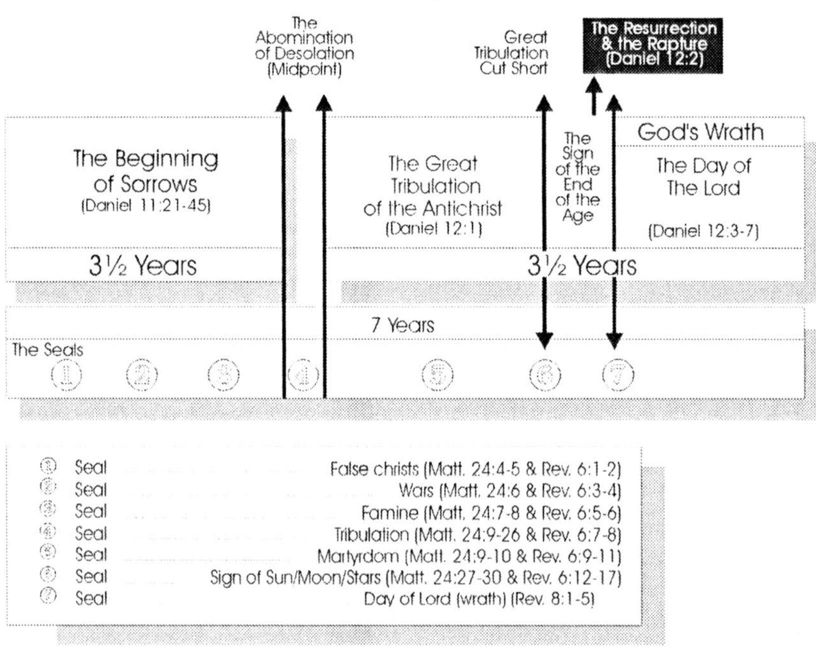

The pattern is extremely simple to follow as Scripture does not ever contradict itself. It may, however, contradict our theology. Unfortunately, this passage in Daniel blatantly contradicts the pre-tribulation rapture view, because it clearly places the resurrection during the very tribulation that the church is not supposed to be around for. To circumvent this passage, many propose that Daniel is speaking of a resurrection of only Old Testament believers. This view is often promoted despite the fact that there is absolutely no Scripture to support a separate resurrection of Old Testament believers. Believers in the Old Testament were saved by their faith in Jesus Christ, as is the case with those of the New Testament. Paul has told us that the dead in Christ shall rise first (1 Thessalonians 4:16). Paul does not specify the dead of the New Testament believers only, but the elect dead, of all the ages, who have put their faith in Jesus for salvation.

In looking at both of these Old Testament passages, it is obvious that they are in complete agreement that the resurrection and rapture, are to occur after the great tribulation, but before God's wrath is poured out. If this is truly the case, then this same scenario should be evident in the New Testament writings of the Apostle Paul.

PAUL'S VIEW

> But now Christ is risen from the dead, and has become the first fruits of those who have fallen asleep. For since by man *came* death, by Man also *came* the resurrection of the dead. For as in Adam all die, even so in Christ all shall be made alive. But each one in his own order; Christ the firstfruits, afterward those *who are* Christ's at His coming. Then *comes* the end, when He delivers the kingdom to God the Father, when He puts an end to all rule and all authority and power. (1 Corinthians 15:20-24)

In this passage, in first Corinthians, the same pattern again seems to emerge. First, Paul states that only those who are in Jesus Christ shall be made alive. This confirms that the Old Testament as well as the New Testament believers will not experience resurrection unless they have put their faith in Jesus. Paul goes on to say that Jesus will glorify those who are alive at His coming. In the Olivet Discourse, Jesus disclosed that these elect believers would be gathered after the sign of the Son of man; which He informed the disciples was the sign of His coming. Finally, Paul reveals that after the resurrection then the end, or the Day of the Lord, would commence. This will be the time when the Lord pours out His wrath on the unbelieving nation of Israel and the kingdom of the Antichrist, in order to establish His eternal kingdom.

Bewilderment at Thessalonica

Probably the most crucial texts on the timing of the rapture are contained in Paul's second letter to the Thessalonians. This was an assembly that was undergoing intense persecution. Paul writes to them, because someone had written a spurious document that stated to the believers in Thessalonica that the rapture had already passed, and they were now in the Day of the Lord. Paul combats this letter by relating to them the proper sequence of events that are to occur before Jesus gathers His elect. Before presenting this chronology, he first comforts them in the midst of their tribulation:

> So that we ourselves boast of you among the churches of God for your patience and faith in all your persecutions and tribulations that you endure, which is manifest evidence of the righteous judgment of God, that you may be counted worthy of the kingdom of God, for which you suffer; since *it is* a righteous thing with God to repay with tribulation those who trouble you, and to *give* you who are troubled rest with us when the Lord Jesus is revealed from heaven with His mighty angels, in flaming fire taking vengeance on those who do not know God, and on those who do not obey the gospel of our Lord Jesus Christ. These shall be punished with everlasting destruction from the presence of the Lord and from the glory of His power, when He comes, in that Day, to be glorified in His saints and to be admired among all those who believe, because our testimony among you was believed. (2 Thessalonians 1:4-10)

Paul states that he has boasted of the Thessalonian believer's perseverance, in the midst of persecution, to the other churches of Christ. He then makes the incredible statement that these tribulations that they are enduring are occurring so that they "may be counted worthy of the kingdom of God." I had often strongly argued that the church would not go through the great tribulation, because God had already forgiven us for our transgressions; so how could persecution make us anymore pure than the blood of Christ? Yet, Paul states that God is using this current tribulation to test the worthiness of those in the assembly at Thessalonica. Often persecution serves to separate the true disciple from the false disciple. While tribulation does not make a believer anymore righteous in God's eyes, it does bring to light who is truly following Jesus. This separation of the true from the false is the primary purpose of God allowing the great tribulation of Antichrist to fall upon His disciples.

Paul next, makes this verse a "near/far prophecy," by applying this church's situation to the great tribulation of the end times. He states that God will eventually unleash His own tribulation upon these persecutors, while also giving rest, or resurrection bodies, to His faithful, when Jesus is revealed from heaven. Paul declares that these will be punished "when He comes, in that Day to be glorified in His saints." Again, the pouring out of God's wrath is to be initiated following His resurrection of the faithful.

In what is probably the single most important set of verses on the timing of the rapture, Paul gives the Thessalonian believers the exact timing of its occurrence.

> Now brethren, concerning the coming of our Lord Jesus Christ and our gathering together to Him, we ask you, not to be soon shaken in mind or troubled, either by spirit or by word or by letter, as if from us, as though the day of Christ had come. Let no one deceive you by any means; for *that Day will not come* unless the falling away comes first, and the man of sin is revealed, the son of perdition, who opposes and exalts himself above all that is all called God or that is worshipped, so that he sits as God in the temple of God, showing himself that he is God. Do you not remember that when I was still with you I told you these things? (2 Thessalonians 2:1-5)

Paul sets the context of these next verses as concerning "the coming of our Lord and our gathering to Him." (2 Thessalonians 2:1). This phrase is a clear indication that Paul will now be addressing the resurrection and rapture of believers. After assuring the Thessalonians that the document they had received was false, he outlines specifically the events that will occur before the Day of Christ and their being gathered to Him.

They are summarized as follows:

> 1. The Day (resurrection/rapture) will not come until the apostasy or the "falling away" comes first.
>
> 2. The Day also will not come until the Antichrist is revealed as he stands in the temple and tells the world that he is God.

Paul is absolutely consistent with all other Scripture that concerns itself with the timing of the resurrection and the rapture. Paul places it after the great "falling away," which are the false christs and false prophets of the first seal (Revelation 6:1) and the Olivet Discourse (Matthew 24:5), and after the "abomination of desolation," where the Antichrist sits in the temple and reveals to the world that he is God (Matthew 24:15). This text proves beyond a shadow of a doubt that Paul believed that the church would not be raptured until after the midpoint of the Seventieth Week, in the midst of the great tribulation. It cannot get any clearer or specific in this passage, as to when the Apostle Paul taught that the rapture would occur. Since he was inspired of the Holy Spirit, I am inclined to believe that what he states here is the only acceptable view on the rapture's timing.

It has been shown that there is absolute consistency in the timing of the resurrection/rapture in the Old Testament prophecies, the Olivet Discourse, and the writings of the Apostle Paul. It then stands to reason that the same sequence of events should be followed in the book of Revelation.

REVELATION AND THE RAPTURE

The 144,000

> **After these things I saw four angels standing at the four corners of the earth, holding the four winds of the earth, that the wind should not blow on the earth, on the sea, or on any tree. Then I saw another angel ascending from the east, having the seal of the living God. And he cried with a loud voice to the four angels to whom it was granted to hurt the earth and the sea, saying, "Do not harm the earth, the sea, or the trees till we have sealed the servants of our God on their foreheads." And I heard the number of those who were sealed. One hundred *and* forty-four thousand of all the tribes of the children of Israel *were* sealed: of the tribe of Judah twelve thousand *were* sealed; of the tribe of Reuben twelve thousand *were* sealed; of the tribe of Gad twelve thousand *were* sealed; of the tribe of Asher twelve thousand *were* sealed; of the tribe of Naphtali twelve thousand *were* sealed; of the tribe of Manasseh twelve thousand *were* sealed; of the tribe of Simeon twelve thousand *were* sealed; of the tribe of Levi twelve thousand *were* sealed; of the tribe of Issachar twelve thousand *were* sealed; of the tribe of Zebulun twelve thousand *were* sealed; of the tribe of Joseph twelve thousand *were* sealed; of the tribe of Benjamin twelve thousand *were* sealed.** (Revelation 7:1-8)

The discussion of Revelation last left off at the end of chapter six, with the breaking of the sixth seal. This seal revealed the sign of the Son of Man, as well as the sign of the sun, moon, and stars. The final verses of Revelation chapter six announced that the Day of the Lord had arrived. If the chronology of Revelation follows the other prophetic texts, we should next see John present the resurrection and rapture of the elect.

Immediately after the opening of the sixth seal, an angel ascends from the east crying out to the four angels who will destroy the earth that they should not begin the judgment until God's elect of national Israel are sealed. This is very likely the voice of the archangel, that is spoken of by Paul, which is to be sounded at the moment of the resurrection and the rapture (1 Thessalonians 4:16). These that are to be sealed are 144,000 of each tribe of the nation of Israel. John gives the name of each tribe to show that these are those of Jewish descent only who are to be sealed. He specifically does this so that one does not assume that he is possibly speaking spiritually of the church. It is later shown, that these who are sealed, are the first of national Israel to come to believe in Jesus as the Messiah (Revelation 14:4). This sealing is much like the sealing that took place in the book of Ezekiel. In Ezekiel, God sealed His righteous servants before His judgment came upon the Jews who worshipped false gods:

> Now the glory of the God of Israel had gone up from the cherub, where it had been, to the threshold of the temple. And He called to the man clothed with white linen, who had the writer's inkhorn at his side; and the Lord said to him, "Go through the midst of the city, through the midst of Jerusalem, and put a mark on the foreheads of the men who sigh and cry over all the abominations that are done within it." To the others He said in my hearing, "Go after him through the city and kill; do not let your eye spare, nor have any pity. Utterly slay old *and* young men, maidens and little children and women; but do not come near anyone on whom is the mark; and begin at My sanctuary." So they began with the elders who *were* before the temple. Then He said to them, "Defile the temple, and fill the courts with the slain. Go out!" And they went out and killed in the city. (Ezekiel 9:3-7).

In this passage, only those who had the seal of God upon their forehead were not killed. In the same manner, as God begins to pour out His wrath, during the Day of the Lord, these 144,000 Jews will be protected. It will be the seal of God that will help them to survive through the entire Day of the Lord. If the seals are part of God's wrath, as many scholars propose, why then does God wait until after the sixth seal to begin His protection of the 144,000? This inconsistency reinforces that fact that the seals cannot be part of the Day of the Lord.

The Twelve Tribes
The Sons of Jacob

Genesis chapters 48-49

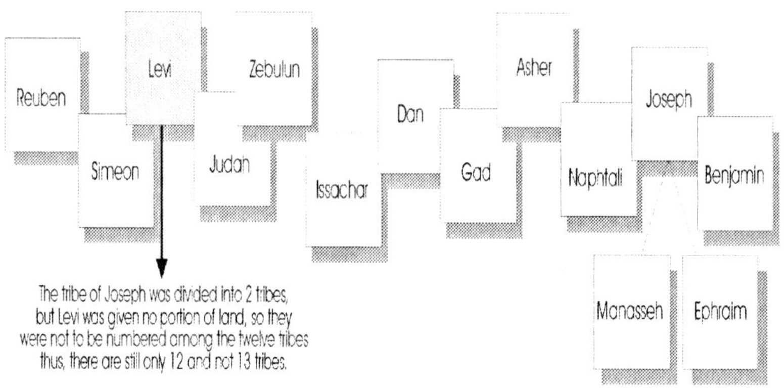

The Twelve Tribes
of the 144,000 in Revelation

Revelation 7:1-8

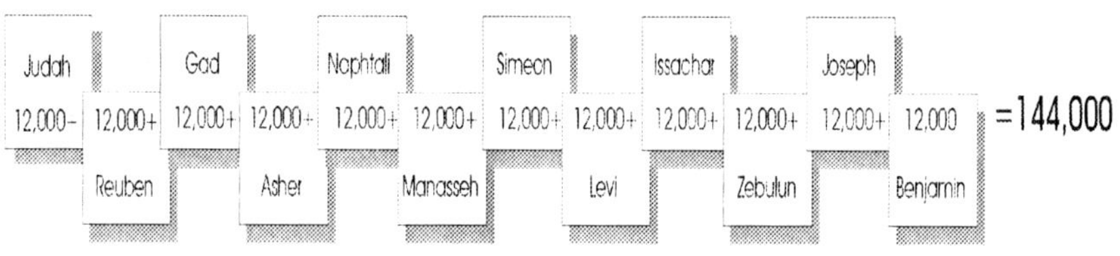

Levi replaces the tribe of Dan, and Joseph replaces the tribe of Ephraim. This is because Dan & Ephraim introduced idolotry to Israel. So they are to be withdrawn from those tribes who will specifically be protected during the Day of the Lord.

These Jews will go into hiding during the last half of the Seventieth Week and be protected during the Day of the Lord.

*They are not Evangelists as some contend.

144,000 Evangelists?

There has been much written declaring that the 144,000 are Jewish evangelists who will witness Jesus to the world, bringing about the greatest revival ever seen. This is a fantastic tale, but unfortunately that is all that it is. I do not mean to be cynical, but there is not one scripture in Revelation, or the entire Bible, that states that these 144,000 will evangelize the world. The story of their great evangelism has been told so many times that believers, as well as most scholars; believe it without checking the word of God to see if it is in fact true. Besides there being no scriptural evidence for their great evangelism, it would actually be next to impossible for these 144,000 to evangelize anyone. This is because God will next begin to pour out His trumpet judgments and they are so powerful and immense, that there will not be any time to evangelize. This is due to the fact that mankind will literally be running for cover. Second, believers are explicitly told that when the Day of the Lord begins, God will send mankind a strong delusion that they should believe the lie (2 Thessalonians 2:11). Once God has taken His church and begins His wrath, there will be no second chances for those who have followed and worshipped the Antichrist, whether they are Jew or Gentile. In fact, as we see these judgments being poured out, it is stated over and over again, by John, that mankind would not repent. This is because they are unable to repent, for God has given them up to their delusion. To say that there will be the greatest revival in history, during the Day of the Lord, is not only inaccurate, but also unscriptural. Another item that should be addressed, concerning the 144,000, is that in John's list the tribes of Dan and Ephraim are not mentioned. Levi and Joseph have been inserted to take their place. The reason for this is because in Deuteronomy 29:18-21 we are told that the man, woman, family, or tribe that should introduce idolatry to the children of Israel shall have their name blotted out from under heaven and be separated out of the tribes of Israel. God also states that they will not be protected from His judgments. We know from 1 Kings 12:25-33 that the tribe of Dan was guilty of idolatry when they permitted Jeroboam to set up golden calves to be worshipped, one at Dan, for the tribe of Dan, and the other at Bethel, for the tribe of Ephraim. However, there are portions of the Holy land that will be allotted to Dan and Ephraim during the Millennium. So while God does not specifically protect them during the Day of the Lord, there will be a remnant from these tribes who will be faithful and survive this period.

THE GREAT MULTITUDE OF THE CHURCH

> **After these things I looked, and behold, a great multitude which no one could number, of all nations, tribes, peoples, and tongues, standing before the throne and before the Lamb, clothed with white robes, with palm branches in their hands, and crying in a loud voice, saying, "Salvation *belongs* to our God who sits on the throne, and to the Lamb!" And all angels stood around the throne and the elders and the four living creatures, and fell on their faces before the throne and worshipped God, saying "Amen! Blessing and glory and wisdom, Thanksgiving and honor and power and might, *Be* to our God forever and ever. Amen." Then one of the elders answered, saying to me, "Who are these arrayed in white robes, and where did they come from?" And I said to him, "Sir, you know." So he said to me, "These are the ones who come out of the great tribulation, and washed their robes and made them white in the blood of the Lamb. Therefore they are before the throne of God, and serve Him day and night in His temple. And He who sits on the throne will dwell among them. They shall neither hunger anymore nor thirst anymore; the sun shall not strike them, nor any heat; for the Lamb who is in the midst of the throne will shepherd them and lead them to livings fountains of waters, And God will wipe away every tear from their eyes."** (Revelation 7:9-17)

After the sealing of the 144,000, John sees something absolutely incredible; a great multitude of men and women suddenly appearing in heaven. This multitude appears after the sixth seal, the sign of the sun, moon, and stars, and after the sign of the coming of the Son of Man. If our hermeneutic is to be consistent with the other passages that were studied, then this great multitude has to be those that were gathered by the angels at the trumpet of God: the resurrected church! This great multitude stands before the throne of God in contrast with the souls of the martyrs who are said to be under the altar (Revelation 6:9). I might point out that nowhere in the text of Revelation is it anywhere stated, or even implied, that this great multitude is made up of martyrs. If we recall, from our earlier study, it was shown that the job of the Seraphim, or the four living creatures, was to purify those who would come before the throne of the Lord. The first four seals of Revelation were initiated by the Seraphim, and they created conditions that would test and purify believers before the rapture, and before the Day of the Lord had begun. Their job has been completed by the sixth seal, and now the church is brought forth purified before the throne of God. John next tells us, that the believers in this great multitude have palm branches in their hands. In order to have hands, one must have a resurrected body. It then becomes obvious this great multitude differs from the martyrs, in that they have bodies. They are not mentioned as merely being souls, as was the case of the martyrs under the altar.

John then asks one of the elders just who, this great multitude is. He seems rather surprised by their sudden appearance in heaven. Up until now, John has only described seeing the four living creatures, the 24 elders, the martyred souls under the throne, and the great myriad of angels. This great multitude is a group of people that appears in heaven, immediately after the sixth seal is opened. In order to make it clear where this great multitude came from, one of the elders, who is distinct from the multitude, tells John that "These are the ones who come out of the great tribulation, and wash their robes and made them white in the blood of the Lamb." This can be none other than the church of Jesus Christ, making up both those who have been resurrected, and those who have been raptured out of the great tribulation. It is a multitude of believers who have put their faith in Jesus, and who have their sins forgiven and robes washed, through His blood that was shed on Calvary. So why is John so surprised by this great multitude? It must be remembered that he lived in a period in history when Christianity was still a small faith amongst thousands of pagan religions. John had no idea the extent, or the amount, of believers that would put their faith in Jesus Christ before His return.

Here is what can be understood about this great multitude:

1. They are standing before the throne, and are distinct from the martyrs who are under the altar.

2. The multitude has bodies, in contrast with the martyrs who are said to be souls.

3. The multitude is said to consist of those who have come out of the great tribulation, and of those who have washed their robes in the blood of the Lamb: Jesus Christ.

4. They appear in heaven after the sixth seal but before the Day of God's wrath unfolds.

This passage in Revelation confirms, and is consistent with every other scripture that has been addressed, concerning the timing of the resurrection and the rapture of the church. If Revelation is to be taken as being both chronological and literal, then the rapture/resurrection must occur exactly where Revelation tells us it occurs. If this view is accurate, then there is no escaping a rapture that occurs after the sixth seal, cutting short the great tribulation, and beginning the Day of God's wrath. To come up with any other view involves twisting, allegorizing, or dispensationalizing Scripture in order to fit a predisposed theological perspective.

THE GREAT HARVEST

Later, in chapter 14 of the book of Revelation, there is another presentation of the rapture of the faithful believers. This passage takes place in the parenthetic chapters which outline God's plan for the ages as well as the outcome for three groups of humanity: national Israel, the church, and the unbelieving world. At the beginning of chapter 14, John presents the salvation of national Israel. Next, he is shown the harvest of the faithful Christians, and finally, the end of those who have followed the Antichrist. In verse six, of Revelation chapter 14, John is shown three angels who go out, at the initiation of the great tribulation, to warn the world of God's impending judgment against those who take the mark of the beast. In verses 12 and 13 John is told that this period will signal a time when believers are called on to persevere, even if it means physical death. In fact, those who die are called "blessed" by a voice from heaven. There is then a new paragraph starting from verse 14, where we see Jesus harvesting the believers from the earth in the resurrection, or the rapture:

> **And I looked, and behold, a white cloud, and on the cloud sat *One* like the Son of Man, having on His head a golden crown, and in His hand a sharp sickle. And another angel came out of the temple, crying with a loud voice to Him who sat on the cloud, "Thrust in Your sickle and reap, for the time has come for you to reap, for the harvest of the earth is ripe." So he who sat on the cloud thrust in His sickle on the earth, and the earth was reaped.** (Revelation 14:14-16)

What John is presenting here is the harvest of the "end of the age," which Jesus spoke of in the parable of the wheat and tares (Matthew 13:24-30 & 36-43). Jesus told His disciples that His angels would first gather the "wheat" into His barn, and then they would commence to reap and burn the "tares." It was also revealed, in other passages, that the Lord Himself would descend, as the "wheat" (believers) was gathered (1 Thessalonians 4:16). The Son of Man, Jesus Christ, does the reaping of the elect believers, while it will be the angels who will do the gathering, as the text of Matthew points out (Matthew 24:31). After the believers have been gathered, it will then be the angel's job to do the reaping, as well as the burning, of the "tares," or the unbelieving world. This will begin with the trumpet and bowl judgments, and culminate with the battle of Armageddon. The destruction of the "tares" by the reapers, or angels, is presented in verses 17 through 20 of Revelation chapter

14. It must be noted that there are two reapings being presented within this text. Many believe that the text is only speaking of the harvest of the wicked. If it is only the wicked who are being reaped, why then are two harvests presented by John? A simple explanation is that the first reaping typifies the Lord descending to the earth to meet His elect who have been gathered by the angels. The second reaping is then carried out by an angel, who is ordered to do so, by another angel who has power over fire (Revelation 14:18). This typifies the reapers, whose fires will burn the "tares," as the "vine of the earth" is harvested (Revelation 14:19). The final verses of chapter 14 will be looked at, more in-depth, as we study the judgments of the Day of the Lord.

In addressing these passages, it becomes apparent that if one really wants to be true to the chronology presented in the book of Revelation, then one must accept that the church will enter the Seventieth Week and suffer through the great tribulation of Antichrist. No one likes persecution or suffering, but we have been forewarned over and over by Jesus, in His letters to the seven churches, that believers must overcome and persevere. Since God is sovereign, I can only accept at face value what the scriptures say, concerning this period of prophetic history. To dispensationalize or allegorize Scripture that does not agree with our own theology does a great injustice to the clear plain meaning of what has been told to us through the prophets, Jesus, Paul, and the book of Revelation.

In presenting this chapter, I have attempted to compare Scripture with Scripture. I have not had to twist or dispensationalize these scriptures to make them coalesce. By merely comparing them, it becomes obvious that they completely complement each other. If what I, and others, have concluded is accurate, then it stands as a grave and fearful warning that the church will undergo a period of trial the likes of which has never occurred. It is my prayer that every believer weighs carefully their faith in Jesus so that they will be able to persevere and overcome the great tribulation.

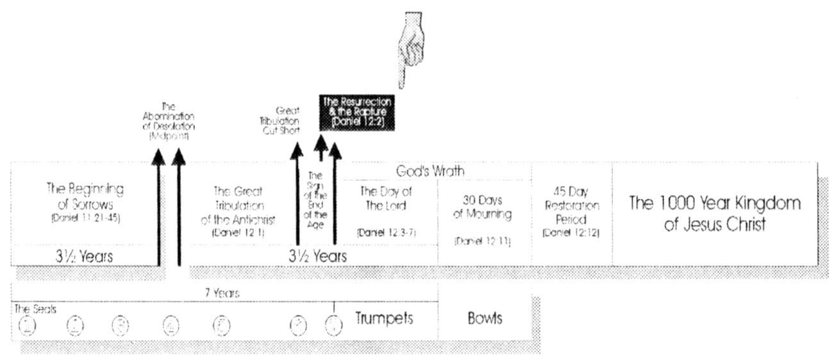

12
THE WRATH OF GOD BEGINS

THE CHURCH HAS BEEN BROUGHT safely to heaven and the 144,000 elect of Israel have been sealed. It is at this point in time where the Day of the Lord unfolds. It is also at this point where the Olivet Discourse culminates. The disciples only asked Jesus to reveal what the events would be that would signal His return. They did not ask Him how Israel would be restored, or how the kingdom of the Antichrist would be overthrown. Revelation is the only book in the New Testament that deals in detail with God's wrath. It outlines in exact chronological order of how these judgments will be accomplished. The Day of the Lord judgments are referred to often in the Old Testament, but it is only the book of Revelation that puts together the exact chronology of how they are to occur.

THE SEVENTH SEAL

After viewing the great multitude in Revelation chapter seven, John now sees Jesus break the last seal on the scroll of God's wrath:

> **When He opened the seventh seal, there was silence in heaven for about half an hour. And I saw the seven angels who stand before God, and to them were given seven trumpets. Then another angel, having a golden**

> **censer, came and stood at the altar. And he was given much incense that he should offer it with the prayers of all the saints upon the golden altar which was before the throne. And the smoke of the incense, with the prayers of the saints, ascended before God from the angel's hand. The angel took the censer, filled it with fire from the altar, and threw *it* to the earth. And there were noises, thunderings, lightnings, and an earthquake.** (Revelation 8:1-5)

The moment of God's judgment is now upon the earth. The fury of God has reached such intensity that there is absolute silence in all of heaven. The Old Testament also refers to this great moment of silence:

> Be silent in the presence of the Lord God; For the day of the Lord *is* at hand, For the Lord has prepared a sacrifice; He has invited His guests. (Zephaniah 1:7)

> Be silent, all flesh, before the Lord, for He is aroused from His holy habitation. (Zechariah 2:13)

The mercy of God has reached its end, and now He will destroy those who have rejected His loving grace. The time of God's grace has ended, and His harsh judgments will now encompass the face of the earth. There will no longer be any question as to whether or not these are divine judgments from God or natural disasters.

It is important to recall that, in the parable of the wheat and the tares, Jesus told His disciples that His holy angels would be in charge of His judgments. True to the word of God, John is now shown seven angels who will be in charge of pouring out God's trumpet judgments upon the earth. In contrast to this, living creatures and not angels revealed the seals. If the angels are to be in charge of God's judgments, it then stands to reason that the seals could not have been the judgments of God. Also, these judgments are initiated once the seventh seal is broken, the scroll opened, and its contents read. Up until this point the contents of the scroll could not have been read. Finally, all these events begin to unfold after the angels, through Jesus, have gathered "the wheat into the barn," or the Christians into heaven, as was revealed by the Lord. The tares have already been separated, and they will now be burned. The Day of the Lord begins with a great judgment of fire cast upon the earth by an angel. This is exactly what the Apostle Peter refers to in his epistle:

> But the day of the Lord will come as a thief in the night, in which the heavens will pass away with a great noise, and the elements will melt with fervent heat; both the earth and the works that are in it will be burned up. (2 Peter 3:10)

Most scholars incorrectly identify this passage as referring to a time, after the 1000-year kingdom of Jesus, in which God will completely annihilate the heavens and the earth. While this is an interesting concept, it does harm to the context of this passage, which is clearly referring to the Day of the Lord. Logic argues that Jesus cannot possibly come as a "thief in the night" after He has been ruling on earth for a thousand years. The Apostle Paul clearly states that Jesus will come as "a thief in the night" to the unbelieving world when the Day of the Lord begins:

> For you yourselves know perfectly that the day of the Lord comes as a thief in the night. For when they say "Peace and safety!" then sudden destruction comes upon them, as labor pains upon a pregnant woman. And they shall not escape. (1 Thessalonians 5:2-3)

I think it is relatively safe to conclude that both these texts concern themselves with the same event: the Day of the Lord. What then is the significance behind Scripture declaring that Christ comes as "a thief in the night?" Our Lord told His disciples in John 10:10, that the "thief comes to steal, kill, and destroy." As a thief, Jesus will come first to "steal" His elect from the hand of Satan; cutting short the great tribulation. He will next "kill" those who have worshipped the beast, and then "destroy" the kingdom of the Antichrist. This all begins with the seven trumpet judgments. Before these trumpet judgments are inaugurated, John sees an angel with a censer containing the prayers of God's saints. These prayers are said to be mixed with fire. The angel hurls the fire down to the earth, beginning the judgment by fire that announces the Day of the Lord. This inferno is accompanied by "noises, thunderings, lightinings, and an earthquake." After this, the seven angels begin to sound the awesome trumpet judgments.

THE TRUMPET JUDGMENTS

The trumpet judgments, while collaterally affecting the whole earth, will be focused primarily on the nation of Israel, and the Mediterranean. Through these judgments God will: One, bring about the repentance of those in Israel who have not yet placed their faith in Jesus as their Messiah, and two, set about to destroy those in Israel who have put their faith in the Antichrist and have received his mark. The prophet Zephaniah speaks of this cleansing of the land of Israel:

> I will utterly consume all *things* From the face of the land, Says the Lord; I will consume man and beast; I will consume the birds of the heavens, The fish of the sea, And the stumbling blocks along with the wicked. I will cut off man

> from the face of the land, Says the Lord. I will stretch out My hand against Judah, And against all the inhabitants of Jerusalem. I will cut off every trace of Baal from this place, The names of the idolatrous priests with the *pagan* priests-- Those who worship the host of heaven on the housetops; Those who worship and swear *oaths* by the Lord, But who *also* swear by Milcom; Those who have turned back from *following* the Lord, And have not sought the Lord, nor inquired of Him. (Zephaniah 1:2-6)

The prophet Zechariah reveals that, in this great judgment, two thirds of Israel shall be cut off and die, while one third would be brought through this period alive (Zechariah 13:8-9). This one third will be composed of the 144,000, and those Jews who heeded the two witnesses' warnings and did not receive the mark of the beast. These Jews will have escaped to the areas of Edom, Moab, Ammon, and Assyria. Daniel states that these are the areas that the Antichrist will not able to control (Daniel 11:41). The Jews, who do not take the mark of the Antichrist, will realize that Jesus was their Messiah as the trumpet judgments unfold. They, along with the 144,000, will make up the remnant of national Israel who will accept Jesus as their Messiah. Unfortunately, they have missed the rapture and will be left on earth to endure the seven trumpet judgments that end the Seventieth Week. The trumpets will be a repeat performance of the time that God delivered His people Israel from the hands of the Pharaoh in Egypt. Only instead of Pharaoh and Egypt, the judgments this time will be against the nation of Israel:

> Therefore the anger of the Lord is aroused against His people; He has stretched out His hand against them And stricken them, And the hills trembled. Their carcasses *were* as refuse in the midst of the streets. For all this His anger is not turned away, But His hand *is* stretched out still." (Isaiah 5:25)

> . . . The end has come upon My people Israel; I will not pass by them anymore. And the songs of the temple Shall be wailing in that day, Says the Lord God--Many dead bodies everywhere, They shall throw *them* out in silence. (Amos 8:2-3)

In Jeremiah we are told that judgments that God will use, to bring Israel to repentance, will surpass those that were done in Egypt:

> Therefore, behold, *the* days are coming, says the Lord, that they shall no longer say, "As the Lord lives who brought up the children of Israel from the land of Egypt," but, "As the Lord lives who brought up and led the descendants of the

house of Israel from the north country and from the countries where I had driven them. And they shall dwell in their own land. (Jeremiah 23:7-8)

During this period, God will passover and protect the elect 144,000 of Israel, while pouring out His wrath on the unfaithful Jews and the unbelieving world. Jesus will then return personally to lead the faithful Jews out of the wilderness in Edom, and back to the Promised Land. This is, in fact, the same wilderness area where they wandered for 40 years. This time it will not take them 40 years. With all this in mind, let's take a look at the trumpet judgments.

THE FIRST TRUMPET

So the seven angels who had the seven trumpets prepared themselves to sound. The first angel sounded: and hail and fire followed, mingled with blood, and they were thrown to the earth; and a third of the trees were burned up, and all green grass was burned up. (Revelation 8:6-7)

The wrath of God begins with incredible fury. As the first angel sounds his trumpet, hail and fire, mixed with blood, are thrown to the earth, burning a third of all the trees and green grass. As evidenced in the text of Revelation, this judgment differs greatly from what occurred during the opening of the seven seals. While the seven seals were common everyday occurrences, in greater intensity, the trumpet judgments are supernatural in nature. It has never, since the plagues of Egypt, rained down hail with fire and blood. This is not what would be referred to as being a natural disaster, rather a supernatural disaster. During this period of the wrath of God, five of the nine plagues of Egypt are repeated. This first judgment is very much like the seventh Egyptian plague that was unleashed from the hand of Moses (Exodus 9:22-26). The difference between this judgment and the one that occurred in Egypt is that there is a reversal as to who is being judged. The judgments in Egypt were against leadership and people of Egypt, but the Day of the Lord judgment's are against the nation of Israel. The Jews who have bowed to the false messiah will now face the wrath of the true Messiah.

THE SECOND TRUMPET

> **Then the second angel sounded: And *something* like a great mountain burning with fire was thrown into the sea, and a third of the sea became blood; and a third of the living creatures in the sea died, and a third of the ships were destroyed.** (Revelation 8:8-9)

John next describes something resembling a mountain that plummets into the sea. This passage is very likely referring to the Mediterranean Sea. This is because these judgments are concentrated primarily in the area surrounding of Israel, as well as the nations bordering the Mediterranean Sea. In the text, John reveals that this great meteoric mass, burning like a volcano, turns to blood one third of the sea, while destroying all life within the one-third area. A third part of the ships in this area also will be destroyed. This plague is very similar to the first plague unleashed upon the land of Egypt (Exodus 7:14-25). In the former plague all the waters of the Nile River were turned to blood. In the second trumpet judgment, only a third of the water is affected. Again, it is evident that this is not a natural common occurrence, but a divine judgment.

THE THIRD TRUMPET

> **Then the third angel sounded: And a great star fell from heaven, burning like a torch, and it fell on a third of the rivers and on the springs of water; and the name of the star is Wormwood; and a third of the waters became wormwood; and many men died from the water, because it was made bitter.** (Revelation 8:10-11)

When the next trumpet is sounded a great star falls from heaven. Specifically what this torch like star is, John is not told. It is known that when God releases it upon the earth, one third of the fresh water in the Mediterranean area will be made excessively bitter and poisonous. This star is named "wormwood" which is an extremely bitter herb used in the manufacture of absinthe.[1] Just as Israel gave Jesus bitter gall to drink when He was crucified (Matthew 27:34), the Lord will now give Israel bitter drink. The prophet Jeremiah speaks of this period also:

> And the Lord said, "Because they have forsaken My law which I set before them, and have not obeyed My voice, nor walked according to it, but they have walked according to the imagination of their own heart and after the Baals, which their fathers taught them," therefore thus says the Lord of

> hosts, the God of Israel: "Behold, I will feed them, this people, with wormwood, and give them water of gall to drink. (Jeremiah 9:13-15)

THE FOURTH TRUMPET

> **Then the fourth angel sounded: and a third of the sun was struck, a third of the moon, and a third of the stars, so that a third of them were darkened; and a third of the day did not shine, and likewise the night. And I looked, and I heard and angel flying through the midst of heaven, saying with a loud voice, "Woe, woe, woe to the inhabitants of the earth, because the remaining blasts of the trumpets of the three angels who are about to sound!"** (Revelation 8:12-13)

This angel strikes a third of the natural lights causing great darkness to come about earlier in the day. This is another cosmic disturbance similar to the sign of the sun, moon, and stars that announced the beginning of the Day of the Lord (Matthew 24:29 & Revelation 6:12-13). The fourth trumpet should not, however, be confused with being the sign of the Day of the Lord. In this judgment only a third of the light is struck, whereas there will be almost complete darkness when the sign of the end of the age, or Day of the Lord, is revealed. The fourth trumpet judgment probably will continue until the culmination of the Day of the Lord. There are other references to this judgment found within the Old Testament:

> In that day they will roar against them Like the roaring of the sea. And if *one* looks to the land, Behold, darkness *and* sorrow; And the light is darkened by the clouds. (Isaiah 5:30)

> And it shall come to pass in that day, says the Lord God, That I will make the sun go down at noon, And I will darken the earth in broad daylight; (Amos 8:9)

After this judgment, John is shown an angel flying in heaven proclaiming three "woes" upon the earth. These "woes" signify that the next judgments are so severe that they will cause unparalleled misery and death for those who are still upon the earth. It will be these last three judgments that will bring to an end Daniel's Seventieth Week.

THE FIFTH TRUMPET (WOE 1)

Then the fifth angel sounded: And I saw a star fallen from heaven to the earth. And to him was given the key to the bottomless pit. And he opened the bottomless pit, and smoke arose out of the pit like the smoke of a great furnace. And the sun and the air were darkened because of the smoke of the pit. Then out of the smoke locusts came upon the earth. And to them was given power, as the scorpions of the earth have power. They were commanded not to harm the grass of the earth, or any green thing, or any tree, but only those men who do not have the seal of God on their foreheads. And they were not given *authority* to kill them, but to torment them for five months. And their torment *was* like the torment of a scorpion when it strikes a man. In those days men will seek death and will not find it; they will desire to die, and death will flee from them. And the shape of the locusts was like horses prepared for battle; and on their heads were crowns of something like gold, and their faces were like the faces of men. They had hair like women's hair, and their teeth were like lions' *teeth*. And they had breastplates like breastplates of iron, and the sound of their wings *was* like the sound of chariots with many horses running into battle. They had tails like scorpions, and there were stings in their tails. And their power *was* to hurt men five months. And they had as king over them the angel of the bottomless pit, whose name in Hebrew is Abaddon, but in Greek he has the name Appollyon. One woe is past. Behold, still two more woes are coming after these things. (Revelation 9:1-12)

With the blowing of the fifth trumpet John sees a star fall from heaven who has a key to the bottomless pit. This star is possibly a fallen angel, of a very high order within the kingdom of Satan. This brings to remembrance Revelation chapter 12 where a third of the stars, or angels, were thrown out of heaven with Satan. It will be one of these fallen angels that God will allow to open the bottomless pit. The bottomless pit that this angel opens should not be confused with Hades, or hell. Hell is the abode of unredeemed humanity, who is awaiting their final judgment from God. The bottomless pit, in contrast, is the abode of a horrific class of evil spirits whom God has consigned to chains until this moment. These evil spirits are very likely the angels who "left their own habitation," as spoken of in the epistle of Jude:

> And the angels who did not keep their proper domain, but left their own habitation, He has reserved in everlasting chains under darkness for the judgment of the great day; (Jude 1:6)

These evil angels are also spoken of in Genesis as those that had cohabited with women, polluting the human gene pool, thus creating a race of evil giants (Genesis 6:1-4). This was Satan's first attempt to thwart God's plan for the redemption of mankind. Since Jesus was to come from the seed of a woman, Satan attempted to pollute man's genes so that Jesus could not be born. God was able to preserve Noah and his family, who were perfect in their generations (Genesis 6:9), while cleansing the earth by the flood. After the time of the flood, God locked up these evil angels. During the sounding of the fifth trumpet, they will again be released and used by God to judge mankind. These demonic, locust-like creatures are sent forth not to kill but to torment men for five months. This torment takes the form of a scorpion's sting that will cause men excruciating pain. This pain will be so intense that men will literally wish to die, but they will be unable to. It is not clear whether those on the earth will be able to physically see these evil beings. It is interesting to note that we are given a time frame of five months for the duration of this judgment. This reveals that the great tribulation of Antichrist cannot last more than three years and one month from the midpoint of the Seventieth Week.

These evil angelic creatures seem to be a type of infernal Cherubim, or Seraphim.[2] They are said to be a combination of a man, a horse, a lion, and a scorpion. Being a twisted type of the "four living creatures" may explain their ability to have cohabited with women. There is a parallel description of these angelic beasts given in the books of Joel and Jeremiah:

> Their appearance is like the appearance of horses; And like swift steeds, so they run. With a noise like chariots Over mountaintops they leap, Like the noise of a flaming fire that devours the stubble, Like a strong people set in battle array. Before them the people writhe in pain; All faces are drained of color. They run like mighty men of war; They climb the wall like men of war; Every one marches in formation, And they do not break ranks. They do not push one another; Every one marches in his own column. And *when* they lunge between the weapons They are not cut down. They run to and fro in the city, They run on the wall; They climb into the houses, They enter at the windows like a thief. (Joel 2:4-9)

> For behold, I will send serpents among you, Vipers which cannot be charmed, And they shall bite you, says the Lord. (Jeremiah 8:17)

These locusts have a king over them who is called "Abaddon" in the Hebrew, and "Appollyn" in Greek. In both languages the word carries the same meaning: destruction. This text cannot be referring to earthly locusts, because it is stated, in the book of Proverbs, that the locusts have no king (Proverbs 30:27). The period of the fifth trumpet will be unbelievably awful for those who have not been sealed by God Almighty. Taking the seal of the Antichrist may have protected one from the great tribulation, but it will be useless during the Day of the Lord. This ends the first woe with the second woe immediately following.

THE SIXTH TRUMPET (WOE 2)

Then the sixth angel sounded: and I heard a voice from the four horns of the golden altar which is before God, saying to the sixth angel who had the trumpet, "Release the four angels who are bound at the great river Euphrates." So the four angels who had been prepared for the hour and day and month and year, were released to kill a third of mankind. Now the number of the army of the horseman *was* two hundred million, and I heard the number of them. And thus I saw the horses in the vision: those who sat on them had breastplates of fiery red, hyacinth blue, and sulfur yellow; and the heads of the horses *were* like the heads of lions; and out of their mouths came fire, smoke, and brimstone. By these three *plagues* a third of mankind was killed-- by the fire and the smoke and the brimstone which came out of their mouths. For their power is in their mouth and in their tails; for their tails *are* like serpents, having heads; and with them they do harm. But the rest of mankind, who were not killed by these plagues, did not repent of the works of their hands, that they should not worship demons, and idols of gold, silver, brass, stone, and wood, which can neither see nor hear nor walk; and they did not repent of their murders or their sorceries or their sexual immorality or their thefts. (Revelation 9:13-21)

As the sixth trumpet is blown, a voice from the altar of God is heard instructing the angel to release four other angels who have been bound at the Euphrates River. That these are evil beings is understood in the very fact that they have been bound. This area, within in the Euphrates basin, was where the seat of Satan was in ancient times. This was the region where the kingdom and religion of Babylon arose. It is also from this area that all of the world's false religions had their beginnings. It will be disclosed later, that this is also where the commercial center of the Antichrist's kingdom will be based. These infernal horsemen, and the river Euphrates, are mentioned by the prophet Jeremiah:

> Who *is* this coming up like a flood, Whose waters move like the rivers? Egypt rises up like a flood, And *its* waters move like the rivers; And he says, "I will go up *and cover* the earth, I will destroy the city and its inhabitants." Come up O horses, and rage O chariots! And let the mighty men come forth: The Ethiopians and the Libyans who handle the shield, and the Lydians who handle *and* bend the bow. For this *is* the day of the Lord God of Hosts, A day of vengeance, That He may avenge Himself on His adversaries. The sword shall devour; It shall be satiated and made drunk with their blood; For the Lord God of hosts has a sacrifice In the north country by the River Euphrates. (Jeremiah 46:7-10)

> *We* looked for peace but no good *came*; And for a time of health, and there was trouble! The snorting of His horses was heard from Dan. The whole land trembled at the sound of the neighing of His strong ones; For they have come and devoured the land and all that is in it, The city and those who dwell in it. (Jeremiah 8:15-16)

The four angels had been prepared for this very hour, day, month, and year to commence their destruction against mankind. They are to slay a third of mankind with an immense army of two hundred million. There has been much speculation that this army is to come from China. There are a number of problems inherit in this belief. First, if one is to remain consistent with the plain meaning of Scripture, then the text must be understood as referring to a spiritual army that is led by these four angels. Second, there is no mention of this army coming from China. And, if this were a human invasion, it would most likely be an army from the nations that surround the Euphrates, and not the Far East. Besides these inconsistencies, there are many other impracticalities of an invasion of two hundred million men from China. These logistical problems, paraphrased below, are outlined by Tim Dailey in his book The Gathering Storm:[3]

> 1. The swiftest movement of troops in history occurred when the United States moved half a million troops into the Middle East within six months. At this same rate it would take two hundred years to move a 200 million-man army from China to the Middle East.
>
> 2. The land route that an army from China would have to take would go straight through the central Asian republics of

the former U.S.S.R.. This is an incredibly hostile territory, and it is not likely that they would be able to pass through with ease.

3. The equipment needed to move this army would consist of a conservative convoy of approximately ten million vehicles containing food, fuel, and supplies. If each vehicle occupied forty yards of road space (including the space between vehicles) the convoy would stretch ten times around the earth to the span of 227,272 miles.

4. Finally, because of the time factor involved, this army would have to begin its movement toward Israel literally decades before the beginning of the Seventieth Week. Since we have not seen any recent troop movements, we are in for a long wait for the Seventieth Week to begin.

I mention these points as evidence that it is often better to understand God's word in its simplest and clearest meaning no matter how supernatural it may seem. These supernatural beings, unlike the last, are given authority to kill with fire, smoke, and brimstone. Even with this mighty show of God's power, it is stated that those who live through this will still not repent. Rather, these men will continue to put their trust and faith in their idolatrous images of the beast. They also will not repent of their sorceries, sexual immoralities, and their thefts. This is because God has sent them a strong delusion that they should believe the lie of Antichrist (2 Thessalonians 2:11). It is, therefore impossible for them to repent. As was stated before, there will not be a great revival during this period. In fact, the total opposite will be occurring. Only the one third of national Israel, the 144,000, and those Gentiles, who were not believers but refused to take the mark, will come to salvation. The rest of mankind will go headlong into destruction. This will be one of the saddest and most bitter moments the world has ever witnessed.

Looking at the beginning of God's wrath one sees a vast difference between the trumpet judgments and what occurred at the opening of the seven seals. The trumpet judgments are literal supernatural events that will be unleashed directly by the hand of God Almighty. He alone will be magnified through these judgments, and everyone will know that it is His power behind them. With the seventh trumpet, John will be shown the end of God's plan of redemption, along with the bodily return of Jesus Christ to the earth. This will be the moment that all creation has longed for, the day when Jesus Christ will finally take possession of the earth and establish His everlasting kingdom.

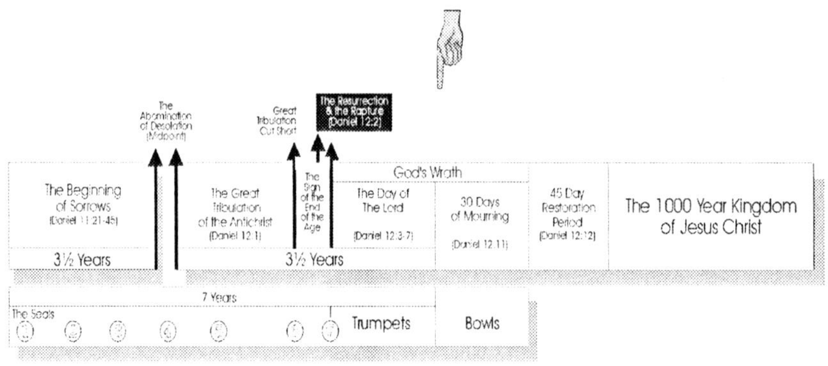

13
THE END OF THE SEVENTIETH WEEK

THE LORD HAS JUST UNLEASHED the first six trumpet judgments, which included the first and second woes. When the seventh and final trumpet sounds, the third woe will be completed and God will have finished His redemptive plan for the nation of Israel and the world. The Seventieth Week will be ended during the second woe, (sixth trumpet) and those of national Israel, who have repented, will be grafted back into God's olive tree, as was declared by the Apostle Paul (Romans 11:23). Israel will then be restored as God's people.

Before the seventh trumpet is sounded, John is presented with some incredible occurrences on planet earth that happen in relation to the nation of Israel during the second woe. In order to fully comprehend what is taking place in Revelation chapters ten and eleven, one must have an understanding of the seven religious feasts given to Israel, by God. It will be during this portion of the Apocalypse that the Lord Jesus Christ will finally fulfill the last of Israel's great feasts. The feasts played a crucial role in the first coming of Jesus, and they will play an equally important role during His second advent.

BACKGROUND ON THE FEASTS

In the Lord's first advent, the first four of these religious feasts were fulfilled in His ministry. There are a total of seven feasts that the nation of Israel was told to observe by God. The instructions pertaining to their celebration are given for us in the book of Leviticus, chapter 23. Their celebration was divided into two periods on the Jewish calendar. The first four were to occur in the spring months of the Jewish calendar, while the last three were celebrated in the fall. They were primarily agricultural feasts that celebrated the harvest in the periods known as the "former rains" and the "latter rains."[1] There were two major rainy seasons in the land of Israel: the spring, known as the former rains, and the fall, referred to as the latter rains. The spring feasts were to celebrate the barley harvests, while the fall feasts celebrated the wheat harvest.

The Jewish Calendars

Civil Calendar	
Tishri (Ethanim)	September-October
Cheshuan (Bul)	October-November
Kislev	November-December
Tevet	December-January
Sh'vat	January-February
Adar	February-March
Nisan (Aviv)	March-April
Iyar (Zif)	April-May
Sivan	May-June
Tammuz	June-July
Av	July-August
Elul	August-September

Religious Calendar	
Nisan (Aviv)	March-April
Iyar (Zif)	April-May
Sivan	May-June
Tammuz	June-July
Av	July-August
Elul	August-September
Tishri (Ethanim)	September-October
Cheshuan (Bul)	October-November
Kislev	November-December
Tevet	December-January
Sh'vat	January-February
Adar	February-March

Jewish Feasts
(Based on religious calendar)
Leviticus 23:4-44)

	Feast	Date
Christ's first advent	1. Pesach/Passover	Nisan (Aviv) 14
	2. Hag Ha Matzah/Unleavened Bread	Nisan (Aviv) 15-21
	3. First Fruits of the Barley Harvest	The first day following the sabbath during Hag Ha Matzah
	4. Shavout/Feast of Pentecost	50 days after First Fruits
Christ's second advent	5. Yom Terah (Rosh ha Shanah)/Trumpets	Tishri (Ethanim) 1
	6. Yom Kippur/Atonement	Tishri (Ethanim) 10
	7. Sukkot/Feast of Tabernacles	Tishri (Ethanim) 15-21
	8. Hanukkah/Feast of Dedication (John 10:22)	Kislev 25

The relevance of these celebrations is that they were decreed to Israel in order to give them understanding and teaching on the first and second advents of the Messiah. These festivals contained pictures and types of what Jesus would accomplish in His ministry to the nation of Israel. It must be stressed that these feasts were to be fulfilled only to the nation of Israel. Therefore, one must not look to their fulfillment in the church. Believers are also specifically told, by the Apostle Paul, that these feasts are to be fulfilled in the ministry of the Messiah:

> Therefore let no one judge you in food or in drink, or regarding a festival or a new moon or Sabbaths, which are a shadow of things to come, but the substance is of Christ. (Colossians 2:16-17).

As stated above, the lessons the festivals teach, concerning the Messiah, were all to be literally fulfilled by His ministry. What the Jewish Rabbis failed to recognize was that these feasts would not all be fulfilled in His first advent, but that there would be two comings of the Messiah. The prophet Hosea clearly teaches that Messiah shall come to Israel as the former and latter rains:

> Let us know, Let us pursue the knowledge of the Lord, His going forth is established as the morning; He will come to us like the rain, Like the latter *and* former rain to the earth. (Hosea 6:3)

This passage also substantiates the fact that the two comings of the Messiah would have some relation to the spring and fall festivals. In fact, in our Lord's first advent, His crucifixion, death, and resurrection brought the complete fulfillment of the spring feasts of the former rains. The spring feasts, which are four in number, take place in the spring months of Nisan and Sivan (our April and June). Taking a look at how these feasts saw their fulfillment in the Lord's ministry, will give a complete picture of how the last three will be fulfilled in His second advent.

PASSOVER/ PESACH

The first of the spring feasts, spoken of in the book of Leviticus (23:4-5), is the feast of Passover. This feast commemorated the time in Egypt when God was going to kill all the firstborn of Egypt. He told the Jewish people that each household was to take a lamb that was without spot or blemish and kill it on the fourteenth day of Nisan at 3 p.m. The blood of this innocent lamb was to be applied to the side post of their doors. When the angel of death came to kill the firstborn, he would passover all the households that had the blood on the side posts. These households would be spared, while those that did not have the blood would not. The amazing fulfillment of this festival is pictured in the crucifixion of Jesus Christ. Jesus the "Lamb of God who takes away the sins of the world!" (John 1:29) was a Lamb without spot and blemish due to His sinless character. Jesus was the Lamb who was to be slain, so that God could passover the sins of those who put their trust in Him.

What the lamb in Egypt was representative of, Jesus was the fulf
Amazingly, our Lord was crucified on the morning of the 14th of N
was nailed to the cross at the third hour (9:00 AM). This was at the
moment that the high priest would bind the lamb to the altar in the Jewish temple. At the ninth hour (3:00 PM) the high priest would kill the lamb pronouncing the words "It is finished."[2] It was at this very moment that we are told Jesus died on the cross yelling, "it is finished" (John 19:30). As the blood of the Passover lamb allowed the angel of death to passover, the blood of Christ allows God to forgive and passover our sins. The Jewish people did not realize that the feast celebrating their deliverance from Egypt also would commemorate their deliverance from sin. Jesus literally fulfilled this feast by being the Lamb who took away the sins of the world. This fulfillment occurred on the exact day and moment that the events of the feast occurred. It is no different with the next three feasts.

UNLEAVENED BREAD/ HAG HAMATZAH

The next feast on the Jewish calendar began on the morning of the fifteenth of Nisan, and was celebrated for seven days. This was the Feast of Unleavened bread (Leviticus 23:6-8). This feast would have begun at 6:00 pm Wednesday, of the same day our Lord was crucified. A Jewish day was reckoned from sunset to sunset. So sunset on Wednesday the fourteenth of Nisan would have been considered the early morning of the fifteenth of Nisan. This day was to be a high Sabbath in which no work could be done (Leviticus 23:7). This is why Jesus who died at 3:00PM Wednesday had to be buried quickly before 6:00PM, which would have signaled the beginning of the high Sabbath day of the fifteenth of Nisan. There are many who mistakenly understand this Sabbath to be the weekly Saturday Sabbath that the Jews would celebrate. This is why Friday is the celebrated day of the Lord's crucifixion. There are two major problems with Friday being the day on which our Lord was crucified:

1. Jesus said that He would remain in the tomb for three days and three nights (Matthew 12:40). This would be impossible if Jesus died at 3:00 pm on Friday.

2. In his gospel, John specifically states that this Sabbath was to occur after the preparation day of Passover, and that this particular Sabbath was a high holy day (John 19:31). The only high holy day that follows the preparation day of Passover and is also a Sabbath day, is the Feast of Unleavened Bread.

During the Feast of Unleavened Bread, God commanded His people to eat only unleavened bread for seven days. Leaven, in Scripture, is often employed as a symbol of sin. As leaven corrupts and permeates dough, so sin corrupts and permeates our life.[3] The celebration of the Feast of Unleavened Bread also included consuming the Passover lamb which was roasted and eaten with bitter herbs. During this meal, a ceremony is celebrated in which a piece of unleavened bread, or matzah, is broken, wrapped in linen, and buried. Jesus had told His disciples, only days before, that this piece of matzah was representative of His body (Matthew 26:26). The bread was unleavened just as Jesus was also unleavened, or sinless. The bread was also striped and pierced through with holes, because of the process needed to bake it. Jesus, Himself, was also pierced on the cross and beaten with many stripes for our transgressions (Isaiah 53:5). [4] This piece of unleavened bread, that was buried in the linen, symbolized our Lord's own burial. Later, during the feast, the piece of bread was brought out while drinking the third cup of wine, called the cup of redemption.[5] It becomes very clear that our Lord's burial fulfilled this feast.

THE FEAST OF FIRST FRUITS

The next feast, First Fruits, is to occur on the day after the weekly Sabbath, following the Feast of Passover (Leviticus 23:9-14). This Feast of the First Fruits would then have been celebrated early Sunday, the eighteenth of Nisan, during the week of our Lord's crucifixion. This third festival commemorated the barley harvest of that year. During the festival, the Israeli farmers were to bring the initial harvest of their barley crops to Jerusalem. A priest would then wave the "first fruits" before the temple.[6] This occurred on the exact day that Jesus was the first to be raised from the dead. He is, in effect, the first fruits of all those who would rise after Him. Just as the priest's blessing on the initial harvest would provide for a greater harvest later, God's blessing during the resurrection of His Son would be the guarantee of a greater future resurrection. Paul, himself, points out that Jesus fulfilled this great feast:

> For as in Adam all die, even so in Christ shall all be made alive. But each one in his own order: **Christ the first fruits**, afterward those *who are* Christ's at His coming" (1 Corinthians 15:22-23) {*Emphasis Mine*}

Our Lord rose from the dead in literal fulfillment the Feast of First Fruits. The next feast that was fulfilled in His first advent was to take place fifty days after the Feast of First Fruits.

Timing of Crucifixion of Jesus and Fulfillment of Spring Feasts

*Hebrew days are reckoned from sunset to sunset

Nisan 14 (Pesach/Passover) Leviticus 23:4-5	6:00p.m. .... 5:59p.m. Tuesday Sunset to Wednesday Sunset Hebrew Wednesday	3rd hour crucified (9:00a.m. Wednesday) 9th hour died (3:00p.m. Wednesday) Jesus had to be buried before 6:00p.m. because next day was a sabbath.
Nisan 15 (Hag Ha Matzah/ Unleavened Bread) Leviticus 23:6-8	6:00p.m. .... 5:59p.m. Wednesday Sunset to Thursday Sunset Hebrew Thursday	A Sabbath Day First night & First day in tomb
Nisan 16	6:00p.m. .... 5:59p.m. Thursday Sunset to Friday Sunset Hebrew Friday	Second night & Second day in tomb
Nisan 17	6:00p.m. .... 5:59p.m. Friday Sunset to Saturday Sunset Hebrew Saturday	The Weekly Sabbath Third night & Third day in tomb
Nisan 18 (Feast of First Fruits) Leviticus 23:9-14	6:00p.m. .... 5:59p.m. Saturday Sunset to Sunday Sunset Hebrew Sunday	The First Day of Week Resurrection
50 days from First Fruits (Pentecost) Leviticus 23:15-22	With the outpouring of the Holy Spirit the fulfillment of Spring Feasts ends	

PENTECOST/SHAVOUT

The final spring feast, Pentecost, was to occur fifty days after the Feast of First Fruits, in the Hebrew month of Sivan (Leviticus 23:15-22). The feast of Pentecost celebrated and brought to remembrance, the giving of the law on Mount Sinai. During this feast, the priest was to wave before God two leavened loaves of bread. This waiving of the two leavened loaves symbolized God's calling out of the world both sinful Jews and Gentiles to be one in the body of Jesus Christ (Galatians 3:28-29). This period, from the Feast of Pentecost onward, signaled the great harvest period, which would culminate in the latter rains of the fall festivals. In the gospels we are told that Jesus was on earth for forty days following His resurrection on the Feast of First Fruits

(Acts 1:3). He then ascended into heaven and told His disciples to wait in Jerusalem for the promise of the Father. Ten days later, on the Feast of Pentecost, the outpouring of the Holy Spirit upon the disciples of Jesus occurred. God then gave a sign to the unbelieving nation of Israel that His Spirit was upon these men who followed Jesus. It is said in the book of Acts, that the disciples spoke with other tongues, and all the Jews who were in Jerusalem, from all over the world, heard these men praising God in their own language. The prophet Isaiah predicted this sign, as the Apostle Paul states in 1 Corinthians:

> In the law it is written: "*With men of other tongues and other lips I will speak to this people; and yet, for all that, they will not hear Me*," says the Lord. Therefore tongues are for a sign, not to those who believe but to unbelievers; but prophesying is not for unbelievers but for those who believe (1 Corinthians 14:21-22)

The sign of tongues would be the last sign God would give to unbelieving Israel, in order to bring them to national repentance, before the Day of the Lord. It was on this very day that Peter, in his great sermon, made the last attempt to offer the Messianic Kingdom to national Israel. Unfortunately, the leadership of Israel did not repent and accept Peter's message. However, there were three thousand who did repent and put their faith in Jesus (Acts 2:41). This is in direct contrast with the first Pentecost in which three thousand were killed at the time the law was given on Mount Sinai (Exodus 32:28). The "letter kills, but the Spirit gives life" (2 Corinthians 3:6).[7] Since Israel did not as a nation repent, God took His plan of salvation primarily to the Gentiles. With the fulfillment of the Feast of Pentecost, God ended his dealings with national Israel, and the great harvest period of the church age began. Yet, God has not forsaken Israel. For during the Seventieth Week He will, again, offer the kingdom to them if they repent.

As the first four spring feasts were fulfilled in our Lord's first coming, the last three will be fulfilled at His second coming. There are some important items to notice concerning the fulfillment of these first four feasts. These items also should be true for the fulfillment of the second set of feasts:

> 1. Their fulfillment will take place specifically to the nation of Israel while the Lord is present on the earth, in bodily form.
>
> 2. As the first four were fulfilled in chronological succession, within exact days of each other, so will the last three. It will not be during the Second Advent, that the first of these feasts will be fulfilled, and then a year or a couple of years later the next one will be fulfilled. Since God is always consistent, the feasts must be fulfilled in the exact

same way as they were at His first coming; within days of each other.

Moving back into the text of Revelation, with the blowing of the sixth trumpet, John is brought to the closing days of the Seventieth Week. It is in this period that the last three feasts will be fulfilled, chronologically and within days of each other. Beginning with chapter ten John describes an incredible sight:

> **And I saw still another mighty angel coming down from heaven, clothed with a cloud. And a rainbow *was* on his head, his face *was* like the sun, and his feet like pillars of fire. And he had a little book open in his hand. And he set his right foot on the sea and *his* left *foot* on the land, and cried with a loud voice, as *when* a lion roars. And when he cried out, seven thunders uttered their voices. Now when the seven thunders uttered their voices, I was about to write; but I heard a voice from heaven saying to me, "Seal up the things which the seven thunders uttered and do not write them." And the angel whom I saw standing on the sea and on the land lifted up his hand to heaven and swore by Him who lives forever and ever, who created heaven and the things that are in it, the earth and the things that are in it, and the sea and the things that are in it, that there should be delay no longer, but in the days of the sounding of the seventh angel, when he is about to sound, the mystery of God would be finished, as He declared to His servants and prophets. Then the voice which I heard from heaven spoke to me again and said, "Go, take the little book which is open in the hand of the angel who stands on the sea and on the earth." And I went to the angel and said to him, "Give me the little book." And he said to me "Take and eat it; and it will make your stomach bitter, but it will be sweet as honey in your mouth." And I took the little book out of the angel's hand and ate it, and it was sweet as honey in my mouth. But when I had eaten it, my stomach became bitter. And he said to me, "You must prophesy again about many peoples, nations, tongues, and kings."**
> (Revelation 10:1-11)

The angel being described here is none other than the Angel of the Lord of the Old Testament: our Lord and Savior Jesus Christ. It is accepted by a majority of biblical scholars that the Angel of the Lord of the Old Testament was a pre-incarnate appearance of Jesus Christ. One may notice that the description of this angel is very similar to the description of Jesus given in

Revelation 1:12-16. The angel is described as being clothed in a cloud of glory with his face shining as the sun and his feet like pillars of fire, much like the burnished brass of Revelation 1:15. Also, it is revealed that this angel has a rainbow around his head, which is very much like the rainbow that was previously seen above the throne of God Almighty (Revelation 4:3). This passage also matches the description given of Jesus Christ by the prophet Ezekiel:

> And above the firmament over their heads *was* the likeness of a throne, in appearance like a sapphire stone; on the likeness of the throne *was* **a likeness with the appearance of a man high above it. Also from the appearance of His waist and upward I saw, as it were, the color of amber with the appearance of fire all around within it; and from the appearance of His waist and downward I saw, as it were, the appearance of fire with brightness all around. Like the appearance of the rainbow in a cloud on a rainy day, so *was* the appearance of the brightness all around it. This *was* the appearance of the likeness of the glory of the Lord**. So when I saw *it*, I fell on my face, and I heard a voice of One speaking. (Ezekiel 1:26-28) {*Emphasis Mine*}

Besides these observations, there are some other major reasons for this Angel being a picture of Jesus Christ as the Angel of the Lord.

> 1. This angel is seen holding a little scroll opened in his hand. As John is shown later, this scroll contains the bowl judgments that will signal the final wrath of God Almighty. In Revelation chapter five, John was told that Jesus alone was worthy to open and hold the scroll containing the trumpet judgments. It is then consistent with God's word that Jesus is also the only one worthy to open, and hold, the little scroll.
>
> 2. In Revelation chapter eleven this angel speaks to John and states "And I will give power to my two witnesses and they will prophecy one thousand two hundred and sixty days clothed in sackcloth." (Revelation 11:3). The angel refers to these men as His "two witnesses," and also declares that He is the one who gives them the power to witness. No mere angel has this type of authority.
>
> 3. In the Old Testament the Jews were led through the wilderness by the Angel of the Lord with a pillar of fire by night and a pillar of cloud by day (Exodus 13:21). The

Angel of Revelation is said to have a cloud of glory surrounding him, and pillars of fire for feet. This same angel will stand upon the earth and as the feasts of Israel are fulfilled, he will lead the faithful Jews out of their hiding in the wilderness areas of Edom, Moab, Ammon, and Assyria back to Israel.

What seems to be presented in this passage of Revelation is Jesus returning to earth, as the Angel of the Lord, to finally take possession of His kingdom. Jesus has already poured out the trumpet judgments on Israel. This occurs in Christ's coming as a "thief to kill." He previously came as a "thief to steal" His elect from the hands of the Antichrist. From this point, until Armageddon, Jesus now comes as a "thief to destroy" those who have persecuted His people Israel, and have taken the mark of the beast. Jesus stands upon the earth and takes possession of it on a very special day.

THE FEAST OF TRUMPETS/ ROSH HASHANAH

The first feast of the fall season, or the latter rains, is the Feast of Trumpets. This festival was to be celebrated on the first day of the Jewish month of Tishri (Leviticus 23:23-25). The feast commemorated the beginning of the Messianic kingdom and the disastrous fate of the unbelieving Gentile nations.[8] From the beginning of Rosh Hashanah until the Day of Atonement are ten days. These ten days are known as "the days of awe," and according to Jewish tradition, are the final period of time that the world and Israel have to repent before God's final judgment is unleashed.[9] The Feast of Trumpets is also believed to be the birthday of the world, the beginning of the Messianic kingdom, and the day in which Messiah will reveal Himself and re-gather Israel back to the land.[10] Since the first day of Tishri was the day in which God created the earth, it seems very appropriate that Jesus, as the Angel of the Lord, stands upon the earth on this same day, reclaiming its possession for His kingdom. The events of this great feast are fulfilled in Revelation chapter 10.

CHRIST'S BODILY RETURN TO EARTH

John sees that this angel sets his right foot on the sea and his left foot upon the land. This will be the first time that Jesus returns physically to earth for the salvation of national Israel. John states that the angel cries out with a loud voice as a lion. The language of these verses's parallels a similar set of verses, in the book of Hosea, which also speak of the Messiah's return for the salvation of Israel:

> They shall walk after the Lord. He will roar like a lion. When He roars, Then *His* sons shall come trembling from the west; They shall come trembling like a bird from Egypt, Like a dove from the land of Assyria. And I will let them dwell in their houses, Says the Lord (Hosea 11:10-11)

Another passage in Isaiah also closely parallels the beginning of Christ's kingdom on the Feast of the Trumpets:

> And it shall come to pass in that day *That* the Lord will thresh, from the channel of the River to the Brook of Egypt; And you will be gathered one by one, O you children of Israel. So it shall be in that day *That* the great trumpet will be blown; They will come, who are about to perish in the land of Assyria, And they who are outcasts in the land of Egypt, And shall worship the Lord in the holy mount at Jerusalem (Isaiah 27:12-13)

In this text is pictured the blowing of the Great Shofar, or Rams horn, which occurs during the celebration of the Feast of Trumpets. Isaiah also states that those who have escaped to the wilderness will come back to worship the Lord at the Holy mount in Jerusalem. This mountain is very likely Holy mount Zion, where Jesus will later be seen standing.

As Jesus returns to the earth and roars to His people to return from the wilderness to Israel it is stated that the seven thunders will sound (Revelation 10:3-4). What these thunders reveal is not described, because John is asked not to record what he hears. They will probably involve some sort of announcement to the world and Israel, regarding what is to occur as Jesus takes possession of His kingdom. Since it is not revealed what the message of the seven thunders is, one can only speculate as to their importance. Jesus then swears before the Almighty Father that there will be no more delay for the establishment of His kingdom. John also states, that in the days of the sounding of the seventh trumpet and final woe, will the mystery of God be completed, which was spoken of by His servants and prophets. This mystery is the completion of God's redemption of national Israel and the establishment of the Messianic Kingdom, as the days of the Seventieth Week come to close. Israel had rejected her Messiah and refused to repent at His first advent. It will be during our Lord's return, that the nation of Israel will finally be redeemed, fulfilling all that was predicted by the prophets. In Romans, Paul speaks of this great mystery:

> For I do not desire, brethren, that you should be ignorant of this mystery, lest you should be wise in your own opinion, that hardening in part has happened to Israel until the fullness of the Gentiles has come in. And so all Israel will be

saved, as it is written: "*The deliverer will come out of Z*
And He will turn away ungodliness from Jacob; For this is My covenant with them, When I take away their sins. (Romans 11:25-27)

As the Lord returns physically to earth, He will cry out to those Jews who have not received the mark that they should repent. As stated in Hebrews, Jesus will come a second time not to put away sin, but for the salvation of Israel (Hebrews 9:28). These compromising Jews will have the ten-day period to accept Christ's offer before the Day of Atonement, which will end the Seventieth Week. Upon their repentance, Jesus will go forth to rescue the 144,000 and the other Jews who are in hiding in the areas of Assyria and Egypt. It will be this great roar of the Messiah that will signal that the Jews should now return to the land of Israel. The prophet Zechariah tells us that there will be great mourning in the land during this period of repentance:

> And I will pour on the house of David and on the inhabitants of Jerusalem the Spirit of grace and supplication; then they will look on Me whom they have pierced; they will mourn for Him as one mourns for *his* only *son*, and grieve for Him as one grieves for a firstborn. In that day there shall be a great mourning in Jerusalem, like the mourning at Hadad Rimmon in the plain of Megiddo. And the land shall mourn, every family by itself: the family of the house of David by itself, and their wives by themselves; the family of the house of Nathan by itself, and their wives by themselves; the family of the house of Levi by itself, and their wifes by themselves; the family of Shimei by itself, and their wives by themselves; all the families that remain, every family by itself, and their wives by themselves. (Zechariah 12:10-14)

This revealing of the Messiah, the calling of the assembly of Israel back to the land, and the beginning of the Messianic kingdom on the first day of the month Tishri, is a perfect fulfillment of the Feast of Trumpets. With its initiation, the ten days of repentance begin, and soon John will be shown the end of the Seventieth Week on the tenth of Tishri. Its culmination will be in fulfillment of the next feast on the Jewish calendar: the Day of Atonement.

THE LITTLE BOOK

Before the next feast is fulfilled, John is told to take and eat the little scroll that is in the hands of the Angel of the Lord. This scroll is said to taste like honey in John's mouth, but becomes bitter in his stomach. The scroll then reveals a bittersweet truth. While it is sweet that the kingdom of Christ has finally come, it will be bitter for all those who will soon suffer the bowl judgments. The bowl judgments contained within the scroll, will vent the final wrath of God Almighty upon those who "dwell upon the earth." John is told that he will again have to prophesy "about many peoples, nations, tongues, and kings." This scroll is, most likely, the same flying scroll that was seen by the prophet Zechariah:

> Then I turned and raised my eyes, and saw there a flying scroll. And He said to me, "What do you see?" So I answered, "I see a flying scroll. Its length *is* twenty cubits and its width ten cubits." The he said to me, "This *is* the curse that goes out over the face of the whole earth: 'Every thief shall be expelled, according *to what is on* this side of *the scroll*; and, every perjurer shall be expelled,' according *to what is on* that side of it." (Zechariah 5:1-3)

This scroll contains within it the final curse, on the earth, against all mankind who have followed after the Antichrist. As the bowls are poured out, in Revelation chapter 16, the final fury of God's wrath will unfold. After John consumes the little scroll, he begins to describe the ministry of the two witnesses from the midpoint of the Seventieth Week until its culmination. Their ministry will be terminated at the end of the Seventieth Week, on the Feast of Atonement.

> Then I was given a reed like a measuring rod. And the angel stood saying, "Rise and measure the temple of God, the altar, and those who worship there. But leave to the court which is outside the temple, and do not measure it, for it has been given to the Gentiles. And they will tread the holy city underfoot *for* forty-two months. And I will give *power* to my two witnesses, and they will prophesy one thousand two hundred and sixty days, clothed in sackcloth. These are the two olive trees and two lampstands standing before the God of the earth. And if anyone wants to harm them, fire proceeds from their mouth and devours their enemies. And if anyone wants to harm them, he must be killed in this manner. These have the power to shut heaven, so that no rain falls in the days of their prophecy; and they have the power over the waters to turn them to blood, and to strike the earth with all plagues as often as they desire. **Now when they finish their testimony, the beast that ascends out of the bottomless pit will make war against them, overcome them, and kill them. And their dead bodies *will lie* in the street of the great city which spiritually is called Sodom and Egypt, where also our Lord was crucified. Then *those* from the peoples, tribes, tongues, and nations will see their dead bodies three and a half days, and not allow**

> **their dead bodies to be put into graves. And those who dwell on the earth will rejoice over them, make merry, and send gifts to one another, because these two prophets tormented those who dwell on the earth. Now after three and a half days the breath of life from God entered them, and they stood on their feet, and a great fear fell on those who saw them. And they heard a loud voice from heaven saying to them, "Come up here." And they ascended to heaven in a cloud, and their enemies saw them. In the same hour there was a great earthquake, and a tenth of the city fell. In the earthquake seven thousand men were killed, and the rest were afraid and gave glory to the God of heaven. The second woe is past. Behold, the third woe is coming quickly.** (Revelation 11:1-14)

I have previously addressed the appearance of these two witnesses at the midpoint of the Seventieth Week. These two men, most likely Moses and Elijah, will preach a message of warning and repentance to those Jews who have not fled Jerusalem. It is very possible that the second witness could be Enoch, but I tend to favor Moses. I am not, however, dogmatic on whom the second of the two witnesses will be. All I am sure of is that they are to prepare the way for the second coming of Jesus. Just as John the Baptist called Israel to national repentance, so likewise, will these two men. These men are said to be given power over weather, the waters of the earth, over plagues, and fire. During the last half of the Seventieth Week, they will, no doubt, perform these great miracles in order to turn away the blindness of Israel. Similar to the 144,000 who fled to Petra in Edom, these two witnesses also will be protected by God from the trumpet judgments. In fact, it is possible that the world will come to believe that it is these two individuals who are behind God's awesome trumpet judgments. So much so, that the Antichrist will attempt to kill them. He will do this after they have finished their testimony, which is to last 1260 days, or three and one half years. The Antichrist will be desperate to kill them knowing that Jesus has now taken possession of the earth, and has called His elect back to meet Him in Israel. This will be the Antichrist's last-ditch effort to consolidate his power, by showing his ability to kill these two men of God. These two witnesses are killed on the Day of Atonement (the tenth of Tishri) exactly 1260 days from the midpoint of the Seventieth Week, thus ending the "ten days of awe."

THE DAY OF ATONEMENT/ YOM KIPPUR

The next feast, which takes place ten days after the Feast of Trumpets, is the Day of Atonement (Leviticus 23:26-32). This is to occur on the tenth day of the month of Tishri. As previously stated, the ten days in between the two feasts are for the repentance of national Israel, as well as the rest of the world. When the Day of Atonement has been reached, those who have not repented and have placed their trust in Jesus, as Messiah will be judged with the rest of the world. This is confirmed in Leviticus where God states that those who do not afflict their soul or repent will be cut off from His people (Leviticus 23:29). The Day of Atonement is considered to be the holiest day of the Jewish year. This was the only day in which the high priest was allowed to enter the inner temple. It was on this day that God would grant or deny redemption to the nation of Israel.[11] It will be on this same day that God will accept the repentance of the nation of Israel and return for their deliverance. It is this period that Daniel refers to in his prophecy of the seventy weeks:

> Seventy weeks are determined for your people and for your holy city, **To finish the transgression, To make an end of sins, To make reconciliation for iniquity, To bring in everlasting righteousness, To seal up vision and prophecy, And to anoint the Most Holy.** (Daniel 9:24) {*Emphasis Mine*}

The Seventieth Week will come to a close as Israel repents and is grafted back into the family of God (Romans 11:23-27). This final redemption of Israel fulfills the Day of Atonement, in exact chronology, precisely ten days after Jesus takes possession of the earth on the Feast of Trumpets.

THE LORD'S MARCH TO ISRAEL

Believing Israel has, upon reaching the Day of Atonement, repented of its sins, and the two witnesses having finished their testimony, are then slain by the Antichrist. The followers of the Antichrist will rejoice greatly for three and a half days thinking that their Antichrist still has the power an authority to stand against God Almighty. It is during the three days of their celebration, that the Lord Jesus will rescue His people and lead them back to the land of Israel. Isaiah reveals that Jesus will come eventually to Mount Zion (Isaiah 59:20). In Hosea we are told that the afflicted, or repentant Jews, will seek the Messiah, after His appearance on the Feast of Trumpets, and He will restore them on the third day after the Day of Atonement:

> I will return again to My place Till they acknowledge their offense. Then they will seek My face; In their affliction they will diligently seek Me. Come and let us return to the Lord; For He has torn, but He will heal us; He has stricken, but He will bind us up. After two days He will revive us; On the third day He will raise us up, That we may live in His sight. Let us know, Let us pursue the knowledge of the Lord. His going forth is established as the morning; He will come to us like the rain, **Like the latter *and* former rain to the earth**. (Hosea 5:15 & 6:1-3) {*Emphasis Mine*}

It was on the third day after Israel accepted the first covenant of God, that the Lord came down from Mount Sinai to speak of His commandments to the nation of Israel (Exodus 19:16-25). [12] In much the same way, three days after Israel accepts the new covenant of God, the Lord Jesus will appear to them in Israel. The parallels are absolutely astounding! It is also confirmed by the scriptures that Jesus, as the Angel of the Lord, will indeed visit Israel. This time it will be for their salvation:

> For He said, "Surely they *are* My people, Children *who* will not lie." So He became their Savior. In all their affliction He was afflicted, And the Angel of His Presence saved them. In His love and in His pity He redeemed them; And He bore them and carried them All the days of old. (Isaiah 63:8-9)

FROM BOZRAH TO JERUSALEM

After the repentance of Israel, on the Day of Atonement, Jesus will first go to Petra in Edom to save the 144,000, leading them on a triumphant march to Jerusalem. Isaiah the prophet speaks of this return to Jerusalem from Edom:

> Who *is* this who comes from Edom With dyed garments from Bozrah, This *One who is* glorious in His apparel, Traveling in the greatness of His strength?-- "I who speak in righteousness, mighty to save." Why is Your apparel red, And Your garments like one who treads in the winepress? I have trodden the winepress alone, And from the peoples no one *was* with Me. For I have trodden them in My anger And trampled them in My fury; Their blood is sprinkled upon my garments, And I have stained all My robes. For the day of vengeance *is* in My heart, And the year of My redeemed has come. I looked and *there was* no one to help, And I

> wondered That *there was* no one to uphold; Therefore My own arm brought salvation for Me; And My own fury, it sustained Me. I have trodden down the peoples in My anger, Made them drunk in My fury, And brought down their strength to the earth. (Isaiah 63:1-6)

In this passage from Isaiah, Jesus is pictured as He heads through Edom Himself destroying those who have come against Israel. In these verses it is emphasized that He is traveling alone. Later, at the battle of Armageddon, the armies of heaven will accompany Jesus. Jesus will also be wearing the very same garment, which becomes soaked with the blood of His enemies. The Lord will pour out great vengeance as He clears the way for the 144,000 to march back to Israel. The prophet Habakkuk speaks of this great march:

> God came from Teman, The Holy one from Mount Paran. Selah His glory covered the heavens, And the earth was full of His praise. *His* brightness was like the light; He had rays *flashing* from His hand, And there His power *was* hidden. (Habakkuk 3:3-4)

> You marched through the land in indignation; You trampled the nations in anger. You went forth for the salvation of Your people. For salvation with Your Anointed. You struck the head from the house of the wicked, By laying bare from foundation to neck. (Habakkuk 3:12-13)

Jesus, as the Angel of the Lord, is viewed marching from Teman and Mount Paran in Edom, with great indignation. He will march for the salvation of His people and will eventually destroy the Antichrist: "the house of the wicked." With those from Edom, Christ will lead His people through the wilderness to Israel, just as He had led them to the Promised Land in the time of Moses (Numbers 14:20-35). Jesus will lead the Jews across the Jordan through the Judean wilderness where, as we are told by Zechariah, He also will gather the faithful from the tribes of Judah before marching into Jerusalem: [13]

> The Lord will save the tents of Judah first, so that the glory of the house of David and the glory of the inhabitants of Jerusalem shall not become greater than that of Judah. (Zechariah 12:7)

As Jesus heads through the Judean hills He also will be joined by the remnant Jews who had fled to Assyria and Egypt and had begun their return as He roared to them on the Feast of Trumpets.[14] The events of this gathering are spoken of in greater detail in Zechariah chapter ten. Jesus, with this great crowd, will again enter Jerusalem through the eastern gate, as He did in His first coming. The gates will swing wide open as Jesus enters Jerusalem. A Lord's first coming into Jerusalem, He was rejected by national Israel. A time He stated that their house would be left desolate, and Israel would see Him no more until they would say, "Blessed is He who comes in the name of the Lord!" (Matthew 23:39). It will be on this day, about three and a half days after the Feast of Atonement, that He will be welcomed by the surviving one-third of the nation of Israel, who now has accepted Him as their Messiah.

As Jesus enters Jerusalem, He will likely come upon the bodies of the two witnesses who have been lying dead in the streets of Jerusalem for three and a half days. It is extremely probable that it will be Jesus, Himself, who breathes the breath life into these men, resurrecting them.[15] I must warn; however, that this cannot be stated dogmatically, since the text of Revelation does not necessitate that it is Jesus who revives these two individuals. The two witnesses are the last of God's faithful disciples who would die by martyrdom. As they ascend toward heaven, there will be a great shout and all of their enemies will view their ascension to heaven. During the hour of their ascension, there will be a mighty earthquake in the land of Israel destroying a tenth of Jerusalem. Seven thousand men will be killed in this earthquake. The rest of the faithful remnant of Israel will have great fear and give glory to God. This is in stark contrast from the response given by those who have taken the mark of the beast, who absolutely refuse to repent during the mighty judgments of the Day of the Lord. The reverence of the faithful remnant is a certification of their salvation and trust in the true Messiah.

THE FEAST OF TABERNACLES/SUKKOT

The last and final feast, which will be fulfilled on the fifth day following the end of the Seventieth Week, will be the Feast of Tabernacles (Leviticus 23:33-43). This feast took place on the fifteenth day of the month of Tishri. It commemorated the time when the Lord led his people through the wilderness to the land of Israel. In remembrance of this period, the Jews were to erect tiny makeshift booths and live in them. This was to remind them that their forefathers had very little shelter during their wilderness trek. This feast also celebrated the commencement of the Messianic kingdom, as well as the end of the fall harvest. It was also traditionally observed atop Mount Zion.[16]

It was revealed by Isaiah previously, that Jesus would head toward Mount Zion as He returns for the salvation of Israel (Isaiah 59:20). Obadiah also prophesies that, "Then saviors shall come to Mount Zion to judge the mountains of Esau, and the Kingdoms shall be the Lord's (Obadiah 1:21). Since Jesus has fulfilled the other six feasts perfectly, He should next be fulfilling the Feast of Tabernacles atop Mount Zion. Amazingly in Revelation chapter 14, which shows the outcome for national Israel in God's conflict of the ages, John is shown Jesus atop Mount Zion with the 144,000:

> **Then I looked, and behold, a Lamb standing on Mount Zion, and with Him one hundred *and* forty-four thousand, having His Father's name written on their foreheads. And I heard a voice from heaven, like the voice of many waters, and like the voice of loud thunder. And I heard the sound of harpists playing their harps. And they sang as it were a new song before the throne, before the four living creatures, and the elders; and no one could learn that song except the hundred *and* forty-four thousand who were redeemed from the earth. These are the ones who were not defiled with women, for they are virgins. These are the ones who follow the Lamb wherever He goes. These were redeemed from *among* men, *being* firstfruits to God and to the Lamb. And in their mouth was found no guile, for they are without fault before the throne of God.** (Revelation 14:1-5)

In the context of Revelation, these verses take place within the parenthetic chapters that the Apostle John pens, after the seventh trumpet has been blown. In these verses, John presents the great conflict of the ages and its final outcome on national Israel, the church, and the unbelieving world. It is at the beginning of chapter 14, that John is again shown the 144,000 who were sealed at the inauguration of the Day of the Lord, preceding the breaking of the seventh seal.

The 144,000 will be divinely protected during the trumpet judgments, and are the first of the tribes of Israel to be redeemed. After being led out of hiding back to Jerusalem, the 144,000 are pictured as standing with Jesus on Mount Zion. Most Bible commentators are presented with serious difficulties in this chapter. This is because Jesus is stated by the text, to be standing on earth before Revelation chapter 19. This is in direct opposition with the opinion of many Bible scholars, who teach that our Lord's first return to earth takes place when He comes at the battle of Armageddon. Therefore, it is argued that this passage cannot possibly be referring to Mount Zion in Israel. They propose that it describes an occurrence that is to take place atop a Mount Zion, which is said to be located in heaven. There are two major flaws in this line of reasoning:

> 1. John is explicitly told that the 144,000 are sealed and will be protected from death during the Day of the Lord. If this is so, what are they doing in heaven? Nowhere, in the text of Revelation, is there any indication that the 144,000 have been transported bodily to heaven.
>
> 2. There also is nothing within the text itself to lead one to conclude that John is even describing an event in heaven. In

fact, stated in verse two, John hears a voice of a multitude singing coming down to him from Heaven. Why does he not state that he hears these voices within heaven, if a heavenly event is indeed occurring?

Fulfillment of Final Fall Feasts

Date	Event
Tishri 1 (Trumpets/RoshHaShanna) Leviticus 23:23-25)	Jesus, as the angel of the Lord, stands upon the earth and reclaims it while calling the assembly of the House of Israel back to the land. (Revelation 10:1-7)
10 Days of Mourning	
Tishri 10 (Atonement/Yom Kippur) Leviticus 23:26-32	Israel repents as they realize Jesus was Messiah. The Two Witnesses are killed as the Seventieth Week ends. Jesus begins to lead Jews from Edom back to Jerusalem. (Revelation 11:1-11)
3½ Days	
Tishri 14	The Two Witnesses are resurrected; possibly by Christ Himself. Jesus then marches toward Mt. Zion.
Tishri 15 (Tabernacles/Succoth) Leviticus 23:33-44	Jesus brings the 144,000 to the summit of Mt. Zion in fulfillment of the Feast of Tabernacles (Revelation 14:1-5)
75 Days from Atonement Kislev 25 (Dedication/Hanukkah) John 10:22	With cleansing of the earth and the temple, the fulfillment of Fall feasts ends.

It is more consistent with the text to understand that the 144,000 are on Mount Zion in Israel, fulfilling the Feast of Tabernacles. Israel has repented and accepted her Messiah, and Jesus has led her through the wilderness triumphantly. The Feast of Tabernacles was a commemoration of the time when Moses led Israel through the wilderness to the Promised Land. It will now be fulfilled in the Lord's leading of the 144,000, as well as the rest of the Jewish remnant, out from Edom to Israel. As the 144,000 ascend Mount Zion they may very well sing Psalm 118, known as the Psalm of ascension.[17] This psalm speaks of Israel's chastening by the Lord, their final salvation, and the recognition of Jesus as their Messiah. It was commonly sung by Israel during the celebration of this great feast.

On top of Mount Zion the 144,000 also will sing a new song. This song is first sung by the redeemed church who sings before the throne of God, the four living creatures, and the elders. This, again, shows the distinction of the great multitude from the elders and the living creatures, who do not join in this song. No one could learn this song except the 144,000 who were on Mount Zion with Jesus. This group seen with Jesus consists of virgins who are said to follow Jesus wherever He goes. They are also said to be the first fruits of the redeemed of Israel, and are without fault before God. Since they have now put their trust in Jesus, their sins are no longer remembered before God. This is a great truth for all who place their faith in Christ's atoning work at Calvary.

The Feast of Tabernacles concludes the fulfillment of the seven feasts of Leviticus. As seen, they will each be fulfilled in exactly the same fashion that they were fulfilled in our Lord's first advent. I hope that throughout, I have remained completely faithful to the text of Revelation not forcing these verses to fit the feasts.

THE SEVENTH TRUMPET (WOE 3)

It will be very likely, that while on Mount Zion, the seventh trumpet will be blown signaling the third woe:

> **Then the seventh angel sounded: And there were loud voices in heaven, saying, "The kingdoms of this world have become *the kingdoms* of our Lord and of His Christ, and He shall reign forever and ever!" And the twenty-four elders who sat before God on their thrones fell on their faces and worshipped God, saying: "We give You thanks, O Lord God Almighty, The One who is and who was and who is to come, Because You have taken Your great power and reigned. The nations were angry, and Your wrath has come, and the time of the dead, that they**

should be judged, And that You should reward Your servants the prophets and the saints, And those who fear Your name, small and great, And should destroy those who destroy the earth." Then the temple of God was opened in heaven, and the ark of His covenant was seen in His temple. And there were lightnings, noises, thunderings, an earthquake, and great hail. (Revelation 11:15-19)

At the seventh trumpet it is proclaimed that the "times of the Gentiles" have come to an end. The kingdoms of the world are now the kingdoms of Jesus Christ. The prophet Daniel had described that a great stone would crush the statue, which symbolized the Gentile empires (Daniel 2:31-45). Jesus Christ, the stone, which the builders rejected (Luke 20:17), will now pour out the bowl judgments crushing the Beast's empire, in fulfillment of the vision. Before He performs this, He will lead the faithful remnant of Israel to the Mount of Olives. The prophet Zechariah discloses what will then occur:

> And in that day His feet will stand on the Mount of Olives, Which faces Jerusalem on the east. And the Mount of Olives shall be split in two, From east two west, *Making* a very large valley; Half of the mountain shall move toward the north And half of it toward the south. Then you shall flee *through* My mountain valley, For the mountain valley shall reach to Azal. Yes, you shall flee As you fled from the earthquake In the days of Uzziah king of Judah. Thus the Lord my God will come, *And* all the saints with You. (Zechariah 14:4-5)

The verses preceding these, tell of the siege of Jerusalem by Antichrist and its deliverance by Jesus (Zechariah 14:1-3). It then moves on to describe the Lord's second advent. As Jesus leads the remnant to the Mount of Olives, it will split in half creating a great gully. The faithful remnant is instructed to flee into this gully to Azal. Azal is an unknown place where the house of Israel will hide as the bowl judgments are poured out. Before the bowls begin, Jesus will return to heaven to give rewards to His saints (Revelation 11:18). It is then stated, by Zechariah, that Jesus will later return to earth with all the saints (Zechariah 14:5).

THE BEMA SEAT JUDGMENT

Jesus, upon returning to heaven, will now judge the elect who have been resurrected and raptured into heaven. Believers will not, at this moment, have their sins judged as these were already judged at Calvary. This will be a judgment of the believer's faithfulness as he or she served God on earth. The Apostle Paul teaches that every believer will have to stand before the Judgment Seat of Christ and receive rewards for the deeds done while on earth (2 Corinthians 5:10). This judgment, known commonly as the Bema Seat Judgment, is outlined more explicitly in first Corinthians:

> For no other foundation can anyone lay than that which is laid, which is Jesus Christ. Now if anyone builds on this foundation *with* gold, silver, precious stones, wood, hay, straw, each one's work will become manifest; for the Day will declare it, because it will be revealed by fire; and the fire will test each one's work, of what sort it is. If anyone's work which he has built on *it* endures, he will receive a reward. If anyone's work is burned, he will suffer loss; but he himself will be saved, yet so as through fire. (1 Corinthians 3:11-15)

Jesus will look at each individual Christian's works that have been performed while on planet earth. Many of these works will have been done unselfishly for the service and building of God's kingdom. Other works will have been performed out of greed and self-ambition. It is these works, done out of self-gain, which will discarded and burned. Though a person's works may be burned, he himself will still be saved; for this is not to be a judgment of a believer's sins. The believer, whose works pass the test, will be given rewards by Jesus as stated in Revelation 11:18. As disciples, it is important that we serve God out of pure motives, and for the furtherance of His kingdom. I believe there will be a number of surprises as Jesus reveals our rewards. Many of those who are looked at as being great men and women of God will, very likely, be eclipsed by lesser known faithful believers. As our Lord said, in the kingdom of God the first shall be last and the last shall be first (Matthew 20:16). After these rewards are distributed to His servants, the last of God's great vengeance will be unleashed.

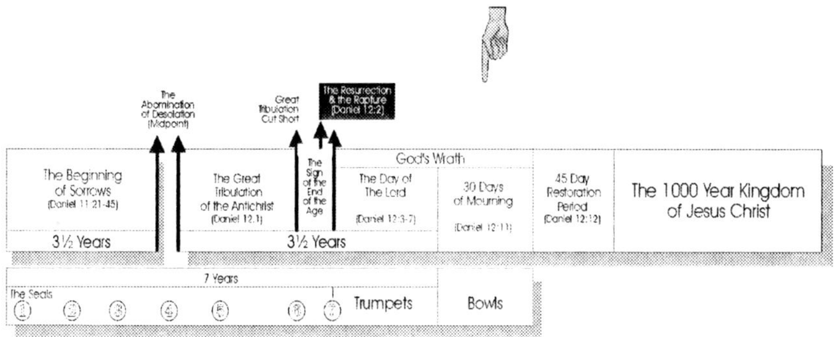

14
BOWLS, BABYLON & BATTLE

IT IS CRITICAL TO UNDERSTAND that the next series of judgments are to take place after the seven-year period of the Seventieth Week has ended. Jesus has already returned physically for the salvation of national Israel following their repentance during the "ten days of awe." While the trumpets were primarily to bring Israel to repentance, the bowls will be initiated against the unbelieving Gentile kingdoms and all who have taken the mark of the beast. The bowl judgments are contained in the little scroll that was open and in the hand of Jesus as He retook possession of the earth. The bowl judgments will herald the destruction of the Gentile kingdoms that have persecuted Israel and the church throughout world history. John is now presented with our Lord's return as a "thief to destroy." Jesus will now bring the kingdom of the Antichrist to a violent end. The prophet Daniel, in a very critical passage, outlines exactly when the bowl judgments are to be poured out and what their duration will be.

DANIEL'S DILEMMA

In the twelfth chapter of the book of Daniel, the prophet is shown the beginning of the great tribulation. He then hears one of the angels cry out that it will be for a time, times, and half a time (3 1/2 years) until all concerning Israel's Seventieth Week will be fulfilled (Daniel 12:7). Daniel, being a bit perplexed, asks what will be the culmination of everything that is to occur. In context, the preceding two chapters of Daniel focused on the Antichrist and his rise to power. Specifically, Daniel would now like to know when the reign of the Antichrist would finally be brought to an end. In response to his inquiry the angel states:

> And from the time *that* the daily *sacrifice* is taken away, and the abomination of desolation is set up, *there shall be* one thousand two hundred and ninety days. (Daniel 12:11)

The angel informs Daniel that from the time that the "abomination of desolation" is set up at the midpoint of the Seventieth Week, until the end of the Antichrist, will be 1290 days. This is thirty days more than the 1260 days given from the midpoint to the end of the Seventieth Week. It will be during this last thirty-day period in which God will bring to an end the rule of the Antichrist. Although the salvation of national Israel has taken place and the mystery of God's redemptive plan is complete, Jesus has not yet taken any direct action against the Antichrist. Upon the completion of the bowl judgments, Jesus will return to the earth with a heavenly army to put to an end, the Antichrist.

Daniel is also advised by the angel that, blessed is the one who makes it to the 1335 days (Daniel 12:12). This now adds on another 45 days to the 1290 days given for the end of the Antichrist. This period is very significant in that it brings us to fulfillment of another of Israel's holidays: Hanukkah. This holiday, although not mentioned in Leviticus, is considered a very special holiday by the Jews. Hanukkah, or the Feast of Dedication, was even celebrated by Jesus in His first advent (John 10:22). It commemorated the time when the Maccabees overthrew the rule of the Syrian king, Antiochus Epiphanes, and cleansed the temple. Antiochus was a type of Antichrist, who desecrated the temple. He did this by sacrificing a pig and erecting an image of Zeus with his face on it in the Holy of Holies. In the same way, after Jesus destroys the Antichrist, the temple will again be cleansed in fulfillment of Hanukkah. This last 45-day period attests to the fact that the Seventieth Week will end on the Day of Atonement. This is because exactly 75 days from the Day of Atonement, Hanukkah is celebrated. If one then adds 75 days to the 1260 days (1260+75=1335), one comes to the 1335 days spoken of by the angel to Daniel. This last period will signal the final cleansing of the temple and the earth, as the kingdom of Messiah begins. Again, every period of time given in Scripture is not without great significance.

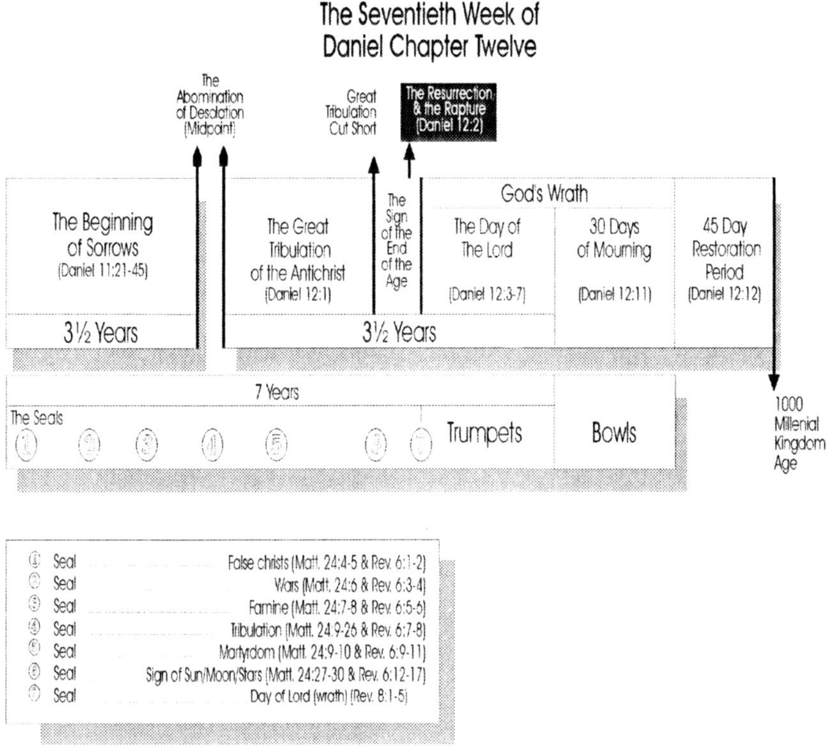

1 Seal	False christs (Matt. 24:4-5 & Rev. 6:1-2)
2 Seal	Wars (Matt. 24:6 & Rev. 6:3-4)
3 Seal	Famine (Matt. 24:7-8 & Rev. 6:5-6)
4 Seal	Tribulation (Matt. 24:9-26 & Rev. 6:7-8)
5 Seal	Martyrdom (Matt. 24:9-10 & Rev. 6:9-11)
6 Seal	Sign of Sun/Moon/Stars (Matt. 24:27-30 & Rev. 6:12-17)
7 Seal	Day of Lord (wrath) (Rev. 8:1-5)

THE BOWLS BEGIN

As stated above, the beginning of the bowl judgments occurs after the Seventieth Week has ended with the seventh trumpet signaling the final culmination of God's redemptive plan. From our study of the feasts it was shown that five days after the end of the Seventieth Week, Jesus celebrated the Feast of Tabernacles with the 144,000 atop Mount Zion. This will then leave 25 days for the bowl judgments to unfold. John reveals that the bowl judgments will take place very quickly, in rapid-fire succession. The word used for bowl, in the text of Revelation, is indicative of a very shallow bowl or goblet which has more breadth than depth.[1] Because of this, the contents of the bowls can be drained quickly. This reveals the swiftness and finality of God's final wrath. Before the bowls begin, John is again shown a great scene in heaven:

> **Then I saw another sign in heaven, great and marvelous: seven angels having the seven last plagues, for in them the wrath of God is complete. And I saw *something* like a**

> **sea of glass mingled with fire, and those who have victory over the beast, over his image and over his mark *and* over the number of his name, standing on the sea of glass, having harps of God. And they sing the song of Moses, the servant of God, and the song of the Lamb, saying: "Great and marvelous *are* Your works, Lord God Almighty! Just and true *are* Your ways, O King of the saints! Who shall not fear You, O Lord, and glorify Your name? For *You* alone *are* holy For all nations shall come and worship before You, For your judgments have been manifested. After these things I looked; and behold, the temple of the tabernacle of the testimony in heaven was opened. And out of the temple came the seven angels having the seven plagues, clothed in pure bright linen, and having their chest girded with golden bands. Then one of the four living creatures gave to the seven angels seven golden bowls full of the wrath of God who lives forever and ever. The temple was filled with smoke from the glory of God and from His power, and no one was able to enter the temple till the seven plagues of the seven angels were completed.** (Revelation 15:1-8)

John is now shown the seven angels who have the seven last judgments. Through these bowls, it is stated that the wrath of God will be completed. John is also given a view of the sea of glass before the throne of God. It is shown to be mixed with fire. In the midst of this sea of glass mixed with fire, are the great multitude of the church who have persevered, and gained victory over the Antichrist. They have been tried by the fire of the Seraphim, and have been found to be pure and worthy of their calling. Because of this, they are enabled to stand before the throne of God Almighty. This great multitude sings the Song of Moses and the Lamb, giving God great glory for His righteous judgments upon the world. After this great hymn, the heavenly tabernacle is opened. It is after this heavenly tabernacle's likeness that the earthly one was patterned after (Exodus chapters 25-27). The seven angels emerge as one of the four living creatures hands them the bowls. Once again, it is apparent that the angels are entrusted with God's judgments, not the living creatures. The temple is so filled with the power, might, and great wrath of God, that no one is able to enter until His judgments are completed. The bowl judgments will be so fierce that there will never be anything similar to them again. The world has now fallen into the hands of an angry God whose long-suffering and patience have come to an end. This final period of wrath will be upon the kingdom of the Antichrist, as well as those who have worshipped the beast, and it will be complete.

THE FIRST BOWL

Then I heard a loud voice from the temple saying to the seven angels, "Go and pour out the bowls of the wrath of God on the earth." So the first went and poured out his bowl upon the earth, and a foul and loathsome sore came upon the men who had the mark of the beast and those who worshipped his image. (Revelation 16:1-2)

The first angel is commanded to pour out the first bowl. As this is done, a foul sore comes upon all those who worship and have the mark of the beast. This judgment is very much like the plague of boils, which God unleashed upon the Egyptians (Exodus 9:8-12). Scholars have no difficulties with that judgment being literal, so there should then be no problem in taking this judgment literally. As with the Egyptians, this plague serves to further harden the hearts of those who have shaken their fists at God. Up to this point in Revelation, there has been no direct judgment on those who have placed their trust in the Antichrist. It will be during this period that they will begin to pay the awesome price for tossing their lot in with the Antichrist. Their great leader, who dared to defy God, will now be unable to save them.

THE SECOND BOWL

Then the second angel poured out his bowl on the sea, and it became blood as of a dead *man*; and every living creature in the sea died. (Revelation 16:3)

At the second trumpet, one third of the Mediterranean Sea was turned to blood. At the second bowl, the entire sea will be affected. As it is turned entirely to blood, every living creature in the sea will die. This will be a judgment of the waters of the Middle East that will eclipse anything that has ever occurred in human history. The severity of this judgment will have a collateral effect on all of the areas of the Middle East that surround the Mediterranean basin.

THE THIRD BOWL

Then the third angel poured out his bowl on the rivers and springs of water, and they became blood. And I heard the angel of the waters saying: "You are righteous,

O Lord, The One who is and who was and who is to be, Because You have judged these things. For they have shed the blood of saints and prophets, And You have given them blood to drink. For it is their just due." And I heard another from the altar saying, "Even so, Lord God Almighty, true and righteous *are* Your judgments." (Revelation 16:4-7)

As the third bowl is poured out, all the rivers and springs of fresh water are turned to blood. This is very similar to the first Egyptian plague (Exodus 7:19-24). It does not seem that this judgment is just limited to the Middle East, as were the previous. Worldwide, all the fresh water will be turned to blood. John hears the cry of the angel, who is given charge over the waters, proclaiming that now God is giving those who have shed the blood of the righteous, blood to drink. It is interesting that God has an angel who is in charge over the waters of the earth. It is comforting to know that the hands of God Almighty control the very water supply of the world. This will truly be a horrifying time for those who have killed God's elect and worshipped the Antichrist.

THE FOURTH BOWL

Then the fourth angel poured out his bowl on the sun, and power was given to him to scorch men with fire. And men were scorched with great heat, and they blasphemed the name of God who has power over these plagues; and they did not repent and give Him glory. (Revelation 16:8-9)

The next bowl is unlike any of the judgments that God unleashed upon Egypt. The heat of the sun will become so intense that its great heat will literally scorch mankind. This burning of men by great heat, is spoken of in the prophets:

Therefore the curse has devoured the earth, And those who dwell in it are desolate. Therefore the inhabitants of the earth are burned, And few men *are* left. (Isaiah 24:6)

For behold, the day is coming, Burning like an oven, And all the proud, yes all who do wickedly will be stubble. And the day which is coming shall burn them up, Says the Lord of hosts, That will leave them neither root nor branch. (Malachi 4:1)

Even with this severe judgment, men will not repent and ask God for forgiveness. Rather, in their intense pain, they will curse and blaspheme the name of God. Those who have followed the Antichrist will continue to remain indignant until the bitter end.

THE FIFTH BOWL

> **Then the fifth angel poured out his bowl on the throne of the beast, and his kingdom became full of darkness, and they gnawed their tongues because of the pain. And they blasphemed the God of heaven because of their pains and their sores, and did not repent of their deeds.** (Revelation 16:10-11)

Immediately following the plague of heat is great darkness. The swiftness of these judgments is borne out in the fact that the sores from the first bowl judgment are still upon these men and women. This fifth bowl is the first judgment that is focused directly against the kingdom of the Antichrist. This will be like the darkness that was upon the land of Egypt during the ninth Egyptian plague (Exodus 10:21-23). The darkness during the Egyptian plague was so thick that no one was able to see anything for three days. It will likely be even worse during this judgment. Imagine the entire world plunged into thick darkness. The Antichrist and his kingdom will be absolutely powerless as this occurs. Yet, men will continue to harden their hearts and blaspheme the name of God.

THE SIXTH BOWL

> **Then the sixth angel poured out his bowl on the great river Euphrates, and its water was dried up, so that the way of the kings from the east might be prepared. And I saw three unclean spirits like frogs *coming* out of the mouth of the dragon, out of the mouth of the beast, and out of the mouth of the false prophet. For they are spirits of demons, performing signs, *which* go out to the kings of the earth and of the whole world, to gather them to battle of the great day of God Almighty. "Behold, I am coming as a thief. Blessed is he who watches, and keeps his garments, lest he walk naked and they see his shame." And they gathered them together to the place called in Hebrew, Armageddon.** (Revelation 16:12-16)

With the pouring of the sixth bowl, the great river Euphrates will be dried up. This will be dried up so that the armies of the east will reach with ease, the valley of Armageddon. Isaiah speaks of this drying up of the Euphrates:

> The Lord will utterly destroy the tongue of the Sea of Egypt; With His mighty wind He will shake His fist over the River (Euphrates), And strike it in the seven streams, And make *men* cross over dry shod. (Isaiah 11:15)

Jesus will bid these armies to challenge Him to battle, and He will not make it difficult for them to assemble. This will not be a battle against Jerusalem, as many propose, but a battle against Jesus as He returns.

John then sees demonic beings, like frogs, come from the mouth of the False Prophet, the Antichrist, and Satan. These spirits will cause these armies to gather to the valley of Megiddo to challenge Jesus. This reveals the absolute depravity and wickedness of man during this moment in history. Even after God's mighty trumpet and bowl judgments, men will still think that they can defeat Jesus. The Antichrist, who has been powerless against these great judgments, will still be able to muster loyal followers. It is no secret that Jesus will return to the valley of Megiddo. It will be here that the Antichrist will make his final stand against God Almighty.

The Lord interjects in this passage that He is coming as a thief. This is His final coming as a "thief to destroy." For He will now end the rule of the Gentiles. The kingdom of God will begin, and it will last for all eternity. Armageddon is just the final step of stamping out the Lord's enemies. Jesus also declares that "Blessed is he who watches, and keeps his garments, lest he walk naked and they see his shame." This seems to be a reference to one of the Lord's parables concerning His wedding to His bride, the church (Matthew 22:1-14). In this parable, a great host of people is invited to witness the wedding. One of the guests, who had come to the wedding, was found to be without a wedding garment. Since he was at the wedding unworthily, he was bound and kicked out into the outer darkness. In the same way, when Jesus returns to set up His kingdom, those who have taken the mark and have survived the Day of the Lord, will be found naked and not be allowed to witness the wedding of Christ to the Church. They will be expelled from His kingdom into the outer darkness of hell. It would not be wise to be found naked before Jesus.

THE SEVENTH BOWL

> **Then the seventh angel poured out his bowl into the air, and a loud voice came out of the temple of heaven, from the throne, saying, "It is done!" And there were noises**

> **and thunderings and lightnings; and there was a great earthquake, such a mighty and great earthquake as had not occurred since men were on the earth. Now the great city was divided into three parts, and the cities of the nations fell. And great Babylon was remembered before God, to give her cup of the wine of the fierceness of His wrath. Then every island fled away, and the mountains were not found. And great hail from heaven fell upon men, *every hailstone* about the weight of a talent. And men blasphemed God because of the plague of the hail, since that plague was exceedingly great.** (Revelation 16:17-21)

The last bowl is poured out, as the angel proclaims, "It is done." God's divine wrath will now culminate with the severest of all the judgments. The greatest earthquake the world has ever witnessed will now occur. It will literally change the face of the entire earth. The city of Jerusalem will be divided into three parts, and every other city in the world will crumble. The world's cities will be rendered into nothing but ash heaps. Many mountains will be leveled, while others will be raised. This will include all islands, because they are really mountains under the ocean. This earthquake also will change the contour of the entire land of Israel. It will raise the Dead Sea, so its waters will flow through the valley created by Jesus when He stood upon the Mount of Olives. This will allow the waters of the Dead Sea to flow again into the Mediterranean Sea (Ezekiel 47:1-12). This incredible earthquake will even destroy the great city of Babylon. John discusses this destruction of Babylon in much greater detail in Revelation chapter 18.

Following the earthquake, great hail is poured out upon mankind, with each stone weighing approximately a hundred pounds. This is much like the hail poured out during the seventh Egyptian plague (Exodus 9:13-35). In the Old Testament blasphemers were to be stoned to death (Leviticus 24:16). These, who have blasphemed the name of God and have killed his servants, will be stoned to death from heaven. The absolute destruction caused by all of these judgments will make the entire earth a wasteland, as the prophet Isaiah states:

> BEHOLD, the Lord makes the earth empty and makes it waste, Distorts its surface And scatters abroad its inhabitants. And it shall be: As with the people, so with the priest; As with the servant, so with his master; As with the maid, so with her mistress; As with the buyer, so with the seller; As with the lender, so with the borrower; As with the creditor, so with the debtor. The land shall be entirely emptied and utterly plundered, For the Lord has spoken this word. The earth mourns *and* fades away, The world

> languishes *and* fades away; The haughty people of the earth languish. (Isaiah 24:1-4)
>
> The earth is violently broken, The earth is split open, The earth is shaken exceedingly. The earth shall reel to and fro like a drunkard, And shall totter like a hut; Its transgression shall be heavy upon it, And it will fall, and not rise again." (Isaiah 24:19-20)

It is possible that untold millions will be killed by this last judgment alone. Those who are fleeing from the earthquake will be met by large hailstones that will crush and kill them. How the armies gathered in the valley of Megiddo will survive this last bowl, I can only speculate. Since they are to be assembled on a flat open plain, there would not be a terrible amount of danger from the earthquake. It also may be that God will not allow the great hail to fall on them, because He has a personal judgment awaiting these armies. All I can state with certainty is that somehow these armies, as well as the Antichrist, will be around to face Jesus at Armageddon. Before the battle of Armageddon begins, John details the destruction of the city of Babylon.

THE END OF BABYLON

> **After these things I saw another angel coming down from heaven, having great authority, and the earth was illuminated with his glory. And he cried mightily with a loud voice, saying, "Babylon the great is fallen, is fallen, and has become a habitation of demons, a prison for every foul spirit, and a cage for every unclean and hated bird! For all the nations have drunk of the wine of the wrath of her fornication, the kings of the earth have committed fornication with her, and the merchants of the earth have become rich through the abundance of her luxury." And I heard another voice from heaven saying, "Come out of her, my people, lest you share in her sins, and lest you receive of her plagues. For her sins have reached to heaven, and God has remembered her iniquities. "Render to her just as she rendered to you, and repay her double according to her works; in the cup which she has mixed, mix double for her. "In the measure that she glorified herself and lived luxuriously, in the same measure give her torment and sorrow; for she says in her heart, 'I sit *as* queen, and am no widow, and will not see sorrow.' Therefore her plagues will come in one day-- death and mourning and famine. And she**

> **will be utterly burned with fire, for strong *is* the Lord God who judges her.** (Revelation 18:1-8)

In the preceding verses we see the announcement that the great city of Babylon has fallen. This city should not be confused with the religious Babylonian system that is to be eradicated when the Antichrist claims that he alone is to be worshipped as god. Notice, the angel uses the phrase "is fallen" twice. This is because there are to be two falls of Babylon, first, of its religious system and second, of its physical existence. The religious system is destroyed at the midpoint of the Seventieth Week. The physical city of Babylon will be destroyed at the seventh bowl, and at the same moment all of the cities of the world are destroyed. It is my firm conviction that Revelation is referring to the actual city of Babylon, and not speaking mystically of Rome, New York, or some other great metropolis. Many scholars, who adhere to a strict interpretation of Revelation, veer off from their hermeneutic when reaching Revelation chapter 18. It has been the thrust of this book to stress the clearest plainest meaning of the text of Revelation. I will not, at this moment, change that approach. As biblical scholar A.W. Pink stated:

> Now what is there to discountenance the natural conclusion that "Babylon" means Babylon? Two or three generations ago, students of prophecy received incalculable help from the simple discovery that when the Holy Spirit spoke of Judea and Jerusalem in the Old Testament Scriptures He meant Judea and Jerusalem, and not England and London; and that when He mentioned Zion He did not refer to the church. But strange to say, few, if any of these brethren, have applied the same rule to the Apocalypse. Here they are guilty of doing the very thing for which they condemned their forebears in connection with the Old Testament they have "spiritualized" . . . What then? If to regard "Jerusalem" as meaning Jerusalem be a test of intelligence in Old Testament prophecy, shall we be counted a heretic if we understand "Babylon" to mean Babylon, and not Rome or apostate Christendom?[2]

Profound words penned from a man who did not live to see the city of Babylon rise out of the ashes, yet believed that it would. Our generation, alone, has witnessed the beginning of the amazing fulfillment of this scripture. Prior to his expulsion, the former "Butcher of Baghdad," Saddam Hussein, among other aspirations, had been busy rebuilding the great city of Babylon. In his book, The Rise of Babylon, author Charles Dyer describes in detail Saddam's rebuilding of the city of Babylon. Hussein, who had believed himself to be the second advent of King Nebuchadnezzar, looked to Babylon as again being a pivotal city in the Arab world. Because of this, he poured literally billions of dollars and thousands of man-hours into restoring the ancient city. The outer walls, along with the palace of King Nebuchadnezzar and the Ninmach Temple have already been erected. And, as with ancient Babylon, the great Euphrates River flows through the rebuilt city.[3]

During the Seventieth Week of Daniel, Babylon will again rise to prominence. It is highly likely that the treaty that the Antichrist confirms with Israel and the Arab world, also will involve an economic alliance. The neutral city chosen for the overseeing of this alliance will be the city of Babylon. This is, of course, only one possible scenario. In any event, Babylon will play a highly important role in the economy of the Antichrist, as well as the entire Middle East. How this is to occur remains to be seen. But after witnessing the collapse of Russia and the instant change of the world's geography, I have no doubt that this event can and will occur. As quickly as Babylon arises, this city whose "sins have reached to heaven," will be pummeled by God Almighty. The kings of the world will then mourn her great destruction:

> **And the kings of the earth who committed fornication and lived luxuriously with her will weep and lament for her, when they see the smoke of her burning, standing at a distance for fear of her torment, saying, 'Alas, alas, the great city Babylon, that mighty city! For in one hour your judgment has come.' And the merchants of the earth will weep and mourn over her, for no one buys their merchandise anymore: merchandise of gold and silver, precious stones and pearls, fine linen and purple, silk and scarlet, every kind of citron wood, every kind of object of ivory, every kind of object of most precious wood, bronze, iron, and marble; and cinnamon and incense, fragrant oil and frankincense, wine and oil, fine flour and wheat, cattle and sheep, horses and chariots, and bodies and souls of men. And the fruit that your soul longed for has gone from you, and all the things which are rich and splendid have gone from you, and you shall find them no more at all. The merchants of these things, who became rich by her, will stand at a distance for fear of her torment, weeping and wailing, and saying, 'Alas, alas, that great city that was clothed in fine linen, purple, and scarlet, and adorned with gold and precious stones and pearls! For in one hour such great riches came to nothing.' And every shipmaster, all who travel by ship, sailors, and as many as trade on the sea, stood at a distance and cried out when they saw the smoke of her burning, saying 'What is like this great city?' And they threw dust on their heads and cried out, weeping and wailing, and saying, 'Alas, alas, that great city, in which all who had ships on the sea became rich by her wealth! For in one hour she is made desolate.' "Rejoice over her,**

O heaven, and you holy apostles and prophets, for God has avenged on her!" Then a mighty angel took up a stone like a great millstone and threw *it* into the sea, saying, "Thus with violence the great city Babylon shall be thrown down, and shall not be found anymore. The sound of harpists, musicians, flutists, and trumpeters shall not be heard in you anymore. And no craftsman of any craft shall be found in you anymore. And the sound of a millstone shall not be heard in you anymore. And the light of a lamp shall not shine in you anymore. And the voice of bridegroom and bride shall not be heard in you anymore. For your merchants were the great men of the earth, for by your sorcery all the nations were deceived. And in her was found the blood of prophets and saints, and of all who were slain on the earth." (Revelation 18:9-24)

As the Antichrist tightens his stranglehold upon the world during the great tribulation period, all items sold in the Middle East will be exported through this great city. The Antichrist will be in complete control of the world's economy by guaranteeing that no one will be able to buy or sell without his mark. To keep control of the outflow of merchandise within the areas of his empire, he will funnel all trade through the city of Babylon. John reveals that many merchants will become rich in this city. The Antichrist will not only be in control of the world's oil reserves, but also of the economy of the entire Middle East area. He will use his power to bring the world to its economic knees buy forcing all to buy and sell through him. Anyone who dares not to bow allegiance to the Antichrist by worshipping him and receiving his mark will not be able to participate in the world economy. History records how Saddam Hussein started an economic panic that brought the armies of the world to his front doorstep when he invaded tiny Kuwait. What will then occur when one man has absolute control over the world's oil reserves, as well as its economy?

In the book of Zechariah we are given more information about the forces driving this wicked city:

Then the angel who talked with me came out and said to me, "Lift your eyes now, and see what this *is* that goes forth." So I asked, "What is it?" And he said, "It *is* a basket (Ephah) that is going forth." He also said, "This *is* their resemblance throughout the earth: Here *is* a lead disc lifted up, and this *is* a woman sitting inside the basket"; then he said, "This is Wickedness!" and he thrust her down into the basket, and threw the lead cover over its mouth. Then I raised my eyes and looked, and there *were* two women, coming with the wind in their wings; for they had wings like the wings of a

> stork, and they lifted up the basket between earth and heaven. So I said to the angel who talked with me, "Where are they carrying the basket?" and he said to me, "To build a house for it in the land of Shinar; when its ready, *the basket* will be set there on its base." (Zechariah 5:5-11)

The basket, or Ephah, is the largest of the Hebrew dry measures, and it is often employed as a symbol of commerce. In the case of these passages it refers to commerce "throughout the earth." The woman inside the basket is called "wickedness." We are told that this basket is to be taken to the land of Shinar, or Babylon, to be placed within the rebuilt city. These verses are disclosing a vision of mass commercialism, characterized by incredible wickedness. The mark of the beast will signal the advent of this wickedest of all economic systems.[4] Men will be required to barter their very souls in exchange for goods from the Antichrist. The city of Babylon will be the physical manifestation of this wicked economic system.

In this period, Babylon will become one of the most influential cities in the world. Yet, its greatness will come to an abrupt end. All those who have gained from the wealth of Babylon will mourn as they witness her destruction. It was in Babylon, where an antichrist named Nimrod tried to unite the world against God (Genesis 11). It will again be in Babylon, that the Antichrist will unite the world in defiance of the Almighty. God will, again, put down man's effort to defy His authority. Man's religious rebellion began at Babylon, and it will be in Babylon where it will end. The destruction of Babylon will be both final and complete, as is indicated by the scriptures:

> And Babylon, the glory of kingdoms, The beauty of the Chaldeans' pride, Will be as when God overthrew Sodom and Gomorrah. It will never be inhabited, Nor will it be settled from generation to generation; Nor will the Arabian pitch tents there, Nor will the shepherds make their sheepfolds there. (Isaiah 13:19-20)

> The sound of a cry *comes* from Babylon, And great destruction from the land of the Chaldeans, Because the Lord is plundering Babylon And silencing her loud voice, Though her waves roar like great waters, And the noise of their voice is uttered, Because the plunderer comes against her, against Babylon, And her mighty men are taken. Every one of their bows are broken; For the Lord *is* the God of recompense, He will surely repay. (Jeremiah 51:54-56)

THE CHORUS OF THE REDEEMED

> **After these things I heard a loud voice of a great multitude in heaven, saying "Alleluia! salvation; and glory and honor and power to the Lord our God! For true and righteous *are* His judgments, because He has judged the great harlot who corrupted the earth with her fornication; and He has avenged on her the blood of His servants *shed* by her." Again they said "Alleluia! And her smoke rises up forever and ever!" And the twenty-four elders and the four living creatures fell down and worshiped God who sat on the throne, saying, "Amen, Alleluia!" Then a voice came from the throne, saying, "Praise our God, all you His servants and those who fear Him, both small and great!" And I heard, as it were, the voice of a great multitude, as the sound of many waters and as the sound of mighty thunderings, saying, "Alleluia! For The Lord God Omnipotent reigns!"** (Revelation 19:1-6)

After the destruction of Babylon, there is exuberant rejoicing in heaven by the great multitude of the redeemed. The first cry of "Alleluia" is in gratitude for the salvation that God has provided. The second "Alleluia" is proclaimed for God's judgment of the false religious system of Babylon: the harlot whose smoke will rise forever. As those on earth weep and mourn over her destruction, the redeemed in heaven will shout for joy. It has been the Babylonian system, in one form or another, that has persecuted the people of God throughout the ages. God has now put to an end this great city, which was the physical manifestation of the evil world system. Another "Alleluia" is proclaimed by the 24 elders and the four living creatures. The fourth "Alleluia" is proclaimed by the redeemed, because now God reigns upon the earth. Interestingly, this text contains the very first occurrences of the word "Alleluia" used in the New Testament. It is a compound Hebrew word, which simply means, "Praise the Lord." In contrast to the three woes announced upon the earth, we have four "Alleluia's" proclaimed in heaven. This is because God's wrath is complete, and the Lord Jesus will now return to the earth, with His heavenly armies, to set up the Kingdom of God. Satan's schemes will finally come to an end because he is no longer the prince of the world system. It is Jesus Christ who will now reign as the rightful and legal ruler of the earth, as well as the universe. This will be the single greatest moment in all of human history. As Jesus takes control, He will begin to right all the wrongs of a sinful and fallen world.

THE MARRIAGE OF THE LAMB

> **"Let us be glad and rejoice and give Him glory, for the marriage of the Lamb has come, and His wife has made herself ready." And to her it was granted to be arrayed in fine linen, clean and bright, for the fine linen is righteous acts of the saints. Then he said to me, "Write: 'Blessed *are* those who are called to the marriage supper of the Lamb!'" And he said to me. "These are the true sayings of God." And I fell at his feet to worship him. But he said to me, "*See that you do not do that*! I am your fellow servant, and of your brethren who have testimony of Jesus. Worship God! For your testimony of Jesus is the spirit of prophecy."** (Revelation 19:7-10)

In the night before His crucifixion, Jesus explained to His disciples that He would not drink of the fruit of the vine again until He had established His Father's kingdom (Matthew 26:29). It will be during the great wedding feast of Jesus to His bride, the church that He will once again partake of the fruit of the vine. This great marriage feast will take place on the earth. All of the surviving repentant remnant of national Israel, as well as those Gentiles who enter Christ's kingdom, will be invited as guests to witness this great event. This gives great insight into the Lord's comment, at the sixth bowl that, "blessed is He who watches, and keeps his garments, lest he walk naked and they see his shame" (Revelation 16:15). As previously explained, those who have followed the Antichrist will be found naked and unworthy to witness the wedding or enter the Millennial Kingdom of Christ.

In the text, it is said of the bride that she "has made herself ready." The elect of God, who have been the overcomers of all the ages, will be arrayed in white garments indicative of the righteous acts performed in their service to God. They will be presented with these bright linen robes after the judgment seat of Christ has taken place. Although they battle sin every day, the reward will be great for those saints who persevere and overcome. The marriage of Jesus to His elect, is one of the great mysteries revealed by the Apostle Paul:

> For we are members of His body, of His flesh and of His bones. "*For this reason a man shall leave his father and mother and be joined to his wife, and the two shall be one flesh.*" This is a great mystery, but I speak concerning Christ and the church. (Ephesians 5:30-32)

> For I am jealous for you with godly jealousy. For I have betrothed you to one husband, that I may present *you as* a chaste virgin to Christ. (2 Corinthians 11:2)

God has called out an elect group of people, throughout all of human history, to have a unique intimate relationship with His Son Jesus Christ. This bride will include believers of all ages, both Jew and Gentile, who have been redeemed by the blood of Jesus Christ. These resurrected and glorified saints will forever serve their Lord and Savior as kings and priests in His eternal kingdom. Because of this marriage, God will hold a great celebration, known as the marriage supper of the Lamb. Imagine God Almighty throwing a celebration for His Son and the church. It will be a festival unequaled in all of eternity. "Blessed are those who are called to the marriage supper of the Lamb!"

Overcome with amazement, John falls down to worship the individual who is speaking to him. Immediately, John is told that he should worship God only, for he, himself, is also a fellow servant of Jesus Christ. This fellow servant then informs John that it is the Lord Jesus who is the spirit, or the sum and substance, of all prophecy.

THE BATTLE OF ARMAGEDDON

> **Then I saw heaven opened, and behold, a white horse. And He who sat on him *was* called Faithful and True, and in righteousness He judges and makes war. His eyes *were* like a flame of fire, and on His head *were* many crowns. He had a name written that no one knew except Himself. He *was* clothed with a robe dipped in blood, and His name is called The Word of God. And the armies in heaven, clothed in fine linen, white and clean, followed Him on white horses. Now out of His mouth goes a sharp sword, that with it He should strike the nations. And He Himself will rule them with a rod of iron. He Himself treads the winepress of the fierceness and wrath of Almighty God. And He has on *His* robe and on His thigh a name written: KING OF KINGS AND LORD OF LORDS.** (Revelation 19:11-16)

The moment of truth has finally arrived for planet earth. Jesus will, again, leave heaven in order to battle the armies of the Antichrist in the last war on planet earth. Jesus comes as one who makes war. He is seated upon on a mighty white horse as He heads toward planet earth. In His first advent Jesus came humbly riding on a lowly colt. This time He will arrive as a warrior on a white stallion to destroy the armies of the Antichrist. Jesus is also said to be wearing a robe that is dipped in blood. This is the same robe that became blood stained as He destroyed Israel's enemies, while leading them from Bozrah to Jerusalem (Isaiah 63:1-6). The very fact that this robe is already blood stained, as He departs heaven toward earth, is proof that this cannot be His first time back to the earth. If this is His first time back, one must ask how did the robe become stained with the blood of His enemies? In His leading of the Jews to Jerusalem, Isaiah states that He will fight alone (Isaiah 63:3). This time, the armies of heaven, who are also upon white horses, will accompany him. It is believed that this army will be composed of millions of Angels (2 Thessalonians 1:7). Whether or not the redeemed saints will be included, is not made clear by the text of Revelation. The epistle of Jude does seem to indicate that the saints also will accompany Jesus:

> Now Enoch, the seventh from Adam, prophesied about these men also, saying, "Behold the Lord comes with ten thousands of His saints, to execute judgment on all, to convict all who are ungodly among them of all their ungodly deeds which they have committed in an ungodly way, and of all the harsh things which ungodly sinners have spoken against Him." (Jude 1:14-15)

Out of the mouth of Christ comes a sharp sword that He will use to destroy the nations that have gathered to battle Him. It will be through the breath of His mouth that He will destroy the Antichrist, as Paul states in 2 Thesalonians:

> And then the lawless one will be revealed whom the Lord will consume with the breath of His mouth and destroy with the brightness of His coming. (2 Thessalonians 2:8)

Paul is not being redundant in this verse. Jesus will, at the battle of Armageddon, consume, or eradicate, the Antichrist. But, at His coming for the church, when the brightness of His glory covers the earth, He will "destroy" the Antichrist. As previously explained, the word used for "destroy" is the Greek word Katargeo, which means: to render inactive or idle. At the Lord's coming, the Antichrist will be rendered inactive, as the great tribulation is cut short and the Day of the Lord begins. The Antichrist will not be able to do much of anything during the period encompassing the trumpet and bowl judgments of the Day of the Lord. Armageddon will be the Antichrist's last effort to stand against God.

John, in this passage, states that Christ will tread the winepress of God Almighty. This treading of the winepress is explained in greater detail in Revelation chapter 14. Contained within this important chapter are the salvation of national Israel (Revelation 14:1-5), and the rapture of the church (Revelation 14:14-16). Presented next, is a glimpse of the fate of those who follow the Antichrist in battle against the Lord Jesus.

> **Then another angel came out from the temple which is in heaven, he also having a sharp sickle. Then another angel**

> **came out from the altar, who had power over the fire, and he cried with a loud cry to him who had the sharp sickle, saying, "Thrust in your sharp sickle and gather the clusters of the vine of the earth, for her grapes are fully ripe." So the angel thrust his sickle into the earth and gathered the vine of the earth, and threw *it* into the great wine press of the wrath of God. And the winepress was trampled outside the city, and blood came out of the winepress, up to the horses' bridles, for one thousand furlongs** (Revelation 14:17-20)

This is the outcome for those who have who have sided with the Antichrist. The imagery here is of a great winepress that is being trampled by Jesus. This is to occur outside the city of Jerusalem, on the plains of Megiddo. As these men are trampled, their blood will fly into the air up to the horse's bridle, which is approximately four feet. The text is not referring to the depth of the flow of blood, but rather how high it splatters as the Son of God tramples these men. Their blood splattering is likened to that of grapes as they are being trampled upon in the winepress. The stains of this decimated armies blood will be seen for 1600 furlongs, or 200 miles. Armageddon will be a most terrible and bloody battle. More details of this battle are given in Revelation chapter 19:

> **Then I saw an angel standing in the sun; and he cried with a loud voice, saying to all the birds that fly in the midst of heaven, "Come and gather together for the supper of the great God, that you may eat the flesh of kings, the flesh of captains, the flesh of mighty men, the flesh of horses and of those who sit on them, and the flesh of all *people*, free and slave, both small and great." And I saw the beast, the kings of the earth, and their armies, gathered together to make war against Him who sat on the horse and against His army. Then the beast was captured, and with him the false prophet who worked signs in his presence, by which he deceived those who received the mark of the beast and those who worshipped his image. These two were cast alive into the lake of fire burning with brimstone. And the rest were killed with the sword which proceeded from the mouth of Him who sat on the horse. And all the birds were filled with their flesh.** (Revelation 19:17-21)

As the battle unfolds, John reveals, in verse 19, that these armies are gathered for the sole purpose to "make war against Him who sat on the horse and against His army." Armageddon will not be the battle for Jerusalem, or a nuclear war of the Antichrist against the kings of the east as some surmise.

This is not a battle in where man is fighting man. The text clearly states that Armageddon is a battle of man against God. Jesus does not return to stop the carnage of the Battle of Armageddon. Rather, He comes to create the carnage and destroy all who dare to oppose Him. It is also clear that this will not even be a battle. Jesus comes down and destroys, without any resistance.

At the beginning of this great battle, an angel will call to the birds of the earth to come and feast on the carcasses of all who are killed. This is called the "supper of the great God." All who are not invited to the "marriage supper of the Lamb" will be forced to attend the "supper of the great God". This is one event I do not want an invitation to.

Presented in the text of Ezekiel chapter 38 is the Antichrist's invasion of Israel at the midpoint of the Seventieth Week (Ezekiel 38:1-16). As Christ returns to inaugurate the Day of the Lord, this invasion is cut short as God rains down the trumpet and bowl judgments (Ezekiel 38:17-23). After these judgments are ended, God states that the Antichrist will be pulled forth again to the mountains of Israel (Ezekiel 39:1-2). It will be in this area, in the valley of Megiddo, where God states that He, Himself, will destroy the Antichrist's armies, and feed them to the birds of prey (Ezekiel 39:3-7). In fact, the very same words are used by John that Ezekiel employs in the calling of these birds to the great feast:

> And as for you, son of man, thus says the Lord God, "Speak to every sort of bird and to every beast of the field: Assemble yourselves and come; Gather together from all sides to My sacrificial meal Which I am sacrificing for you, A great sacrificial meal on the mountains of Israel, That you may eat flesh and drink blood. You shall eat the flesh of the mighty, Drink the blood of the princes of the earth, Of rams and lambs, Of goats and bulls, All of them fatlings of Bashan. (Ezekiel 39:17-18)

Ezekiel, chapters 38 and 39, parallel perfectly: the Antichrist's invasion of Jerusalem, the judgments of the Day of the Lord, and the final destruction of him and his armies. Ezekiel is not referring to some mythical invasion of the Middle East by Russia, as many suppose. If Ezekiel is portraying a different battle, other than Armageddon, then there is going to need to be two suppers of the great God. This is because the supper in Ezekiel has too many similarities with the supper presented in the text of Revelation.

Ezekiel also discloses that Gog, or Antichrist, is to come to his end on the mountains of Israel. The prophet Daniel confirms this:

> And He (Antichrist) shall plant the tents of his palace between the seas and the glorious holy mountain; yet he shall come to his end, and no one will help him. (Daniel 11:45)

John is also shown that both the Antichrist and the False Prophet will be captured and thrown alive into the lake of fire. They will not be able to put up any resistance, because they are powerless against Jesus Christ. All the great miracles and power that these two will have perpetrated upon the world are nothing more than a clever deception by the very hand of Satan. The Antichrist was never any big threat to God, for He is in control of all things at all times. This beast, who brought the world to its knees comes to a very insignificant ending. He is merely captured, and tossed into the lake of fire. He will not be given the dignity of burial for the earth will cast him out, as Isaiah states:

> Those who see you will gaze at you, *And* consider you, *saying*: "*Is* this the man who made the earth tremble, Who shook kingdoms, Who made the world as a wilderness And destroyed its cities, *Who* did not open the house of his prisoners?" All the kings of the nations, All of them sleep in glory, Everyone in his own house; But you are cast out of your grave like and abominable branch, *Like* the garment of those who are slain, Thrust through with a sword, Who go down to the stones of the pit, Like a corpse trodden underfoot. You will not be joined with them in burial, Because you have destroyed your land *And* slain your people. The brood of evildoers shall never be named. (Isaiah 14:16-20)

As Jesus was the "first fruits" of the resurrection to life, the Antichrist will be the "first fruits" of those who are resurrected for eternal death. With the defeat at Armageddon, the reign of the Antichrist is ended and his armies defeated. Jesus will begin to restore a nearly decimated earth, and have the dead of this great slaughter buried (Ezekiel 39:12). It is interesting that Ezekiel says that the weapons of this army will be burned by Israel for fuel for seven years (Ezekiel 39:9). Many struggled with how to explain how Israel could burn up modern weaponry. A simple consistent explanation would be that this army would not be armed with modern weaponry. Remember, there will be incredible destruction on earth during the trumpet and bowl judgments. Most military weaponry will be destroyed or rendered absolutely useless. It is likely that, given the state of things, this army will be armed with wooden clubs, sticks, arrows, spears, and other simple weapons, against Christ (Ezekiel 39:9). If this is the case, Armageddon is going to be one real sad battle. It is specifically stated in Ezekiel 39:3 that God will cause the army's arrows to fall out of their hands. Why can't these be literal arrows? Whatever the case, Armageddon will be a very one-sided battle in which Antichrist will be utterly defeated.

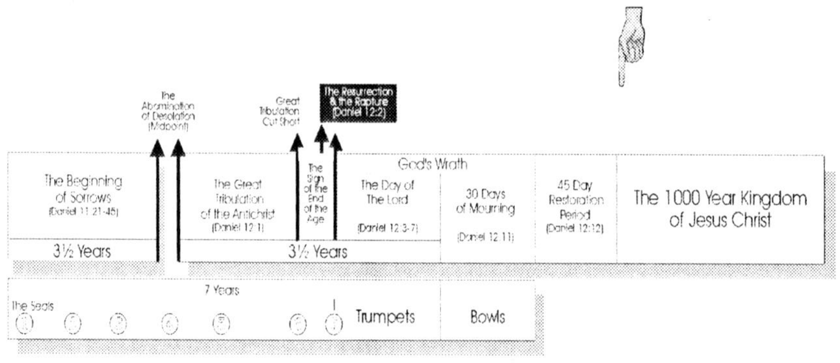

15
THE END AND THE BEGINNING

THE ANTICHRIST, along with those who have opposed the return of Jesus, has been vanquished by the sword of His mouth. In Revelation chapter 20, John begins to describe what takes place as the kingdom of Christ begins. This kingdom will first begin with a 45-day period of a cleansing of the earth. This was the last 45-day period revealed to Daniel the prophet (Daniel 12:12). This final allotment of time will bring the fulfillment of another of Israel's feasts.

THE FEAST OF DEDICATION/ HANUKKAH

As discussed in the previous chapter covering these feasts, Hanukkah takes place seventy-five days after the Feast of Atonement, on the twenty-fifth day of the Hebrew month of Chislev. The last half of the Seventieth Week will last for a period of three and a half years or 1260 days (Daniel 12:7). The final day of the Seventieth Week will culminate on the Jewish Day of Atonement. Thirty days after the end the Seventieth Week, on day 1290, the Antichrist will be defeated (Daniel 12:11). Forty-five days after the defeat of the Antichrist, on the 1335th day, will be the Feast of Dedication (Daniel 12:12). Hanukkah or the Feast of Dedication continues to be an important holiday for the Jewish people. Celebrated by Christ (John 10:22-23) during His first advent, the feast commemorated Israel's deliverance from a forerunner of the Antichrist: Antiochus Epiphanes. Antiochus Epiphanes, as explained previously, was the Syrian ruler of one of the four divisions of the Grecian empire. The Jews signed a covenant with him, much like what they will do with the Antichrist. This evil ruler turned on the Jews and marched into Jerusalem desecrating their temple. A Hebrew leader named Judas Maccabeus led a revolt against Antiochus. Antiochus was eventually defeated, and the temple was cleansed. On the twenty-fifth day of the month of Chislev, the temple was rededicated in a celebration that lasted eight days, known as Hanukkah. In similar manner, during the forty-five day period following the defeat of the Antichrist, Jesus will cleanse the earth in preparation for the dedication of His kingdom. This cleansing period and dedication will be the ultimate fulfillment of the Feast of Dedication. Again, it is fulfilled exactly as the other Jewish festivals have been fulfilled. Moving back, into the final chapters of Revelation, John sees this great cleansing along with the complete restoration of the heavens and the earth. He then discloses some important events that occur as the Millennial Kingdom begins.

SATAN LOCKED UP

> **Then I saw an angel coming down from heaven, having the key to the bottomless pit and a great chain in his hand. He laid hold of the dragon, the serpent of old, who is *the* Devil and Satan, and bound him for a thousand years; and he cast him into the bottomless pit, and shut him up, and set a seal on him, so that he should deceive the nations no more till the thousand years were finished. But after these things he must be released for a little while.** (Revelation 20:1-3)

The first great event that immediately follows the battle of Armageddon is the capture and detainment of Satan. In this passage, it is revealed that this great adversary of God, who has plunged the world into darkness, is locked up by some unnamed angel. Satan, the entity who has dared to take on God Almighty in the battle of the ages, is not even worthy of being captured personally by Jesus Christ. This shows the absolute authority that God has always had over Satan. God, in His divine wisdom, has chosen not to end Satan's reign until His plan for the redemption of the nation of Israel and mankind has come to a close. Once God's plan is completed, He will send forth one of His angels to capture Satan, and lock Him up in the bottomless pit. Satan is not yet thrown into the lake of fire, for at the end of the thousand year kingdom, God will allow him to be freed for a short period of time. Why God allows this will become evident as John moves forward in his end-time chronology.

THRONES AND JUDGMENT

> **And I saw thrones, and they sat on them and judgment was committed to them. And *I saw* the souls of those who had been beheaded for their witness to Jesus and for the word of God, who had not worshipped the beast or his image, and had not received *his* mark on their foreheads or on their hands. And they lived and reigned with Christ for a thousand years. But the rest of the dead did not live again until the thousand years were finished. This *is* the first resurrection. Blessed and holy is he who has part in the first resurrection. Over such the second death has no power, but they shall be priests of God and of Christ, and shall reign with Him a thousand years.** (Revelation 20:4-6)

The next event to occur is the establishing of the Lord's government, as the kingdom of God gets underway. Resurrected believers will all have responsibilities in Christ's kingdom. The most important of these thrones that are mentioned by John, will be those that are set up for the twelve Apostles. It will be upon these twelve thrones that the Apostles will judge the entire house of Israel, deciding who is worthy to enter the kingdom of God. Christ stated this, Himself, in the gospels of Matthew and Luke:

> So, Jesus said to them, "Assuredly I say to you, that in the regeneration, when the Son of Man sits on the throne of His glory, you who have followed Me will also sit on twelve thrones, judging the twelve tribes of Israel." (Matthew 19:28)

> And I bestow upon you a kingdom, just as My Father bestowed one upon Me, that you may eat and drink at My table in My kingdom, and sit on thrones judging the twelve tribes of Israel. (Luke 22:29-30)

The thrones that are set up for the judgment of Israel are twelve in number. Notice, that they are in direct contrast with the 24 thrones of the elders that were seen previously in heaven. One of the most debated questions is who will be the twelfth Apostle, Matthias or Paul? I tend to lean in favor of Paul for a couple of reasons:

> 1. Jesus personally chose the first twelve, and also personally chose the Apostle Paul, while on the road to Damascus (Acts 9:1-9). Matthias was not chosen directly by Christ, but by Peter and the other disciples (Acts 1:15-26).

> Since Jesus was the one who originally chose the Apostles, and Himself chose Paul, it seems consistent that Paul is the rightful twelfth Apostle.
>
> 2. Jesus had instructed His disciples not to do anything, but to wait in Jerusalem for the promise of the Holy Spirit (Luke 24:49). It is likely that Peter may have jumped the gun by selecting Matthias before the Holy Spirit had been poured out.

Whatever the case, there will be twelve thrones and the Apostles of Jesus will judge Israel as the Millennium begins. Those Jews who have worshipped the beast, and have survived the Day of the Lord, will not be permitted to enter the kingdom of the true Messiah. This is their reward for following the false messiah.

THE SHEEP AND GOAT JUDGMENT

Those of the Gentiles, who have survived the Day of the Lord, will be brought before the throne of Christ to be judged by Him personally. This is referred to by Matthew as the sheep and goat judgment:

> When the Son of Man comes in His glory, and all the holy angels with Him, then He will sit on the throne of His glory. All the nations will be gathered before Him, and He will separate them one from another, as a shepherd divides *his* sheep from the goats. And He will set the sheep on His right hand, but the goats of the left. Then the King will say to those on His right hand, "Come, you blessed of My Father, inherit the kingdom prepared for you from the foundation of the world: for I was hungry and you gave Me food; I was thirsty and you gave Me drink; I was a stranger and you took Me in; I *was* naked and you clothed Me; I was sick and you visited Me; I was in prison and you came to Me." Then the righteous will answer Him, saying Lord, "when did we see You hungry and feed *You*, or thirsty and give *you* drink? When did we see You a stranger and take *You* in, or naked and clothe *you*? Or when did we see You sick, or in prison, and come to You?" And the King will answer and say to them, "Assuredly, I say to you, inasmuch as you did *it* to one of the least of these My brethren, you did *it* to Me. Then He will say to those on His left hand, "Depart from Me, you cursed, into the everlasting fire prepared for the Devil and his angels: (Matthew 25:31-41)

With the awesome destruction of this period, it is safe to conclude that not very many people will be alive to attend this judgment. Those who do survive will be gathered before the throne of Christ. Jesus will then divide the worthy from those who are found to be unworthy to enter the Millennial Kingdom. Gentiles who have taken the mark, or have worshipped the Antichrist, will immediately be found to be unworthy to enter. Those who have not taken the mark will then be separated as to how they treated the Lord's disciples during the great tribulation. The Gentiles, who helped to feed, clothe, and shelter, the remnant Jews and the Christians during the great tribulation of Antichrist will be allowed to enter the kingdom of Jesus Christ. Although these "sheep" do not become believers in Christ until after His return, they will still be allowed to be part of His kingdom. They are not saved merely by their works, but rather their works are the evidence of their hearts toward God and His people. By not taking the mark and helping to shelter the people of God during this time, they show the acts of a righteous heart. Jesus states that for these the kingdom had been prepared "from the foundation of the world." They are therefore found worthy because of God's election, and not because of the works they performed. Their works are merely the evidence of God's election. Paul clearly states that by the works of the law no flesh will be justified (Galatians 2:16). God, as He does in every age, will prompt these Gentiles to have saving faith as Christ returns. God is the only one who knows each individual's heart and how he or she will respond to His free gift of salvation. Obviously, in contrast with the rest of the unbelieving world, these Gentiles will respond positively. They will enter the kingdom of God and begin to repopulate a restored and refurbished planet earth. The "earth dwellers" that do not respond to God, nor helped His disciples during the great tribulation, will be found unworthy to enter Christ's kingdom. They will be consigned to hell to await the final judgment. The earth will be completely rid of all men and women who have not put their trust in Christ. As the thousand-year period begins, only those who believe in Jesus will enter. Even though the kingdom of Jesus will begin only with believers, John is shown that things will change toward the end of the Millennium.

THE RESURRECTION OF THE MARTYRS

After the setting up of the thrones, John then concerns himself with the resurrection of the martyrs who were last seen as souls before the throne of God (Revelation 6:9-11). The martyrs were informed that they were to wait until all of their fellow brethren, who would be killed in the same manner as they were, would be completed. The last of those who will be martyred in their service to Jesus will be the two witnesses who are killed on the last day of the

Seventieth Week. Their martyrdom occurs after the rapture and resurrection has already taken place. Because of this, the martyrs will not receive their resurrection bodies until the kingdom of Christ begins. As the author of Hebrews states, these martyrs will obtain a better resurrection (Hebrews 11:35). John discloses that they also will reign with Christ for a thousand years. This is the culmination of the first resurrection. Those in the first resurrection will never be harmed by the second death. As Paul confirms:

> So when this corruptible has put on incorruption, and this mortal has put on immortality, then shall be brought to pass the saying that is written: "*Death is swallowed up in victory.*" "*O Death, where is thy sting? O Hades, where is your victory*?" (1 Corinthians 15:54-55)

The elect of the ages will all be given bodies that can never die. They will be glorious bodies that will never grow old, tired, or sick. Jesus will redeem our bodies from the curse of sin and we will live and reign with Him forever. Those who have been chosen to be numbered among the redeemed will be the most blessed of all of God's creation. It will make the enjoyments and pleasures of our current stay on earth pale by comparison.

THE FINAL FATE OF SATAN AND THE UNREDEEMED

Before John moves on to describe the restoration of the earth by Jesus, he pens the final doom awaiting Satan and all his followers. John has already introduced the resurrection of life, and the fate of the redeemed. He will now speak of the resurrection of the dead and their fate, along with the end of Satan. John has to catapult us forward to the end of the Millennium, in order to reveal how the end of Satan and his followers comes about.

> **Now when the thousand years have expired, Satan will be released from his prison and will go out to deceive the nations which are in the four corners of the earth, Gog and Magog, to gather them together to battle, whose number *is* as the sand of the sea. They went up on the breadth of the earth and surrounded the camp of the saints and the beloved city. And fire came down from God out of heaven and devoured them. And the devil, who deceived them, was cast into the lake of fire and brimstone where the beast and false prophet *are*. And they will be tormented day and night forever and ever. Then I saw a great white throne and Him who sat on it, from whose face the earth and the heaven fled away. And**

> **there was found no place for them. And I saw the dead, small and great standing before God, and books were opened. And another book was opened, which is *the Book* of Life. And the dead were judged according to their works, by the things which were written in the books. The sea gave up the dead who were in it, and Death and Hades delivered up the dead who were in them. And they were judged, each one according to his works. Then Death and Hades were cast into the lake of fire. This is the second death. And anyone not found written in the Book of Life was cast into the lake of fire.** (Revelation 20:7-15)

At the close of the thousand years God will let Satan out of his prison in Hell. When he is released it quickly becomes evident that he has not learned any lessons, for he will once again try to lead a revolt against God Almighty. I believe God allows this to put to rest two main arguments that man has often made concerning his sinful nature:

> 1. Man has always argued that he is not born sinful, but rather is a product of his environment. If given a better environment, humanity would not experience sinfulness.
>
> 2. Many also believe that if God were around, in tangible form, they would then gladly believe and worship Him.

At the end of Christ's thousand-year reign, God will show the inaccuracy of these, along with many other arguments man has made concerning his nature. During the Millennium, man will be put into a perfect environment where there will be no more hunger, sickness, disease, war, or famine. All nations will live peacefully under the rule of Jesus Christ. Since Jesus will be ruling from the New Jerusalem, it will be very easy for the people of earth to go to Jerusalem to see the glory of the resurrected Son of God. God's very presence will be upon the earth in a literal tangible way. Yet, even with all of this, Satan is still able to gather many people to lead a revolt against God. This shows, as God has often revealed, that man's sinful nature lies within his very heart. The nature of unregenerate man is always against God. It does not make any difference how good his environment is, or that he is able to see God. Man's sinful nature is in opposition to God. This period also reveals the complete unrepentant and black heart of Satan. Even though he has spent a thousand years in the bottomless pit, Satan has still not changed his evil nature or repented.

At the end of the Millennium, all who have served Jesus out of duty rather than devotion will believe the final lies of Satan. Satan will amass a final rebellion and bring literally millions of people up against the New Jerusalem. This will be the city where Jesus and His redeemed saints will rule from. All who were born during the last thousand years, who have not truly put their faith in Jesus Christ for their redemption, will follow Satan. This is God's way of finally ridding the universe of those who will not truly serve Him. It is important to note that John specifies that this great multitude come up against the "beloved city," or New Jerusalem during the Millennium (Revelation 20:9). There are many commentators who are of the opinion that the New Jerusalem does not descend to earth until after the Millennium ends. This is incorrect, as later; it is evident that John describes the New Jerusalem as it descends to earth at the beginning of Christ's kingdom. This final rebellion against the city of God will not last very long. John is shown that God will send fire from heaven, and it will completely destroy these nations who have participated in Satan's final rebellion. Satan's first rebellion took place in the paradise of Eden, where he convinced Adam and Eve to follow his cunning lies. His second rebellion will occur in the paradise of the Millennium, and man again will believe his lie. As is often stated, the only thing man learns from history is that he never learns anything from history. These words hold very true as Satan, again, is able to get man to believe his lie rather than God's truth. Humanity will believe everything but the truth, and it will be no different at the end of the Millennium. This rebellion comes as no surprise to Jesus. For we are told by Paul that ". . . He must reign till He has put all enemies under His feet." (1 Corinthians 15:25) This period becomes God's great object lesson to mankind, confirming the fact that he is born with a sinful nature, and only through obedience to Jesus Christ can he be freed. Rebellion only brings death, and following this event we are shown the final and ultimate death this rebellion brings.

THE GREAT WHITE THRONE JUDGMENT

Once God stamps out this final rebellion, Satan will be seized and thrown into the lake of fire, where he will never escape. An important aspect concerning the lake of fire is that, although it has intense and tormenting heat, those cast into it are not annihilated. John is told that the false prophet and the Antichrist are still alive as Satan, himself, is cast in. The false prophet and the Antichrist have already been tormented in the lake of fire for one thousand years and yet, they still exist. There are a couple of observations that can be made concerning the lake of fire:

> 1. It will be a literal lake of fire that will burn white hot forever and ever. There is no reason to understand this lake as being symbolic, since we have attempted throughout to remain consistent with a literal interpretation of Revelation.

> 2. Those who are cast into the lake of fire will suffer torment. This torment will last forever and ever. There will be no reprieves or pardons, as the fate of those who are sent there is final.
>
> 3. Those within the lake of fire will not be consumed or annihilated by its flames. Rather, they will exist in an eternal conscious state completely aware of their torment.

John the Baptist said that there would be two baptisms by Jesus: one with the Holy Spirit, and the other by fire (Matthew 3:11). Those who are not baptized into the body of Christ by His Holy Spirit will be baptized out of the body of Christ in the lake of fire. The lake of fire will be the place where all who have rejected God will be forever banished. This judgment is so horrifying that there are no words appropriate to describe it. Its fires are so terrifying, that the Son of God crossed into our universe, in the body of a man, to pay for the sins of all mankind. Only one who was fully man and fully God, could pay for the sins of humanity that were committed against an infinite God. Jesus came so that man would not suffer the second death, for the lake of fire was never God's intention for man. Yet, there are many that will suffer the fate that John describes as the books are opened during the great white throne judgment of God.

The final fate of these who have rejected God's gift of salvation is seen before this great white throne. It is stated that there was found no place for these dead of the ages (Revelation 20:11). God is the author of the creation, and to reject God is to cut oneself off from all that He created. Since God created all things, there is no place in creation for these who have rejected Him. They are now to be eternally separated from their Creator; this will culminate in what is called spiritual death. Those that are judged here are said to be the significant, as well as the insignificant, of all of human history. Their status, while on the earth, will mean nothing before God. Each person will be brought up individually before the throne of God Almighty, and the record of their lives will be read before them. Each one will be judged according to the works that they have done in while in the body. This is not to discover whether or not they will escape the lake of fire, for by works will no flesh be justified before God (Galatians 2:16). Their fate of being cast into the lake of fire was determined the moment they, forever, rejected Jesus Christ. They are now being judged as to what degree of punishment they will receive. Just as believers receive degrees of status and rewards in Christ's kingdom; these also will receive degrees of judgment. Jesus stated this in the gospel of Luke:

> And that servant who knew his master's will, and did not prepare *himself* or do according to his will, shall be beaten with many *stripes*. But he who did not know, yet committed things worthy of stripes, shall be beaten with few. For everyone to whom much is given, from him much will be

required; and to whom much has been committed, of him they will ask the more. (Luke 12:47-48)

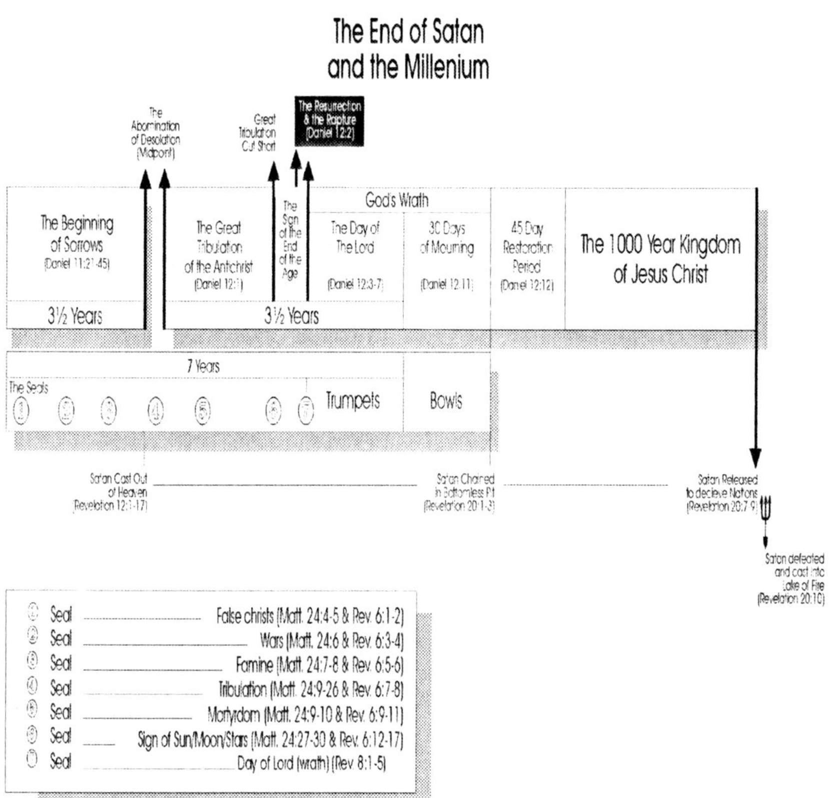

God is just, even in this final judgment of the dead. Those who have known the way of Christ, but have refused to follow Him will pay dearly. Those who have not known the way of salvation but still have sinned against God will be punished, but not as harshly. It is up to each individual to use what light God has bestowed on him or her. Each person is personally responsible for his or her actions and will answer for himself or herself to God concerning their lives. It is said by John that the Book of Life is to be opened, and all whose names are not written in the Book of Life will be cast into the lake of fire. It will, at this moment, not matter how much money or how successful one was while on planet earth. All that will matter is, did one put their faith in the salvation that Jesus paid for on the cross. For those that have not, no place will be found for them, except the lake of fire which is the second death. Concerning the second death, Jesus stated to " . . . not fear those who kill the body but cannot kill the soul. But rather fear Him who is able to destroy both soul and body in hell (Matthew 10:28). John discloses that death and hell, itself, also will be cast into the lake of fire. Sin, death, and hell will no longer be a part of God's universe, since all the enemies of God have been vanquished forever.

In the second death, there will be no second chances, no reprieves, and no pardons. It is the final and ultimate ending for all who have rejected Jesus Christ. Each one will, on this day, come to the realization that Jesus was God's only provision for eternal life. As Paul stated:

> Therefore God also has highly exalted Him and given Him the name which is above every name, that at the name of Jesus every knee should bow, of those in heaven, and of those on earth, and those under the earth, and *that* every tongue should confess that Jesus Christ is Lord, to the glory of God the Father. (Phillippians 2:9-11)

RESTORATION OF THE EARTH

> **And I saw a new heaven and a new earth, for the first heaven and the first earth had passed away. Also there was no more sea.** (Revelation 21:1)

Having now informed us of the fate of those who will not rank among the redeemed, John now shifts back to events that will immediately follow the Battle of Armageddon. Presented next is not a description of eternity future, as many scholars propose. Contextually, John is still writing about the beginning of the Messianic Kingdom. What John has done, in the preceding verses, is to propel us forward to a time after the Millennium, revealing how the fate of Satan and unregenerate humanity is to come about. After doing this, he then shifts back (Revelation 21) to give greater insight and details concerning the thousand-year period. This contextual style is nothing new for John. Remember how John describes the final bowl judgment upon Babylon (Revelation 16:17-21), and then follows with two chapters that give even greater details of the rise and fall of Babylon, although, contextually, Babylon has already been destroyed (Revelation 17 & 18). The same thing is occurring in Revelation chapters 20 and 21.

It would seem on the surface that the text indicates that God will create a whole new heaven and earth, while destroying the previous heaven and earth. This, however, would be in direct contradiction to God's word, for He has told us that the earth would exist forever:

> *One* generation passes away, and *another* generation comes;
> But the earth abides forever. (Ecclesiastes 1:4)

> *You who* laid the foundations of the earth, So *that it* should not be moved forever. (Psalm 104:5)

The answer lies in the Greek words used for "new" and "passed away." The term used for "new" is the word Kainos which means: new as to form, or a quality of a different nature from what was before.[1] The term for "passed away" is the word Parerchomai which means: to pass from one form of existence into another.[2] Parerchomai does not imply annihilation, or termination of existence.[3] It then becomes apparent that we are to understand that there will be a new quality or nature to the earth as its old form of existence is done away with. This is the very hope of the creation that was spoken of by the Apostle Paul:

> For the earnest expectation of the creation eagerly awaits for the revealing of the sons of God. For the creation was subjected to futility, not willingly, but because of Him who subjected *it* in hope; because the creation itself also will be delivered from the bondage of corruption into the glorious liberty of the children of God. (Romans 8:19-21)

During the wrath of the Day of the Lord, the earth will be renovated by fire and its old existence will be transformed by Jesus (2 Peter 3:10). The Lord will then restore the earth as His kingdom begins. Man will again live in an earthly paradise. The prophet Isaiah provides greater insight into this period of history:

> For behold, I create new heavens and a new earth; And the former shall not be remembered or come to mind. But be glad and rejoice forever in what I create; For behold, I create Jerusalem *as* a rejoicing, And her people a joy. I will rejoice in Jerusalem, And joy in My people; The voice of weeping

> shall no longer be heard in her, Nor the voice of crying. No more shall an infant from there *live but a few* days, nor an old man who has not fulfilled his days; for the child shall die one hundred years old, but the sinner *being* one hundred years old shall be accursed (Isaiah 65:17-20)

It is important to notice that in this passage Isaiah is speaking of the new heaven and earth in terms of the Millennium, and not eternity future. This is obvious in that he speaks of short lives for those who are sinful and long lives for those who are not. So there will be death for those who are sinful during this period. It will not be until the end of the Millennium that God will throw death into the lake of fire (Revelation 20:14). Isaiah then goes on to list the blessings that will occur during the rule of the Messiah (Isaiah 65:21-25). From understanding both Isaiah's and John's text, it can be determined that the restored heavens and earth will occur immediately after the Day of the Lord, at the commencement of the Millennium. Finally, it is stated by John that "there was no more sea" (Revelation 21:1). This does not mean that there will be no major bodies of water on earth. Rather this is a reference to the renovation of the Mediterranean Sea. Revelation focuses primarily on events that will occur in and around the Mediterranean basin. At the second trumpet, the Mediterranean Sea received a severe judgment. John now informs us of the fate of this great body of water. According to both John and the prophet Zechariah, the Mediterranean will be cleansed from the blood judgment, and its waters will run into the Dead Sea (Zechariah 14:8). The waters of the Mediterranean will be healed and will no longer be salty (Ezekiel 47:9), for it is no longer to be a sea. Saltiness is what makes a sea a sea. Since the Mediterranean will now consist only of fresh water, John correctly states that there will be no more sea. Its fresh waters will give life to the trees that will be growing along the banks of the river that will flow from the Mediterranean to the Dead Sea (Ezekiel 47:1-12 & Revelation 22:1-2). This will, most definitely, solve all the fresh water problems of the entire area of the Middle East.

> **Then I, John saw a holy city, New Jerusalem, coming down out of heaven from God, prepared as a bride adorned for her husband. And I heard a loud voice from heaven saying, "Behold, the tabernacle of God is with men, and He will dwell with them, and they shall be His people, and God Himself will be with them *and be* their God. And God will wipe away every tear from their eyes; there shall be no more death, nor sorrow, nor crying; and there shall be no more pain, for the former things have passed away." Then He who sat on the throne said, "Behold I make all things new." and He said to me, "Write, for these words are true and faithful." And He said to me, "It is done! I am the Alpha and the Omega,**

> **the Beginning and the End. I will give the fountain of the water of life freely to him who thirsts. He who overcomes shall inherit all things, and I will be his God and he shall be My son. But the cowardly, unbelieving, abominable, murderers, sexually immoral, sorcerers, idolaters, and all liars shall have their part in the lake which burns with fire and brimstone, which is the second death.** (Revelation 21:2-8)

John now describes the descent of the New Jerusalem into the atmosphere of planet earth. In the gospel of John, Jesus told His disciples that He would go to prepare a place for His elect, and that when He returned they would dwell with Him forever (John 14:1-4). The New Jerusalem is the place that Jesus has been preparing for the elect of the ages. Only those who have been redeemed and resurrected will inhabit the New Jerusalem. God will now dwell with men in this great city, and it will become the "camp of the saints" (Revelation 20:9). It will be against this very city that Satan will attempt to lead his final rebellion at the expiration of the thousand years (Revelation 20:9). The redeemed within its gates are told that for them there will be no more death, crying, or pain. Isaiah also states that no weeping shall be heard ever again within the New Jerusalem (Isaiah 65:19). All the trials and tribulations of our physical lives will no longer be remembered. Our Lord, as the Alpha and Omega, promises living waters to all who thirst, and that "he who overcomes" will inherit all these things. Again, a reference is given by Jesus to the overcomer, as was the case in His letters to the seven churches. Those who do not overcome, but are cowardly and sinful, are to have their part in the lake of fire. They will never be allowed to share in the rewards of those who have faithfully followed Jesus. The happiness that will be in the New Jerusalem will eclipse anything that Satan or the world could ever hope to offer. Satan tried to offer his petty kingdom to Jesus (Matthew 4:8-9), but it could not even begin to compare to the kingdom that the Father would eventually bestow upon Him. In the following verses, John is given a very detailed description of this awesome city.

The Splitting of the Dead Sea

THE NEW JERUSALEM

Then one of the seven angels who had the seven bowls filled with the seven last plagues came to me and talked with me, saying, "Come, I will show you the bride, the Lamb's wife." And he carried me away in the Spirit to a great and high mountain, and showed me the great city, the holy Jerusalem, descending out of heaven from God, having the glory of God. And her light
was **like a most precious stone, like a jasper stone, clear as crystal. Also she had a great and high wall with twelve gates, and twelve angels at the gates, and names written on them, which are *the names* of the twelve tribes of the children of Israel: three gates on the east, three gates on the north, three gates on the south, and three gates on the west. Now the wall of the city had twelve foundations, and on them were the names of the twelve apostles of the Lamb. And he who talked with me had a gold reed to measure the city, its gates, and its wall. And the city is laid out as a square, and its length is as great as its breadth. And he measured the city with the reed: twelve thousand furlongs. Its length, breadth and height are equal. Then he measured its wall: one hundred *and* forty-four cubits, *according* to the measure of a man, that is, of an angel. And the construction of its wall was *of* jasper; and the city *was* pure gold, like clear glass. And the foundations for the wall of the city *were* adorned with all kinds of precious stones: the first foundation *was* jasper, the second sapphire, and the third chalcedony, the fourth emerald, the fifth sardonyx, the sixth sardius, the seventh chrsolite, the eighty beryl, the ninth topaz, the tenth chrysoprase, the eleventh jacinth, and the twelfth amethyst. And the twelve gates *were* twelve pearls: each individual gate was of one pearl. And the street of the city *was* pure gold, like transparent glass. But I saw no temple in it, for the Lord God Almighty and the Lamb are its temple. And the city had no need of the sun or the moon to shine in it, for the glory of God illuminated it, and the Lamb is *its* light. And the nations of those who are saved shall walk in its light, and the kings of the earth bring their glory and honor into it. Its gates shall not be shut at all by day (there shall be no night there). And they shall bring the glory and the honor of the nations into it. But there shall by no means enter it anything that defiles, or causes an abomination**

> **or a lie, but only those who are written in the Lamb's Book of Life.** (Revelation 21:9-27)

John is brought to a high mountain (most likely Mount Zion) for a better perspective on the New Jerusalem. He is told that this city is the bride, the Lamb's wife. This is because; the city is the abode of the elect of the ages who make up the bride of Christ. There are said to be twelve gates, each with the name of one of the tribes of Israel written on top. There are to be three of these gates on each of the four sides of the city. This is exactly what Ezekiel describes as He details the Jerusalem of the Millennium (Ezekiel 48:30-34). Also, John reveals that the city shall have twelve foundations; with each foundation bearing the one of the names of the twelve Apostles. John then gives the incredible dimensions of this city, which is said to be 12,000 furlongs by 12,000 furlongs by 12,000 furlongs. 12,000 furlongs is approximately 1380 square miles. The city is said to be 1380 miles in width, height, and depth.[4] If laid down at the edge of the eastern sea board of the United States, this city would occupy more than one half of its land area. From Maine to Florida lengthwise, and from the Atlantic Ocean to 600 miles west of the Mississippi breadth wise.[5] It will be structured in either a cube or pyramidal form. It is most likely a pyramid, because a wall 144 cubits (216 feet) would not be able to support a wall 1380 miles high, as would have to be the case if it were a cube.[6] The surface area of this city will be absolutely immense. There will be enough room for the redeemed of the ages to fit comfortably within its gates. The walls, as well as the foundations, are said to be laid with precious stones, as God has spared no expense in the construction of the New Jerusalem. That the city is made out of precious stones is also confirmed by the prophet Isaiah (Isaiah 54:11-12). Also, the structures, as well as the streets are said to be constructed of pure transparent gold, while each gate entrance is carved out of a single giant pearl. No doubt, the reflection of the glory of God from this city will light up the entire area of the Middle East. In fact, John discloses that the city, itself, will not have need of the moon or the sun, because of the brightness of God's glory. There will never be darkness or night within the New Jerusalem. This is not to say that the sun and the moon will no longer exist, just that their light will not be needed to illuminate the New Jerusalem. It is also revealed that the nations and the kings of the earth will bring the glory and the honor of its peoples into it. These nations are the descendants of those who survived the Day of the Lord, and were allowed to enter the kingdom of God. The people of these nations will be required to go to Jerusalem to worship during the great Hebrew feasts:

> And it shall come to pass *that* everyone who is left of all the nations which came against Jerusalem shall go up from year to year to worship the King, the Lord of Hosts, and to keep the Feast of Tabernacles. And it shall be *that* whichever of the families of the earth do not come up to Jerusalem to

> worship the King, the Lord of hosts, on them there will be no rain. (Zechariah 14:16-17)

John states that there is no temple within the New Jerusalem. This is because the Millennial temple is to be built on Mount Zion. At the earthquake of the seventh bowl, Mount Zion will be made the highest of all the mountains of Israel:

> Now it shall come to pass in the latter days *That* the mountain of the Lord's house Shall be established on the top of the mountains, And shall be exalted above the hills; And all the nations shall flow to it. Many people shall come and say, "Come, and let us go up to the mountain of the Lord, To the house of the God of Jacob; He will teach us His ways, And we shall walk in His paths." For out of Zion shall go forth the law, And the word of the Lord from Jerusalem. (Isaiah 2:2-3)

The New Jerusalem shall descend into the earth's atmosphere, levitating, with its center encompassing the Millennial temple atop Mount Zion.[7] The prophet Ezekiel gives great details concerning the temple that will be the throne of Messiah on top of Mount Zion (Ezekiel chapters 40-48). There are so many details that it would be completely out of the scope of this book to describe everything. As Bob Van Kampen pointed out, in his book The Sign, there are some major similarities that need to be addressed, that make it very evident that these passages in both Ezekiel and Revelation are referring to the Millennium: [8]

> 1. Within both the Millennial temple, and the New Jerusalem is said to be the throne of God and Jesus Christ. (Revelation 22:1-3 & Ezekiel 43:7)
>
> 2. Both thrones will seat a King who rules forever. (Revelation 22:5 & Ezekiel 43:7-9)
>
> 3. The throne in the New Jerusalem and the throne in the Millennial temple will display the glory of God. (Revelation 21:23-24 & Ezekiel 43:4-5)
>
> 4. Both thrones have water flowing through them, upon the banks of which are said to be trees that will grow for the healing of the nations. (Revelation 22:1-2 & Ezekiel 47:12)
>
> 5. Only those whose names have been written in the Book of Life shall enter, while the unrighteous will be excluded (Revelation 21:27 & Ezekiel 44:9)

It should then be safe to conclude that the throne room in the description of the New Jerusalem is one and the same with the Millennial Temple that sits upon Mount Zion. Ezekiel also states that this temple will have priests who will perform sacrifices that will continually bring to remembrance the Lord's atonement on Calvary (Ezekiel chapters 44 & 45). The sacrifices in the Old Testament were never for the remission of sins, but for the Jewish people to comprehend the price that had to be paid for sin. During the Millennium, the nations will be continually reminded of the Lord's sacrifice, as they come to worship Him on Mount Zion.

It is then revealed that no one who is sinful or unclean, will be allowed to enter the city; only those who have been written in the Book of Life. As discussed before, there will be those of these nations who will reject Jesus and His kingdom, and side with Satan at the end of the Millennium. These unbelievers will not be allowed access to the New Jerusalem.

The angel next shows John the river of life:

> **And he showed me a pure river of water of life, clear as crystal, proceeding from the throne of God and of the Lamb. In the middle of its street, and on either side of the river, *was* the tree of life, which bore twelve fruits, each *tree* yielding its fruit every month. And the leaves of the tree *were* for the healing of the nations. And there shall be no more curse, but the throne of God and of the Lamb shall be in it, and His servants shall serve Him. They shall see His face, and His name *shall be* on their foreheads. And there shall be no night there: They need no lamp nor light of the sun, for the Lord God gives them light. And they shall reign forever and ever.** (Revelation 22:1-5)

This river was created when Christ split the Mount of Olives and raised the Dead Sea, at the seventh bowl judgment. It shall flow through the throne room and into the city. Ezekiel tells us that the water will flow under the threshold of the temple from the right side of the altar toward the east (Ezekiel 47:1). Both John and Ezekiel, also state that trees will grow along this river's banks, and that they will bear fruit every month (Ezekiel 47:12 & Revelation 22:2). These trees shall be medicine for the healing of the nations who live on the earth, outside of the New Jerusalem (Ezekiel 47:12 & Revelation 22:2). Most importantly, the tree of life, which was taken away from man when sin began, is now restored to the earth. Those who have overcome will be able to eat freely from the tree of life, as was stated in Christ's letter to the church at Ephesus (Revelation 2:7). In fact, many of the things promised to the faithful of the seven churches are now fulfilled. There will no longer be any curse upon the earth, and the very name of Jesus shall be written upon His servant's foreheads. God will reign over the earth and the redeemed of the ages, shall reign with Him forever and ever. The Millennial Kingdom, and the period following, will be an unprecedented time of blessing that will right all of the wrongs that have occurred because of Satan, sin, evil, and death. A few of the characteristics of the kingdom of Christ are as follows:

1. It will be a period of peace, for there will be no more wars (Isaiah 2:4)

2. It will be a period of great joy, longevity, and health (Isaiah 12:3, 33:24 & 65:20)

3. It will be an unequaled time of prosperity and ease of labor (Isaiah 35:1-2 & 65:21-22)

4. It will be a time when the knowledge of God will cover the earth (Isaiah 11:9 & 66:19-20)

Despite all of these tremendous blessings, there will still be those who will side with Satan to try and revolt against the government of Jesus (Revelation 20:7-9). Fortunately, as Isaiah states, nothing will ever bring an end to the kingdom of Jesus Christ:

> For unto us a Child is born, Unto us a Son is given; And the government will be upon His shoulder. And His name will be called Wonderful, Counselor, Mighty God, Everlasting Father, Prince of Peace. Of the increase of *His* government and peace *There will be* no end, Upon the throne of David and over His kingdom, To order it and establish it with judgment and justice From that time forward, even forever. The zeal of the Lord of Hosts will perform this. (Isaiah 9:6-7)

THE FINAL WORDS OF REVELATION

> **Then he said to me, "These words *are* faithful and true." And the Lord God of the holy prophets sent His angel to show His servants the things which must shortly take place. "Behold, I am coming quickly! Blessed is he who keeps the words of the prophecy of this book." Now I, John, saw and heard these things. And when I heard and saw, I fell down to worship before the feet of the angel who showed me these things. Then he said to me, "See *that you do* not *do that.* For I am your fellow servant, and of your brethren the prophets, and of those who keep the**

> **words of this book. Worship God." And he said to me, "Do not seal the words of the prophecy of this book, for the time is at hand. He who is unjust, let him be unjust still; he who is filthy, let him be filthy still; he who is righteous, let him be righteous still; he who is holy, let him be holy still." "And behold, I am coming quickly, and My reward is with Me, to give to everyone according to his work. I am the Alpha and the Omega, *the* Beginning and *the* End, the First and the Last." Blessed *are* those who do His commandments, that they may have the right to the tree of life, and may enter through the gates of the city. But outside *are* dogs and sorcerers and sexually immoral and murderers and idolaters, and whoever loves and practices a lie. "I, Jesus, have sent My angel to testify to you these things in the churches. I am the Root and the Offspring of David, the Bright and Morning Star. And the Spirit and the bride say, "Come!" And let him who hears say, "Come!" And let him who thirsts come. And whoever desires, let him take the water of life freely. For I testify to everyone who hears the words of this prophecy of this book; if anyone adds to these things, God will add to him the plagues that are written in this book; and if anyone takes away from the words of the book of this prophecy, God shall take away his part from the Book of Life, from the holy city, and *from* the things which are written in this book. He who testifies to these things says, "Surely I am coming quickly." Amen. Even so, come, Lord Jesus! The grace of our Lord Jesus Christ *be* with you all. Amen.** (Revelation 22:6-21)

The angel next assures John that words in Revelation are true, and that they will come to pass. Jesus then interjects that He is coming quickly, and pronounces a blessing to those who put into practice what has been written in Revelation. John, again, states that he heard and saw these things, indicating that the prophecies outlined did not arise out of some weird dream that he had. These events were in actuality taking place as he witnessed them.

After this, John surprisingly begins to worship the angel who brought him the Revelation. Immediately, the angel tells John that he is to worship only God. The angel's instruction captures the overall focus of Revelation: that man should worship God, and God alone. All those who do not, will have their part in the lake of fire. As Jesus states, He has His rewards, and each one will be given according to his or her works. Those who obey and keep His commandments will have access to the tree of life and the New Jerusalem. Those who do not will be left outside never to enter or enjoy the rewards that God has for His redeemed.

Jesus, again, puts forth His credentials as being of the lineage of David, as well as the "Bright and Morning Star." This title of the Lord's is contrasted with Satan, or Lucifer's title, which is the "son of the morning" (Isaiah 14:12). The "Morning Star" brings with Him eternal life, while the "son of the morning" brings eternal damnation. Jesus also discloses that the things in Revelation are for "the churches." This indicates that the words of the text of Revelation are for the entire body of Christ, throughout all the ages, and not just specifically for the seven churches of Asia Minor. However the words of Revelation will have their greatest significance for the churches that enter the Seventieth Week.

John then gives a severe warning to those who add or take away anything from what has been written in Revelation. This should be a sober warning for all those who teach the message of Revelation: including the author. Believers must be extremely careful when approaching the study of any portion of God's precious word, especially the book of Revelation.

REVELATION UNSEALED

The angel then instructs the Apostle John that the book of Revelation is not to be sealed. Ironically, Revelation has been unsealed since the very day it was penned by John. God has always been willing to give men understanding of its contents, as well as its implications for His children. Yet, many are unwilling to come to study its prophecies. Revelation's message is frightening and glorious, bitter, yet sweet. God will one day right all the wrongs, but it will be a long tough road of faith and trust in Jesus Christ to get there. I pray that the body of Christ will be overcomers and persevere. For the gates of hell will never prevail against the church of Jesus Christ. As we face the trials and tribulations ahead, the words continually upon our lips should be

EVEN SO, COME LORD JESUS!

Book of Genesis	Book of Revelation
Genesis, the book of The beginning	Revelation, the book of the end
Earth is created (Gen. 1:1)	Earth passes away (Rev. 21:1)
Satan's first deception (Gen. 3:1-24)	Satan's last deception (Rev. 20:3 & 7-10)
A river for the Earth's blessing (Gen. 2:10-14)	A river for the New Earth (Rev. 22:1-2)
Man in God's Image (Gen. 1:26)	Man headed by one in Satan's image (Rev. 13)
Entrance of Sin (Gen. 3)	Development and end of sin (Rev. 21,22)
Curse pronounced (Gen. 3:14-17)	No more curse (Rev. 22:3)
Death entered (Gen. 3:19)	No more death (Rev. 21:4)
Man driven out of Eden (Gen. 3:24)	Man restored to Eden (Rev. 22)
Tree of Life guarded (Gen. 3:24)	Right to Tree of Life (Rev. 22:14)
A Flood from God to destroy an evil Generation (Gen. 6-9)	A flood from Satan to destroy an elect generation (Rev. 12)
The Bow, the token of God's covenant with the Earth (Gen. 9:13)	The Bow for God's remembrance of His covenant with Earth (Rev. 4:3, 10:1)
Sodom & Egypt, places of corruption (Gen. 13,19)	Sodom & Egypt again (representing Jerusalem) (Rev. 11:8))
A confederacy against Abraham's people (Gen. 14)	A confederacy against Abraham's seed (Rev. 12)
Marriage of First Adam (Gen. 2:18-23)	Marriage of Last Adam (Rev. 19)
Man's dominion ceased; Satan's begun (Gen. 3:24)	Satan's dominion ended and Man is restored (Rev. 22)
The old serpent causing Sin, Suffering, & Death (Gen. 3:1)	Old serpent bound for 1000 years (Rev. 20:1-3)
The doom of old serpent pronounced (Gen. 3:15)	The doom of old serpent executed (Rev. 20:10)

16
EPILOGUE

AS DEMONSTRATED, THE BOOK OF REVELATION is not a tall tale or an allegory of past historical events. It is a manuscript that contains the final destiny of God's plan for humanity. Within its pages are great truths concerning the end of death, evil, sin, and Satan. God in His divine Sovereignty will bring to a close the darkest chapter of the universe's history. The cosmos will finally be rid of all the things that have caused the suffering of mankind. The question is not if these events will happen, but when they will happen. Everything written by the Apostle John will come to pass, and the world, today, is on a fast paced collision course toward its initiation.

In light of this, each individual must decide how he or she will respond to the message of Revelation. For those who already bear the name of Jesus, Revelation sounds a call of introspection and examination as to how genuine their faith truly is. To those following Christ merely out of religious affiliation, rather than true dedication, Revelation speaks strongly, and its consequences are harsh. On the other hand, true disciples must be prepared to face terrible persecution and possible martyrdom for their faith in Jesus. As the world grows darker their light must shine brighter. The church has the obligation to rouse up and get prepared for the greatest trial it will ever face.

For those who do not know Jesus, Revelation reveals their final destiny. One could choose to dismiss its contents as the fanciful writings of an old exiled Apostle. To those who do not, God has provided a way to escape the events outlined in Revelation. Scripture states "that if you confess with your mouth the Lord Jesus and believe in your heart that God has raised Him from the dead, you will be saved." (Romans 10:9). This is not speaking of a mere intellectual ascent to believing that Jesus is Lord and Savior, rather, it is of putting one's trust of salvation solely on the redemptive work of Jesus Christ on the cross of Calvary. True discipleship begins with a commitment to the Lord Jesus, as well as renouncement of one's former sinful practices. Christianity means a commitment to following Jesus. Those who are truly His disciples are those that follow and obey His words (John 14:23). They are the "overcomers" of the book of Revelation. By repenting and asking Jesus to be your Lord and Savior, you can rank among the redeemed of the ages. All the blessings of eternity future will be your reward. Following Jesus is not always easy, but it is the only way to receive eternal life. To those that reject the message of the cross, the lake of fire is their final and ultimate destination.

Finally, although the study of end-time events is extremely interesting, one should not look to every world event as being the fulfillment of prophetic Scripture. I have, for the most part, stayed away from integrating what is currently happening in the world into my interpretation of Revelation. This is because Revelation itself should dictate what events will come to pass. Jesus has outlined very clearly the events that are to unfold. All we need to do is understand and recognize them when they occur. Jesus did not order believers to quit their jobs, build bomb shelters, store food, and wait for Armageddon's arrival. Rather, He told His disciples to preach the gospel to all nations. This should be the ultimate calling of all believers: to preach salvation through Jesus to a lost and dying world, that will one day come to know the fierceness of God's terrible wrath. The responsibility is great, but the rewards are even greater.

ENDNOTES

Chapter 1. The Significance of Revelation

1. Trent Duller Ed., Holman Bible Dictionary (Nashville: Holman Publishers, 1991) 180.

Chapter 2. Some Prophetic Background

1. Josh McDowell, Evidence That Demands a Verdict (San Bernadino: Here's Life Publishers, 1990) 167.

2. McDowell, Evidence That Demands A Verdict 275.

3. Mcdowell, Evidence That Demands A Verdict 275-277.

4. James Strong, "A Concise Dictionary of the Words of the Greek New Testament & A Concise Dictionary of the Words in the Hebrew Bible," Strong's Exhaustive Concordance (Iowa Falls: World Bible Publishers, 1986) 147.

5. Sir Robert Anderson, The Coming Prince (Grand Rapids: Kregel Publication, 1988) 124.

6. Grant Jeffrey, Armageddon Appointment With Destiny (Toronto: Frontier Research Publications, 1988) 38-42.

Chapter 3 Revelation Unsealed

1. Robert Thomas, Revelation 1-7: An Exegetical Commentary (Chicago: Moody Press, 1992) 21.

2. E.W. Bullinger, Commentary On Revelation (Grand Rapids: Kregel, 1984) 6.

3. Thomas, Revelation 1-7: An Exegetical Commentary 10.

4. W.E. Vine, The Expanded Vines Expository Dictionary of New Testament Words (Minneapolis: Bethany House Publishers, 1994) 1043.

5. Thomas, Revelation 1-7: An Exegetical Commentary 87.

6. Clarence Larkin, The Book Of Revelation (Glenside: Reverend Clarence Estate, 1919) 9.

7. Thomas, Revelation 1-7: An Exegetical Commentary 118.

8. Thomas, Revelation 1-7: An Exegetical Commentary 117.

9. Thomas, Revelation 1-7: An Exegetical Commentary 115.

Chapter 4. The Seven Churches

1. Duller Ed., Holman Bible Dictionary, 425.

2. Thomas, Revelation 1-7: An Exegetical Commentary 159.

3. Thomas, Revelation 1-7: An Exegetical Commentary 180.

4. Thomas, Revelation 1-7: An Exegetical Commentary 207.

5. Thomas, Revelation 1-7: An Exegetical Commentary 242.

6. Thomas, Revelation 1-7: An Exegetical Commentary 271.

7. Thomas, Revelation 1-7: An Exegetical Commentary 298.

8. Strong, A Concise Greek Dictionary 66.

9. Thomas, Revelation 1-7: An Exegetical Commentary 199.

10. Thomas, Revelation 1-7: An Exegetical Commentary 201.

11. Thomas, Revelation 1-7: An Exegetical Commentary 308.

Chapter 5. The Throne

1. Thomas, Revelation 1-7: An Exegetical Commentary 337.

2. Thomas, Revelation 1-7: An Exegetical Commentary 342.

3. Thomas, Revelation 1-7: An Exegetical Commentary 347.

4. Robert Van Kampen, "A Biblical Examination of the Revelation of Jesus Christ," Grace & Truth Tapes: 1993.

5. William Schlegel, "The Scroll of Revelation," Zions Fire November/December 1992: 16.

6. Schlegel, "The Scroll of Revelation," 16.

7. Schlegel, "The Scroll of Revelation," 16.

8. Thomas, Revelation 1-7: An Exegetical Commentary 392.

9. Thomas, Revelation 1-7: An Exegetical Commentary 347.

10. Thomas, Revelation 1-7: An Exegetical Commentary 410.

Chapter 6. The Seventieth Week Begins

1. Vine, The Expanded Vines Expository Dictionary of New Testament Words 201.

2. E.W. Bullinger, A Critical Lexicon & Concordance to the English and Greek New Testament (Grand Rapids: Zondervan Publishing, 1975) 169.

3. Larkin, The Book Of Revelation 56.

Chapter 7. The Rise of Antichrist

1. A.W. Pink, The Antichrist (Grand Rapids: Kregel, 1988) 11

2. Clarence Larkin, The Book of Daniel (Glenside: Reverend Clarence Larkin Estate, 1929) 163.

3. Pink, The Antichrist 298.

4. Pink, The Antichrist 301.

5. Strong, Concise Hebrew Dictionary 112.

6. Archer Gleason, "Daniel." The Expositors Bible Commentary Edited by Frank E. Gaebelein. (Grand Rapids: Zondervan Publishers, 1985) 86.

7. Gleason, Daniel 86.

8. Tim Dailey, The Gathering Storm (Tarry Town: Chosen Books, 1992) 166.

9. Tim Dailey, The Gathering Storm 167.

10. Duller Ed., Holman Bible Dictionary, 1213.

11. Tim Dailey, The Gathering Storm 171.

12. Yohanan Aharoni, Michael Avi-Yonah, Anson F. Rainey and Ze'ev Safrai, The Macmillian Bible Atlas (New York: Macmillain Publishing Company, 1993) 21;89.

13. Duller Ed., Holman Bible Dictionary, 951.

14. Duller Ed., Holman Bible Dictionary, 1376.

15. George Roux, Ancient Iraq (New York: Penguin Books, 1966) 272.

16. Hal Lindsey, and Chuck Missler, The Magog Factor: A Special Report (Palos Verdes: Hal Lindsey Ministries, 1992) 9.

17. Lindsey, and Missler The Magog Factor: A Special Report 10.

Chapter 8. The Midpoint

1. Larkin, The Book of Revelation 151.

2. Vine, The Expanded Vines Expository Dictionary of New Testament Words 1053.

3. Pink, The Antichrist 53-55.

4. Robert Van Kampen, "A Biblical Examination of the Revelation of Jesus Christ," Grace & Truth Tapes: 1993.

5. William Wilson, Old Testament Word Studies (Peabody: Hendrickson Publishers, 1961) 219.

6. Wilson, Old Testament Word Studies 416.

7. Larkin, The Book of Revelation 101.

8. N.W. Hutchings, Petra in History and Prophecy (Oklahoma: Hearthstone Publishing, 1991) 11-12

Chapter 9. The Great Tribulation

1. Vine, The Expanded Vines Expository Dictionary of New Testament Words 1127.

2. Thomas Ice and Randall Price, Ready to Rebuild (Eugene: Harvest House Publishers, 1992) 105-109.

3. Bob Rosio, Hitler and the New Age (Lafayette: Huntington House Publishers, 1993) 83-91.

4. Van Kampen, The Sign 216-222.

5. Michael Strassfield, The Jewish Holidays: A Guide and Commentary (New York: Harper & Row, 1985) 24-25.

6. Strassfield, The Jewish Holidays: A Guide and Commentary 13.

Chapter 10. The Great Sign of the End

1. Vine, The Expanded Vines Expository Dictionary of New Testament Words 1037.

2. Van Kampen, The Sign 315.

3. Vine, The Expanded Vines Expository Dictionary of New Testament Words 5.

Chapter 11. The Resurrection & The Rapture

1. "The Teachings of the Twelve Apostles," The Ante Nicene Fathers: Volume 7 (Grand Rapids: Erdmore Publishing Company, 1989) 382.

2. Tertullian, "On the Resurrection of the Flesh," The Ante Nicene Fathers: Volume 3 (Grand Rapids: Erdmore Publishing Company, 1989) 563.

3. Irenaeus, "Against Heresies" The Ante Nicene Fathers: Volume 1 (Grand Rapids: Erdmore Publishing Company, 1989) 555.

4. Justin Martyr, "Dialogue With Trypho," The Ante Nicene Fathers: Volume 1 (Grand Rapids: Erdmore Publishing Company, 1989) 253-254.

5. Hippolytus, "Treatise on Christ and Antichrist," The Ante Nicene Fathers: Volume 5 (Grand Rapids: Erdmore Publishing Company, 1990) 217.

6. Hippolytus, "Treatise on Christ and Antichrist," 217.

7. Alan Johnson, "Revelation." The Expositors Bible Commentary Edited by Frank E. Gaebelein. (Grand Rapids: Zondervan Publishers, 1981) 522.

8. Marvin Rosenthal, "Paralambano," Zions Fire July/August 1992: 6-7.

9. Strong, Concise Greek Dictionary 73.

10. Vine, The Expanded Vines Expository Dictionary of New Testament Words 1117.

11. Rosenthal, "Paralambano," 11.

Chapter 12. The Wrath of God Begins

1. Larkin, The Book of Revelation 72.

2. Larkin, The Book of Revelation 76.

3. Tim Dailey, The Gathering Storm 176-177.

Chapter 13. The End of the Seventieth Week

1. Good, Rosh Hashanah and the Messianic Kingdom to Come 17.

2. Good, Rosh Hashanah and the Messianic Kingdom to Come 37.

3. Tom McCall, and Zola Levitt, Raptured (Eugene: Harvest House Publishers, 1975) 33.

4. McCall, and Levitt, Raptured 33.

5. McCall, and Levitt, Raptured 34.

6. McCall, and Levitt, Raptured 34.

7. McCall, and Levitt, Raptured 36.

8. Good, Rosh Hashanah and the Messianic Kingdom to Come 97.

9. Strassfield, The Jewish Holidays: A Guide and Commentary 95.

10. Good, Rosh Hashanah and the Messianic Kingdom to Come 83-84.

11. Good, Rosh Hashanah and the Messianic Kingdom to Come 43.

12. Van Kampen, The Sign 336.

13. Van Kampen, The Sign 336-337.

14. Van Kampen, The Sign 337.

15. Van Kampen, The Sign 339.

16. Van Kampen, The Sign 406.

17. Van Kampen, The Sign 407.

Chapter 14. Bowls, Babylon & Battle

1. Bullinger, A Critical Lexicon & Concordance to the English and Greek New Testament 847.

2. Pink, The Antichrist 257.

3. Charles Dyer, The Rise Of Babylon (Wheaton: Tyndale House Publishers, 1991. 25-32.

4. Larkin, The Book of Revelation 159-161.

Chapter 15. The End and the Beginning

1. Vine, The Expanded Vines Expository Dictionary of New Testament Words 781.

2. Larkin, The Book of Revelation 200.

3. Marvin Rosenthal, "A New Heaven-A New Earth-A New Jerusalem," Zions Fire May/June 1993: 7.

4. Rosenthal, "A New Heaven-A New Earth-A New Jerusalem," 11

5. Larkin, The Book of Revelation 205.

6. Larkin, The Book of Revelation 205.

7. Van Kampen, The Sign 396.

8. Van Kampen, The Sign 503-504.

SELECTED BIBLIOGRAPHY

Aharoni, Yohanan, Michael Avi-Yonah, Anson F. Rainey, and Ze'ev Safrai. The Macmillian Bible Atlas. New York: Macmillan Publishing Company, 1993.

Alnor, Willian. Soothsayers of the Second Advent. Old Tappan: Fleming H. Revell Company, 1989.

Anderson, Robert. The Coming Prince. Grand Rapids: Kregel Publications, 1988.

Bickerman, Elias. The Jews in the Greek Age. Cambridge: Harvard University Press, 1988.

Boice, James. Daniel: An Expositional Commentary. Grand Rapids: Zondervan Publishing, 1989.

Brooke, Tal. When the World Shall be as One. Eugene: Harvest House Publishers, 1989.

Bruce, F.F. The Canon Of Scripture. Downers Grove: Intervarsity Press, 1988.

Bullinger, E. W. A Critical Lexicon & Concordance to the English and Greek New Testament. Grand Rapids: Zondervan Publishing, 1975.

Bullinger, E. W. Commentary on Revelation. Grand Rapids: Kregel Publications, 1984.

Bullinger, E.W. The Companion Bible. Grand Rapids: Kregel, 1990.

Bultema, Harry. Commentary on Daniel. Grand Rapids: Kregel Publications, 1988.

Burkett, Larry. The Coming Economic Earthquake. Chicago: Moody Press, 1991.

Carr, Joseph. The Twisted Cross. Lafayette: Huntington House Publishers, 1985.

Cumbey, Constance. The Hidden Dangers of the Rainbow. Lafayette: Huntington House Publishers, 1983.

Dailey, Tim. The Gathering Storm. Tarry town: Chosen Books, 1992.

Duller, Trent, Ed. Holman Bible Dictionary. Nashville: Holman Publishers, 1991.

Dyer, Charles. The Rise of Babylon. Wheaton: Tyndale House Publishers, 1991.

Ellison, Stanley. Biography of a Great Planet. Wheaton: Tyndale House Publishers, 1975.

Ellison, Stanley. Who Owns the Land?. Portland: Multnomah Press, 1991.

Flavius, Josephus. The Works of Josephus. Peabody: Hendrickson Publishers, 1987.

Glasser, Mitch, and Zhava Glasser. The Fall Feasts of Israel. Chicago: The Moody Bible Institute of Chicago, 1987.

Gleason, Archer. "Daniel." The Expositors Bible Commentary. Edited by Frank E. Gaebelein. Grand Rapids: Zondervan Publishers, 1985.

Good, Joseph. Rosh Hashanah and the Messianic Kingdom to Come. Port Arthur, Hatikva Ministries, 1989.

Green, Jay P. The Interlinear Bible: Hebrew-Greek-English. Peabody: Hendrickson Publishers, 1986.

Hanegraaf, Hank. Christianity in Crisis. Eugene: Harvest House Publishers, 1993.

Hindson, Ed. End Times, the Middle East and the New World Order. Wheaton: Victor Books, 1991.

Hutchings, N.W. Petra in History and Prophecy. Oklahoma: Hearthstone Publishing, 1991.

Ice Thomas, and Randal Price. Ready to Rebuild. Eugene: Harvest House Publishers, 1992.

Jeffrey, Grant. Apocalypse. Toronto: Frontier Research Publications, 1992.

Jeffrey, Grant. Armageddon Appointment with Destiny. Toronto: Frontier Research Publications, 1988.

Jeffrey, Grant. Messiah: War in the Middle East. Toronto: Frontier Research Publications, 1991.

Jeffrey, Grant. Prince of Darkness. Toronto: Frontier Research Publications, 1994.

Johnson, Alan. "Revelation." The Expositors Bible Commentary. Edited by Frank E. Gaebelein. Grand Rapids: Zondervan Publishers, 1981.

Kirban, Salem, and Gary Cohen. Revelation Visualized. Huntingdon Valley: Salem Kirban Inc., 1971.

Larkin, Clarence. The Book of Daniel. Glenside: Reverend Clarence Larkin Estate, 1929.

Larkin, Clarence. The Book of Revelation. Glenside: Reverend Clarence Larkin Estate, 1919.

Larkin, Clarence. The Greatest Book on Dispensational Truth in the World. Glenside: Reverend Clarence Larkin Estate, 1918.

Lindsey, Hal. The Late Great Planet Earth. Grand Rapids: Zondervan Publishing, 1970.

Lindsey, Hal, and Chuck Missler. The Magog Factor: A Special Report. Palos Verdes: Hal Lindsey Ministries, 1992.

Marrs, Texe. Mystery Mark of the New Age. Westchester: Crossway Books, 1988.

Martin, Malachi. The Keys of this Blood. New York: Simon and Schuster, 1990.

McCall, Tom and Zola Levitt. Coming: The End. Chicago: Moody Press, 1992.

McCall, Tom, and Zola Levitt. Raptured. Eugene: Harvest House Publishers, 1975.

McConnel, D.R. A Different Gospel. Peabody: Hendrickson Publishers, 1988.

McDowell, Josh. Evidence That Demands a Verdict. San Bernadino: Here's Life Publishers, 1990.

Moriarity, Michael. The New Charismatics. Grand Rapids: Zondervan Publishers, 1992.

Owen, Jim. Christian Psychology's War on God's Word. Santa Barbara: East Gate Publishers, 1993.

Peters, George. The Theocratic Kingdom. 3 Volumes. Grand Rapids: Kregel, 1988.

Pink, A.W. The Antichrist. Grand Rapids: Kregel, 1988.

Poland, Larry. The Coming Persecution. Grand Rapids: Here's Life Publishers, 1990.

Robertson, Pat. The New World Order. Dallas: Word Publishing, 1991.

Rosenthal, Marvin. The PreWrath Rapture of the Church. Nashville: Thomas Nelson, 1990.

Rosio, Bob. Hitler and the New Age. Lafayette: Huntington House Publishers, 1993.

Roux, George. Ancient Iraq. New York: Penguin Books, 1966.

Spaulding, Mark. Heartbeat of the Dragon. Sterling Heights: Light Warrior Press, 1992.

Strassfield, Michael. The Jewish Holidays: A Guide and Commentary. New York: Harper & Row, 1985.

Strong, James. "A Concise Dictionary of the Words of the Greek New Testament & A Concise Dictionary of the Words in the Hebrew Bible." Strongs Exhaustive Concordance of the Bible. Iowa Falls: World Bible Publishers, 1986.

The Ante-Nicene Fathers. 10 Volumes. Grand Rapids: Erdmore Publishing Company, 1989-1990.

Thomas, Robert. Revelation 1-7: An Exegetical Commentary. Chicago: Moody Press, 1992.

Van Kampen, Robert. The Sign. Wheaton: Crossway Books, 1992.

Vine, W.E. The Expanded Vines Expository Dictionary of New Testament Words. Minneapolis: Bethany House Publishers, 1994.

Walvoord, John. The Prophecy Knowledge Handbook. Wheaton: Victor Books, 1990.

Wilson, William. Old Testament Word Studies. Peabody: Hendrickson Publishers, 1961.

Wood, Leon J. Daniel: Bible Study Commentary. Grand Rapids: Zondervan Publishers, 1975.

Woodrow, Ralph. Babylon Mystery Religion: Ancient and Modern. Riverside: Ralph Woodrow Evangelistic Association, 1966.

Periodicals, Articles, & Tapes

AP Wire. "Violence Spreads in Germany" The Chicago Tribune 5 September 1992.

Howlett, Debbie. "Gays, Opponents Engage in a War of Video Images." USA Today: in Christian Action Network Newsletter 1993.

Niebutt, Gustav. "The Lords Name." The Wall Street Journal LXX III no. 137: 27 April 1992.

Rosenthal, Marvin. "A New Heaven-A New Earth-A New Jerusalem." Zions Fire 4 no. 3 (May\June 1993): 5-11.

Rosenthal, Marvin. "Paralambano." Zions Fire 3 no. 4 (July\August 1992): 3-11.

Schlegel, William. "The Scroll of Revelation." Zions Fire 3 no. 6 (November\December 1992): 16-21.

Van Kampen, Robert. "A Biblical Examination of the Revelation of Jesus Christ." Grace & Truth Tapes: 1993.

For comments, questions, and inquiries about Revelation Unsealed, or for speaking engagements, please contact Donald A. Salerno Jr at telephone number (708) 738-4730 or email him at Brondar1@msn.com.

Printed in the United States
25554LVS00005B/106-108

9 781589 395411